UNREDACTED

FEDERAL BUREAU OF INVESTIGATION

...dated 12/13/2018 regula...
...nt and invoice payment should...

Submitted By:
First Level Approved By:
Second Level Approved By:

STEELE advised that the information in this report was derived
his primary subsource's visit to ...
2016. The primary subsource had ...

...never heard of AGALAROV prior to this report ...
...never heard of EMIN AGALAROV ...
music. STEELE did not know much about AGALAROV as he had not crossed
paths with him professionally.

Company Intelligence Report 2016/112

STEELE believed that the information in this report was derived ...
his primary subsource's interaction with one of ...

STEELE believed that this report was produced after STEELE's meeting
with FBI representatives in Rome, which had happened the week prior,
and after ... attended by his primary subsource.

During ... the primary subsource also spoke to a
Russian Federal Security Service (FSB) officer at a party. One of the
topics brought up during the primary subsource's conversation with the
FSB officer was EDWARD SNOWDEN. This contact with the FSB officer was
direct -- it was not brokered through another individual.

for the final paragraph of the report (paragraph 4), STEELE was unsure
if the information was derived from the "SNOWDEN source" but thought
it was unlikely to have been the FSB officer.

STEELE advised that his primary subsource had not had official contact
with the FSB, though STEELE believes that his primary subsource may
have talked to a local FSB officer.

Company Intelligence Report 2016/132 (dated 13 October 2016)

STEELE indicated that ...
information in this report ...
primary subsource's visit ... 2016. The information was collected during the
... 2016 -- the same trip

...concern, following the public release of the dossier, that NYT situation
involving the provision of funds can be a dangle to a controlled
operation, STEELE has heard, and it is his understanding that the
situation involving CODY SHEARER and the ... parallels something that
the US Government has been involved with, but he plans on talking about
that in more detail (see below). STEELE added that there are some "dark
web" aspects to this, and STEELE asked about who was handling or analyzing
"dark web" issues for the FBI.

STEELE did not provide funds to his primary subsource for payment to sub-
subsources. STEELE said that he provided a monthly retainer to his
primary subsource, and said that a primary subsource might, in turn, pay
for food or drinks while collecting information from his or her sub-
subsources, but the sub-subsources are not paid for information. STEELE
also advised that he sometimes paid for his primary subsource's trip
expenses, save for the primary subsource.

... STEELE, an important point when it came
... the issue of reporting quality ... STEELE advised that the lack of
payment meant there was no incentive for sources to exaggerate their
connection. In one situation, STEELE advised that his company and/or
FUSION GPS were involved in obtaining ... for one of his primary
subsource's sub-subsources. ... STEELE recalled
that ORBIS may have provided ...
...ION GPS ... were ... STEELE ... were then procured by
... (FBI) ...

STEELE provided some overall comments regarding the election-related
dossier reports. The time between Steele's receipt of information to report
... location was generally quick -- the time could vary, but often a report
generated two days to one week after the debriefing of the primary
source. In some cases where the difference between the date of
...mation and the date of published report was within a day, the
...mation for the report had most likely been received ...
directly with his primary subsource ... rather than through an in-person ...

... election-related dossier reports, STEELE said that the commentary
and "Company Comments" was generated by FUSION GPS. The first report
ORBIS to FUSION GPS was sent via direct courier; however, reports
typically encrypted and sent via email.

September 2017, CHRISTOPHER
...viewed at ... by the Operation...
... and SEN...
STEELE indicated ...
... the United States ...
ORBIS subsection ...
... in September ...
... and ...
...ty of ...

...expressing conc...
...d that he and ...
...to want the re...
...to get
...tract with ...
...her with STEELE
...contractual

...the fall ...
... they as...
...d ...
...velied
...at their
...rished
...and
...but
...they,

Continuation of FD-302 of Steele   Interview ...

...individual who origin...
Carter-related inform...
...followed up...
...of the three people ...

STEELE said that he ha...
GEORGE PAPADOPOULOS be...
which STEELE said got ...
...before this...
...in greater detail later...

When asked by intervi...
...subsource, STEELE ...

UNREDACTED

Russia, Trump, and the Battle for Democracy

CHRISTOPHER STEELE

MARINER BOOKS

New York   Boston

HarperCollins books may be purchased for educational, business, or sales promotional use. For information, please email the Special Markets Department at SPsales@harpercollins.com.

FIRST EDITION

Library of Congress Cataloging-in-Publication Data has been applied for.

ISBN 978-0-06-337343-3

24 25 26 27 28 LSC 10 9 8 7 6 5 4 3 2 1

To

Katherine, my love, rock, and guiding star.
And Chris, my business partner, friend, and the
wise older brother I never had.

Contents

AUTHOR'S NOTE — ix

INTRODUCTION: Ringing the Bells — 1

Part One: Russia Calling

CHAPTER 1: Lessons of the Valleys — 11

CHAPTER 2: The Recruitment Liaison Office — 27

CHAPTER 3: Midnight in Moscow — 37

CHAPTER 4: Windows on the West — 59

CHAPTER 5: The French Direction — 73

CHAPTER 6: The Beating of Wings — 79

CHAPTER 7: Pastures New — 89

CHAPTER 8: Foul Play — 105

Part Two: The Dossier

CHAPTER 9: Project SNAKE — 123

CHAPTER 10: Company Intelligence Report 2016 / 080 — 137

CHAPTER 11: Raising the Alarm — 149

CHAPTER 12: The FBI Will See You Now — 161

CHAPTER 13: Comey Agonistes   171

CHAPTER 14: Going Badly   175

CHAPTER 15: "Will You Look After My Cat?"   185

CHAPTER 16: "An Enemy of Mother Russia"   191

CHAPTER 17: Collateral Damage   195

CHAPTER 18: Three Strikes   203

CHAPTER 19: The Durham Farce   217

CHAPTER 20: The Long Arm of the Kremlin   225

CHAPTER 21: Lawfare   231

Part Three: The Quiet Fight

CHAPTER 22: Silver Linings   243

CHAPTER 23: 2020   249

CHAPTER 24: The China Challenge   275

CHAPTER 25: The New World Disorder   295

EPILOGUE: 2024—High Noon For Western Democracy   309

ACKNOWLEDGMENTS   317

Author's Note

UNREDACTED HAS BEEN written by me as an intelligence professional, in good faith, with the intent to inform as well as provoke further discussion of the key challenges facing leading Western democracies from our corrupt, and corrupting, authoritarian state adversaries. It aims to highlight the weaknesses in Western political, security, regulatory, and legal institutions, as I have experienced them, and to make suggestions as to how these institutions could be strengthened and improved for the common good. In so doing it draws on my work and experiences in connection, in particular, with (1) Russian interference in US presidential elections; (2) the possibility that Russia or other adversaries may have access to "kompromat" in respect of Donald Trump; and (3) the ways in which powerful individuals are able to use political and legal processes to undermine criticisms of them and avoid accountability including, in the UK, by taking advantage of claimant-friendly legal rules and opportunities for what I describe in the work as "lawfare."

These are matters of substantial and important ongoing public debate in which my own involvement is now a matter of public record and renown since the publication of the so-called "Steele Dossier" (or "Trump-Russia Dossier"). I believe that this book can make an important contribution to that debate by recording my firsthand account and experiences of events since the "dossier," as well as my involvement in and assessment of attempts by others to investigate the matters raised in my intelligence reporting.

I believe it is in the public interest, in that context, for me to revisit matters raised in the dossier and republish them in the form I have decided to in this work so that readers are able fully to understand my account of the events described; my criticisms of the investigative efforts which followed; and my ongoing concerns that matters raised in the dossier (including the issue of Russian kompromat) have not been resolved and so remain a threat.

I have also written this book definitively to set the record straight and to counter the lies and disinformation about me and my work which has been propagated and disseminated in recent years by various adversaries, both domestic and foreign. I believe it is in the public interest that I take the opportunity to reply to these attacks and give my side of the story.

THIS BOOK IS, as I have said, the product of extensive research and intelligence work.

It draws extensively on intelligence collected by my associates and me over several years, mainly from established sources judged previously reliable. I am limited in what I can say about this intelligence because of my obligations to the Crown and because of the vital need to protect my sources of information, who would be at risk of serious retribution if exposed. I have given some account of my investigative and intelligence efforts in the work itself and so I think it is unnecessary to address this in more detail here.

In general, since the Trump-Russia Dossier was published

without my knowledge or approval by *Buzzfeed* in 2017, it has not been possible to meet or further debrief the original sources, many of whom have been subsequently unmasked and punished by the Russian regime and its facilitators, both inside the country and abroad. We have, however, been approached by independent sources on the issues involved, who have shared their intelligence and other information with us. Some of this is referenced in the work.

I have also drawn on a wide range of other source material, intelligence, investigative journalistic reporting, and official investigations. Again, some of this is explicitly referenced in the work.

In relation to Russia, in terms of the Kremlin's evolving and extensive interference in the US, the UK, and Europe, I have drawn on (including re-reading relevant extracts) the 2017–2018 Mueller Investigation; the US Senate Select Committee on Intelligence report on Russian interference in 2016; the published work of the inspector general of the US Department of Justice; the 2020 US criminal trials of Michael Sussmann and Igor Danchenko; the UK Parliament Intelligence and Security Committee's Russia Report of 2020; and statements made, particularly on "lawfare" issues, by members of the British Parliament. Much of this has been explicitly cross-referenced in the text.

On China, the arguments in this book have been informed by reports from the UK Parliament's Intelligence and Security Committee, Foreign Affairs Committee, and the work of the Inter-Parliamentary Alliance on China, as well as the published academic work of former British government expert sinologists. On Europe, there has been less official, governmental open-source material to draw on, but Russian and other sanctions designations since 2022 have been instructive, as has our ongoing dialogue on Russia and other threats with the governments and intelligence and security services of various EU member states.

And in the journalistic sphere, I have drawn upon (and frequently referenced) the excellent investigative work done by Luke Harding, Paul Wood, Nina dos Santos, Ed Lucas, and John Sweeney, as well as Mark Hosenball, Natasha Bertrand, and John Sipher in the US.

GIVEN THE NATURE of the (mis)governance of democracy's adversaries—Russia, China, Iran, and North Korea—I have been highly alert to the issues of double agents, disinformation, and the dishonesty generally inherent in authoritarian political systems, and always alive to the possibility that a source may just be embellishing or fabricating information for money. The discourse, arguments, and assertions in this book have all those considerations firmly baked in. Intelligence is rarely 100 percent accurate, sources are motivated by different things and make genuine mistakes, but ultimately they need to be protected at all costs given the terrible retribution that is unleashed on them (and their families) if they are exposed. This has led me here to sanitize or even omit important information and detail which otherwise would have been germane and merited for inclusion to strengthen my arguments and better inform the reader.

Where I am not certain about something in the text, e.g., intelligence on Russia from a source I judge credible but whose reporting might be difficult to corroborate, I have caveated this accordingly. My discussion in these pages of the main subject matter—the integrity and vulnerability of Western democracy and the Rule of Law, which is the bedrock of our form of government but sadly in retreat overall in today's world, and the increasingly brazen aggression and interference of our adversaries like Russia and China—I would argue, is firmly in the public interest.

Donald Trump

The sections of the work which deal with Donald Trump are concerned generally with (1) Russian interference in the elections in which Trump has stood for US president; (2) the possibility that Russia could exert improper influence over Trump because it possesses compromising material in respect of him; and (3) my experiences of being sued by Trump in the US and UK in respect of the dossier.

These parts of the work have drawn in particular on:

1. The original intelligence reporting which appeared in the dossier;

2. Proceedings and investigations in the US as summarized above;

3. Other journalistic investigations and reporting.

I am of course conscious of the fact that Trump has brought proceedings against me and my private intelligence company, Orbis Business Intelligence, challenging the accuracy of information included in the dossier including, in particular, in respect of the kompromat allegations. I have considered carefully whether it is in the public interest to repeat or refer back to that material in light of Trump's denials and previous legal challenges. I am firmly of the view that it is in the public interest to do so in the way in which I have done in the work. That includes for the following non-exhaustive reasons that I set out in outline only:

1. I remain of the view that the original intelligence was obtained from credible sources.

2. That is not only my view but one shared by other intelligence professionals including the FBI, in their testimony in support of Igor Danchenko as a high-quality source on Russia during the John Durham–instigated perjury trial in the US.

3. The veracity of the intelligence I obtained is supported by other evidence as set out in the work. In addition there are various other relevant independent sources of intelligence/information of which I am aware and are built into the judgments and statements I make in the book. These include former US Homeland Security Department official Anthony Ferranti's expert witness report on hacking of the 2016 US election by Russia which was presented at the *Gubarev v. Buzzfeed* trial in the US in 2018.

4. Trump's denials were not tested in court because his claim against me was struck out. It is a relevant factor that a person in Trump's position would have no option but to deny the allegations and, although he has done so repeatedly, he has not refuted them in the sense of demonstrating them to be untrue, despite his being in perhaps a unique position to be able to do so. For example, his claim not to have stayed overnight at the Ritz Carlton Hotel in Moscow in November 2013 appears to be untrue, thus calling into question his other denials relating to this event.

5. The substance of these allegations is now firmly established in the public domain as a result of the extensive

official investigations, reporting and legal proceedings which have followed. Much of the relevant material was in fact declassified and published by Trump himself and so was put into the public domain by him. Given Trump is running once again for the US presidency, I would contend there is a clear public interest in reporting these matters (including where there are questions to be asked as to the efficacy of these investigations). I also have regard to these factors when assessing the likely harm which Trump may suffer from repetition of these allegations if, in fact, they are untrue.

6. It is essentially indisputable that Russia has sought to influence past US elections in Trump's favor. This is information of important contemporaneous and future relevance given the forthcoming US presidential election.

7. I reflect Trump's denials in the book and included his denials given under oath in the English data protection law case.* I believe the work means only that it is possible that Russia has compromising material in respect of him. I believe that conclusion is supported by the evidence and intelligence which I have reviewed.

---

* We did not contact Donald Trump with a request for comment prior to publication because his views on the matters covered in the book are already well known (as reflected in the text), and most unlikely to change; because he would be likely to (ab)use his political platform in the US relentlessly and dishonestly to attack me and the work for several months prior to publication, something it would be very difficult for me to counter in the interim; and because he remains in breach of an English High Court costs order in connection with a previous data-protection case he brought against me and my company, Orbis, and which he appears to have no intention of paying.

I have considered, before publishing, what further enquiries and checks I could undertake to try to establish the veracity of the claims I am repeating in respect of the alleged kompromat. I do not believe there are any steps reasonably open to me to conduct further investigations now. That is because many of the events covered are now a minimum of eight years old; most of the information and sources involved are known to the Russian regime which will have taken active steps to suppress and cover-up anything significant; because the operational methods required e.g. geolocation would be beyond our technical means and only legal for government services to employ; and as the cost of this additional research would be prohibitive for a small company like Orbis.

Having considered all the material available to me, the risk of harm to Trump and the public interest if the allegations I reference in the work are untrue, and the practical impossibility of further investigation, my view is that the public interest in publishing this material in the work very strongly outweighs the risks. I am satisfied that it is in the public interest that I publish.

—Farnham, Surrey, England, July 30, 2024

UNREDACTED

Introduction

RINGING THE BELLS

He says, "You're not going to be a dictator, are you?"
I said: "No, no, no, other than day one."

—*Donald Trump, December 2023*

MY FIRST PAID job was as a church choirboy. I sang at St. Paul's in the small suburban English town of Wokingham, thirty-five miles west of London. Singing quickly led to bell ringing, also known as campanology, an ancient and uniquely Anglican denominational art.

At my first practice, I wrapped my hands around the rope and pulled. High above me in the tower, the heavy bronze bell tipped and the hammer inside struck the thick metal sides. Sound filled the church and pealed far across the rooftops of the town and beyond to the countryside. I loved making such a loud noise, thrilled at the idea that it could be heard for miles around in every direction. That day I became a dedicated bell ringer, and I continued this passion during my school and university years.

In many ways being a bell ringer is like being a member of an orchestra or a band. You ring bells in a team, coordinating your rope pulling. You create a particularly mathematical form of music. But the original, primary purpose of English bell ringing was not to create a form of harmony, magical though that is. It was rather to communicate important and often urgent news to the local population. Bells call people to prayer. They warn of impending deaths and announce recent ones. They celebrate harvest and marriages. They fall silent during times of war, as they did throughout much of World War II. They celebrate victory, as they did when the war ended. They were used to drive out demons. As a boy I would become absorbed in the togetherness of the effort and the sound—and I liked the sense of connection to history, to the countless times over the centuries that bell ringers have played a role in communicating important messages to the community and to the country. Nowadays, I reflect on one further crucial message the bells have in the past sent out into the streets and fields: an attack is incoming, and it's time for us to take up arms.

If this book serves any purpose, it is as a warning of an ongoing attack and the impending intensification of that danger. And it is a call to arms.

I began my career working in intelligence and diplomacy at the age of twenty-two in 1987. During this career, the West has faced three obvious great security threats: nuclear war with the Soviet Union, extreme Islamist terrorism, and Vladimir Putin's Russia. As a government servant I worked on all three of these. But by far the greatest threat is Putin's Russia. This book will hopefully explain why.

Let us take the Islamists first. Putin has military power that dwarfs anything Al Qaeda, ISIS, or any Islamist group could ever dream of possessing. He has now easily matched their brutality and tactics. He has ordered assassinations, bombings, poisonings, civilian massacres, and more. He has repeatedly started major wars and has invaded other countries. The Islamists terrified the West for many years after the events of September 11, 2001. But they were never a strategic threat or had significant military power, and they have now largely been defeated.

The Soviet Union was a much more potent foe than the Islamists. It ran proxy wars around the world. It conducted relentless espionage campaigns against the West. It maintained secret and illegal biological and chemical weapons programs that could have devasted its enemies. And most of all, it nearly initiated a catastrophic nuclear war on several occasions.

The Soviet Union, however, was a relatively structured and rational entity. It had effective party and state architecture. In most ways, its leaders respected geopolitical rules and norms. By contrast, Putin's Kremlin is fluid and lacks structure, like a medieval court, and thus is unpredictable in ways the Soviet Kremlin was not. And he retains roughly the same strategic military capability—easily enough nuclear weapons to destroy the planet.

Putin's unpredictability has been shaped by his own desperate need to survive. By invading Ukraine in 2014 and again, full-scale, in 2022 he has fought himself into a corner. Dictators who start and then lose wars tend not to last. Putin is haunted, multiple sources say, by the much-circulated smartphone video of the public humiliation and beating of Muammar Gaddafi that was filmed shortly before the Libyan dictator was brutally killed in 2011. Putin has long regarded himself as being in a fight to the death, a fact willfully misunderstood by many Western leaders until very recently.

But the Russian leader is himself not, in fact, the greatest current threat to our way of life. Nor is the ruthless, ambitious, increasingly powerful Xi Jinping and his Communist Party of China. Nor is the increasingly aggressive Islamic Republic of Iran. The West, led by the United States, has always been able to stand up to authoritarian powers and rogue states and would, under normal circumstances, still retain that power. But today we face a threat to democracy on a scale we have never confronted before—the threat from *within*. Presently the gravest threat to Western democracy and the rule of law comes from Donald Trump and the US Republican Party, increasingly the willing handmaidens for Putin.

In November 2024, American voters will choose a new president. That vote will represent Putin's best and possibly only shot at saving his regime and likely his life. As a result, he will be doing all he can to get a Republican isolationist elected to the White House. Again. It is sometimes easy to forget that Putin helped Trump to become president before, in 2016, as the report by Special Counsel Robert Mueller made clear. And in 2016 the stakes for Putin were much lower. He is now desperate to have Trump back in the White House. And a second Trump presidency would be incomparably worse than the first.

If Putin succeeds in helping Trump get reelected, I am convinced that the global political and economic order will be utterly changed. We shall have entered a new historical era of strategic chaos, a "new world disorder."

The potential consequences of Trump winning the election are catastrophic. A second Trump administration would likely result in the end of funding for Ukraine, the almost inevitable Russian victory that would follow, and the occupation of that country. We would also see the emboldening of Trump-like autocrats around the world, increasingly close alliances with other undemocratic regimes, the withdrawal from climate change commitments and action, and a needless confrontation with China that could lead to a war.

What qualifies me to offer my thoughts on any of this?

My own life and the journey Russia has been on for the past four decades have been rather interwoven. I have been a diplomat and an intelligence professional working on Russia since before the fall of the Soviet Union. I was there when the putsch against Mikhail Gorbachev took place and when Boris Yeltsin took over the newly independent Russia. I also worked on Russia in Paris and London, and later became one of the lead government Russia experts involved in the investigation into the Kremlin-ordered murder of Alexander Litvinenko. In 2016 I wrote a series of reports about the then presidential candidate Donald Trump and his links to Russia. And hellish though the period was for me and my family when those reports—the so-called Steele Dossier, or Trump-Russia Dossier—became one of the biggest stories in the world, it did have an unexpected upside: since then I have had even better access to sources of information and intelligence on Russia that arguably give me a rather privileged view of what's going on inside the Kremlin— and how much we should worry about it. I have continued to collect that information over the past eight years.

In the chapters that follow I will share for the first time what that inside view looks like, how I came to the point of gaining such a level of insight, and what Western governments— and all of us—can and should do to counter this generational threat.

I will also describe for the first time how I am part of a well-coordinated but informal group of Western intelligence professionals outside government who are pushing back against Putin's Russia, including its oligarch allies and beholden organized crime groups. We have more latitude than government intelligence services in many respects, and we have decades of experience between us. None of us does it for the money. But, in ways that I will describe in this book, we hope that we have helped protect Western democracy in our own quiet way.

Unredacted reflects a journey of discovery in which my professional intelligence work over the years has illuminated and crystallized mainly baleful developments in world geopolitics. For most of my time serving in government, 1987–2009, the West was not only in the ascendancy on the international stage but also enjoyed close alliances, both military (NATO) and economic (the EU), and a strong liberal consensus prevailed, regardless of which party happened to be in office. That consensus was in favor of democracy, human rights, the rule of law, free trade, a free press with recognized standards of journalism, transparency, and tolerance in civil society.

If this book can help widen an understanding of where we are and how we reached this dangerous point, then it will have achieved something of value.

I should make one further point here—about what I can't write about in this book and why.

Unlike in the United States, where even former officers of the Central Intelligence Agency's National Clandestine Service (NCS) can speak with some freedom after they have left government service, there is a strict rule in the UK that former officers of the foreign intelligence service (MI6 or SIS) and Security Service (MI5) are not allowed to avow in public the fact that they were ever even employed by those government departments. Only the heads of these services are declared or "avowed" public figures. There are good reasons for this, including the ongoing security of intelligence sources and operations.

As far as possible my business partner, Chris Burrows, and I have always respected this rule, including when under hostile cross-examination in the English High Court during civil suits brought against Orbis Business Intelligence, the private intelligence company we cofounded in 2009.

The non-avowal rule is, however, rather academic in our

cases. We were both publicly identified as MI6/SIS officers on the internet in 1999 and then by the news media in the aftermath of the leaking and publication of the Trump-Russia Dossier in 2017. Also, the then British prime minister, Theresa May—with whom we had both met informally soon after she was appointed home secretary in 2010—unadvisedly mentioned to George Stephanopoulos of ABC News in a live interview in 2017 that I was someone "who was no longer employed by the British Intelligence Services." Apart from being inaccurate, the comment implied that I had worked for them in the past. So in that moment, I was once again avowed—by none other than the serving British prime minister.

Despite all this, Chris and I try to respect the rules on avowal as far as possible, although that seems, and often feels, rather ridiculous. Regardless, I will continue to do so as much as is feasible in this book. Consequently, parts of the story that follows may seem to the reader like biographical gaps. I have signaled in those moments in the book that these are matters— or time periods—that I'm not at liberty to describe.

But there is a lot that I can.

Part One

RUSSIA CALLING

Chapter 1

LESSONS OF THE VALLEYS

THREE VALLEYS MEET at the Welsh town of Pontypridd. The Glamorganshire Canal runs through it, meandering all the way to the sea at Cardiff, the capital city of Wales. From the middle of the nineteenth century the town was also linked to the outside world by train. For an out-of-the-way place in Wales it was remarkably well-connected. That was because of what lay buried in the hills that gazed down on the town and in those beyond: coal. There were vast amounts of it. Such was the demand for this resource throughout Great Britain—for many decades, the industrial superpower of the world—that at one point the train platform at Pontypridd station was believed to be the longest in the world.

My paternal grandfather, Arthur Steele, was a coal miner. Born in 1903, on June 24 like me, he lived in Ynysybwl, one of the many villages that peppered the hills outside Pontypridd. By the time he had become a father, he had decided that he had one main duty to his children: to make sure they were well-educated and then got out. That became his mantra to his son Perris, my father.

Arthur had good reason to say that. My grandfather had left school at the age of fourteen to start work in the mines. There were few other ways of making a living in a Welsh mining town in the 1920s. Working conditions were deplorable, and the work was extremely dangerous. Undetected gas could build up and explode, causing pits to collapse. In 1894, a massive explosion ripped through the nearby Albion Colliery in Cilfynydd, killing 290 people.

Sometimes the miners would chip away at a seam of coal that proved unstable and the black mass above their outstretched bodies would collapse. My grandfather's brother died in one such accident. His widow could never again look at my grandfather without crying because the resemblance to her late husband was so strong. Water pipes in the mines were another hazard; sometimes they burst. My grandfather once stood watching floodwater in the pit rising over his boots, up his legs, up his torso, and toward his head. He knew there was no way out. And then just before it drowned him, the water suddenly stopped rising and receded.

Like all miners, he returned home each day from a ten-hour shift covered in soot and dust. Each night the side of the drained bath in the house would be caked with the insides of the Welsh hills. I imagine his lungs would have been likewise.

The pay for working in these conditions was meager. The house my father grew up in had one light bulb. There was only an outside toilet. By the 1920s there were economic pressures on the British mining industry, and the pit owners tried to impose wage cuts and to extend the working hours of the country's 1.2 million miners. So pit workers—my grandfather included—went on strike in May 1926. Hundreds of thousands of workers from other industries supported them in what became known as the General Strike. The support of the other workers, how-

ever, lasted only nine days. The miners remained on strike for
months, their families becoming increasingly desperate. By
November they had almost all returned to work, by this time
cowed, paid less than before, and forced to work longer hours.

So my father had ample motivation to do as his father im-
plored him. He worked hard at school, gaining entrance to
a selective state high school that gave him an education and
qualifications he would not have obtained at the regular local
institution. It was his route out, his way to avoid a life down
the mines.

But after World War II, my grandfather decided he would
take matters into his own hands. Now in his forties, he decided he would leave the pits—and Wales—behind. His older
brother, George, had walked the 150 miles from Wales to London to find work. My grandfather and my grandmother followed, moving the family to the South of England. It was a
risk—to move away from steady mining work and their close-
knit community—but my grandparents made a home in the
gentler world of Hertfordshire in southern England. Psychologically, though, the mining culture of Wales and all its hardship and insecurities lived on within our family's culture.

* * *

I WAS BORN on June 24, 1964, quite some distance from the
Home Counties of England—in Aden, a British armed forces
base and port on the Arabian peninsula. Aden was established,
once the Suez Canal had been completed in the 1860s, as the
main staging post en route to what was then British India. India had years earlier gained its independence, but the British
military remained in Aden. My father worked as a weather fore-
caster and climatologist, and in this instance he was attached

to the Royal Air Force, which was fighting an Arab nationalist insurgency up-country in Yemen. The UK's Meteorological Office was then part of the British Ministry of Defense. (My parents had met while they were both working at the Met Office, although my mother, Janet, later became a librarian.)

The Aden posting was formative for my family. What we would now call terrorist attacks were launched against the British forces there; Yemeni nationalist insurgents once threw grenades at the British governor on the airport runway and even into a British military children's birthday party. This was just one of several experiences of living with the threat of terrorism that my father faced during his career. We were a family who knew the threat of political violence—and we learned to be resilient in the face of it.

We returned to the UK from Aden in 1965 and lived in the South of England for around a decade. I had a lucky escape in 1970 when I was run over by a car outside our house. My mother had called me back home for tea from the playground opposite where we lived. If I had stepped out into the road a split second earlier, I would have been killed. My mother saw the whole incident and initially thought I had died. She blamed herself and apparently had nightmares about it for years. I suppose the incident gave me a sense that there is danger all around—but equally that I could live to tell the tale, even from brushes with death. It did nothing to take the edge off my willingness to take risks, though, a trait I still have.

In 1974, one of my childhood heroes came to visit us in the UK for the first time. This was my American uncle Les. I have never spoken publicly before about my close American family ties. They are something that binds me to the United States in a personal and emotional sense, far beyond just the professional or political ties. Uncle Les had served in the famous 101st Airborne and fought in World War II, including in Normandy, and could trace his ancestry back to the Pilgrim Fathers. When stationed in England before D-Day, Uncle Les had met and fallen in love with my aunt Marge, then a nurse treating his injured comrades. Les's war journey mirrored almost exactly that of Easy Company in the renowned TV drama *Band of Brothers*. They married after the war and settled in the United States.

When I first met him and Aunt Marge, as an impressionable ten-year-old boy in 1974, they seemed so wealthy compared with us. And glamorous. Marge wore a fur coat and striking jewelry. She was focused on the genealogy (ancestry) of her English family, however, and Les no less so. I recall he particularly enjoyed visiting English National Trust properties and historical archives and, what seemed odd to me at the time, eating our wholemeal bread because unlike loaves in America it contained no preservatives. By profession he had become a painter and decorator, owning his own business in Rochester, New York. I recall him repapering our hallway single-handedly in less than a day. Years later, when working in the British embassy in Paris, I had the honor of hosting Marge and their son Drew on a tour of the Normandy battlefields where Les had fought so bravely, and visiting the 101st Airborne's regimental museum and memorial at St. Mere Eglise.

In 1976 my father was posted to Lerwick in the Shetland Isles, the northernmost point in the British Isles. Our time there was sadly reduced from three years to one when my father was promoted, but during that year we lived on a remote climatological research station and enjoyed the wild outdoors. I spent much of my time bird-watching and climbing on the steep mountains and cliffs of the Shetlands. I liked the thrill of knowing I could slip and fall. I sought out ever-steeper rock faces.

After a further year back in the Home Counties, my father was posted to RAF Akrotiri, Cyprus, in 1978 for a three-year tour. We arrived four years after the Turkish invasion and occupation of the north of the island. Cyprus was a strategic ally, an important place then as now; it is almost within touching distance of Turkey, Lebanon, Syria, Israel, and Egypt.

For me, the island became something of a teenage playground. I was into punk rock, cigarettes, and booze. I mixed with some rather rough characters, many of whom later went into the toughest British army units like the Parachute Regiment and Royal Green Jackets.

By this stage my father, although technically a civilian, was the equivalent of a senior military officer, and we lived accordingly, attending many Officers' Mess and Club events and playing golf at the spectacular raised beach links course in "Happy Valley," where you were regaled by the haunting cries of the colony of griffon vultures that inhabited the steep cliffs above. Our own bungalow at Akrotiri was about half a mile from the beach, where we went every day to swim in the summer.

My father returned to Akrotiri for a second posting in the mid-1980s when I was at university. Perhaps unsurprisingly, I suddenly became very popular with my Cambridge peers who fancied a cheap vacation, albeit one that meant sleeping on the floor. In return I expected their vote and support in the Cambridge Union, which would come to play a central role in my years at university.

Terrorism continued to shatter the Cyprus idyll. After the US bombing of Libya in 1986, the country's dictator, Col. Muammar Gaddafi, ordered attacks on NATO targets, including Akrotiri. One Sunday afternoon in August, when my father was on duty in the Akrotiri operations center, he heard what he thought were fireworks near the office. Going outside to look, he realized that they were in fact mortar bombs being fired from outside the perimeter fence of the base. Several hit their target, and he had to shelter with colleagues under a table. It was a close shave. The Libyan team, who were using civilian aircrew cover to get into and off the island, also shot at a British forces vehicle towing a horse box back to Akrotiri from the other British base area at Dhekelia, on the southeast of the island. Fortunately, no one was killed.

I suspect my father took with him from the valleys a trace of fear from the mining life as well as relentless determination. He had grown up in the war and now he was living a much more comfortable but still challenging work life. We were newly middle class, but we never had money to spare. My father always seemed a bit on edge. It was like he sensed that one mishap could see us all return to the sort of poverty trap he had escaped from. As if he was always looking over his shoulder.

His family had not been alone in fleeing from the mining communities of South Wales; large numbers of bright children from the region moved to England and became teachers, scientists, academics, and lawyers. Those generations of strivers tended to have some common traits: they were exceptionally hardworking as they broke through Britain's calcified class system and moved from the working classes into the professional middle classes. I grew up in a household that was acutely political and where conversation around the dinner table routinely focused on the rights and wrongs of society, and on injustices playing out in the country and around the world.

But our family's brand of left-of-center politics was not revolutionary. My father was a patriot. As a meteorologist attached to the military, he had a deep sense of service and loyalty to his country. He believed that for all its faults the United Kingdom was a force for good, and his duty was to help keep it strong while working to improve it from within. Some on the British left see the institutions, traditions, and structures of the state as inimical to fairness. Others, like my father—and myself—are as patriotic and committed to serving the nation as they are determined to right wrongs.

When I was a child I probably exhibited the early stirrings of the mix of respect for tradition with antiestablishment views that my parents modeled. I was a choirboy and a bell ringer—but I was also a punk rocker and a troublemaker. On a Sunday I would be singing hymns and ringing the bells in church; on a Friday or Saturday night I might be pogo dancing and drinking at a Clash concert. My friends and I could also push things a little far at times, getting into occasional trouble with the police for various misdemeanors.

I liked to push myself in nearly every way—except school-work. I was distinctly not studious. So often it seems to take a single teacher to change the life trajectory of wayward kids. For me that teacher was Lynn Harrison, who taught me geography at St. John's (British armed) forces school in Cyprus when I was fifteen. Something opened up for me in her class. She was patient and enthusiastic, and she made what had for years seemed utterly dull to me suddenly become compelling and absorbing. She filled all her students with enthusiasm. She had spent much of her career doing fieldwork and research abroad, and that gave her real authority and made geography feel alive and relevant. We hit it off well, and she was instrumental in my decision to apply to Cambridge University, something that would have been unthinkable in my family a generation earlier. As part of my preparation for the Cambridge entrance exam, in late 1982 I entered an essay competition on development issues in India run by the *Guardian* newspaper. There were eight hundred entries and unexpectedly I won. First prize was a trip to India for two, with all expenses paid. I was thrilled and asked my dad if he would come with me.

Before we left, I was interviewed by the BBC World Service, which made it all the more exciting, but that was rather routine compared to what happened soon after we arrived in New Delhi. Our hosts told us that we had to be up early the next morning for an important meeting. It was only when our car was leaving the hotel's grounds the next day that they told us: we were on our way to meet the prime minister of India, Indira Gandhi, at her official residence on Safdarjung Road. I felt rather daunted, to put it mildly.

The meeting with Mrs. Gandhi lasted around thirty minutes. We sat on a sofa and talked with her about our trip and about India's various challenges. I still have a photograph of the occasion. The prime minister was quite reserved and a good listener but remarkably generous with her time. She wished us well.

Less than eighteen months later, Mrs. Gandhi was assassinated in this same residence by a Sikh bodyguard, after an armed uprising in Punjab by some of his fellow coreligionists had been brutally suppressed by the Indian army.

The murder was a shock. It was sobering to think that we had drunk tea with her in the home where she was killed. But the trip was, for me, formative. I had loved traveling to a very distant and different place—and I had enjoyed encountering one of the world's most influential people and, in a small way, brushing up against history.

* * *

I WAS ACCEPTED into Cambridge, and in 1983 I matriculated at Girton College to study social and political sciences.

As a result of the various postings my father had had when I was growing up, I had needed to learn to adapt and make new friends quickly in changing environments. My two sisters and I knew what it was like to show up at a new school, and we understood how to study its rules and its social currents. So I found Cambridge, for all its history, tradition, and abundant sense of privilege, to be relatively easy to navigate. I made friends quickly, many of whom remain so to this day.

Academically, however, I was not self-confident. I was aware that I had not sailed into Cambridge. All around me were Old Etonians and Old Harrovians who had elided effortlessly from their elite schools to this top university—and weren't shy about telegraphing their apparent academic superiority to the likes of me. So I worked hard. And at the end of the first year I made sure I was there early to see the results of Tripos, a form of examination specific to Cambridge. I had achieved first class honors, the highest level at Cambridge. This conferred upon me the title of "exhibitioner," with a modest stipend as a reward. It was, perhaps, not mature or generous of me, but I did not dislike that the poster boy for the privileged in my year at Cambridge, Prince Edward—the Queen's third son, who was in my classes—had achieved a rather unimpressive lower second grade. Did I have a chip on my shoulder? Maybe.

My group of friends, mainly men—the Cambridge student body in those days was about 75 percent male, overwhelmingly white, and flooded with the sons of lords, earls, and magnates— found common ground in feeling excluded from the elite social stratum that seemed to be the dominant force among the undergraduates at the university.

Why did that matter? Why did we care about the posh boys who had it easy? Well, while you can certainly attend Cambridge purely for its stellar education, it has also always offered other opportunities that can be shortcuts to certain careers that are otherwise hard to break into. Here's one example: the number of prominent or powerful British journalists who worked on the student newspapers and magazines of Oxford and Cambridge is remarkable. I wrote for the student newspaper, *Stop Press*, and I kept an eye on a possible future career in journalism. But we all knew that the most reliable springboard to future success at Cambridge—and at Oxford—was its famous debating society, the Cambridge Union.

To the outsider the intense focus around a student debating society may seem a little out of proportion. Surely students had other things to focus on—like their studies, the sporting battles between Oxford and Cambridge, or even just their social lives. But few, if any, of those activities offered what the Union did. Each term the Union stages debates that feature, on each side, student debaters and guest speakers, who are invited by the president of the Union. These guest speakers are usually prominent in public life and are always influential in their fields and well-connected. This was one thing being involved in the Union had going for it—an early professional networking opportunity, getting to know some of the most influential people in the world and enjoying the privilege of debating with them.

But there was, and is, another factor at play: it was a very public testing ground for at least four key traits that elite employers look for. To get to a senior position at the Union, and especially to be elected its president, requires a student to be highly effective at politicking; that student must then be a good leader, to continue rising through the ranks and to organize the prominent debates; they will almost inevitably be confident, intelligent, good at public speaking, and, in a respectful manner, effective at persuading an audience that their position is the correct one. Elite employers, certainly in my day, knew all this, and, perhaps unfairly to others, they tended to regard involvement in the Union as a signal that someone was worth taking seriously as a job candidate. There's no question that being elected to senior positions in the Union created great opportunities for those graduates, and still does.

My friends and I understood all that. And we also knew something else—that the wealthy, landed, and titled establishment figures who floated among but apart from us considered themselves as having a God-given right to control the Union. They were entitled—but often also complacent.

For each of the three terms in a university year the members of the Union elect a new president, and below the president there were three other officers and a Standing Committee of six, the Union's main managerial body. All of those positions are elected by the student members. Some are more senior than others. And so the aim of any student wishing to hold influence over the Union is to get elected to the Standing Committee and then, through further elections over subsequent terms, work their way up to becoming president.

It wasn't party politics that brought my friends and me together to try to take control of the Union; one of my best friends then, as now, was Graham Davies, a well-known British public speaking coach who has always been a committed supporter of the Conservative Party. There were other Conservatives in our group. But we all felt like antiestablishment outsiders, and we all shared a dislike of the unconcealed and glib sense of entitlement the establishment, as we came to see our opponents, exuded. These young men were, we felt, assuming they would ascend to the presidency of the Union—and as a result would benefit, at our expense, from the contacts and opportunities being senior in the Union bestowed. This had, by and large,

been the way of things at Cambridge—and at Oxford—for decades.

I don't mean to make too big a deal out of what is, after all,
just a student debating society. It was hardly a life-and-death
political struggle. But it did matter to me. I did not see why the
already rich and powerful should have their future lives made
even easier by being ushered by their privileged voting peers in
the Union to these positions. It was perhaps the first time in my
life that I had had a direct opportunity to prevent what I felt
was an injustice in the making. And, not for the last time in my
life, I fought my battle inside the system rather than from the
outside on a literal or metaphorical picket line. My grandfather
fought unfairness in his own way. I fought it in mine.

So my friends and I organized. And one by one, we got ourselves elected to the Standing Committee. And, of course, we
debated.

I loved debating. It was a challenge and a thrill and required
a degree of confidence—whether real or manufactured—that
tended to help successful debaters in later life. I suspect debating helped me in the life that lay ahead of me after university, one that would require me to perform in public and
social settings rather regularly and often, not least as a way of
shielding my real duties.

Debating also gave me an avenue for tackling some of the
big issues of the day that I felt personally passionate about.

The most significant debate I took part in was held in 1985
and was about South Africa. It was the height of the West's
awareness of apartheid. The chamber was full. The debate was
even televised. On the opposing side was the South African
ambassador—representing the apartheid regime—and his fellow debater from the Union. I was on the other side, with the
anti-apartheid South African journalist Donald Woods, who

would later be portrayed by Kevin Kline in the Richard Attenborough movie *Cry Freedom*. There were probably a thousand people inside. The atmosphere was electric. I was the first speaker. We won. And that got me noticed.

Soon afterward I was elected to Committee, worked my way up through five elections, and was president in my ninth and final term at Cambridge. My counterpart that term at the Oxford Union was, incidentally, now former British prime minister Boris Johnson. One evening he and a group of fellow Oxford students traveled to debate us in Cambridge. As I shall explain later in this book, when Johnson became prime minister many years later, I would come to have grave concerns about his decision-making in relation to Russia, and the negative impact he had on British public and political life more generally.

Also in 1985, I took part in a debate that would give me a passing acquaintance with someone else I would cross paths with—from afar—much later in life. I was one of four speakers arguing that US president Ronald Reagan's SDI Star Wars program was a mistake that would destabilize the then highly volatile nuclear relationship between the West and the Soviet Union. My guest debating partner that evening was a young Soviet official called Sergei Lavrov. It's been hard to pin down, but I imagine the chances are very high that he was the same Sergei Lavrov who has been Vladimir Putin's foreign minister since 2004 and who, in the mid-1980s, was a senior disarmament advisor to the Soviet mission at the United Nations in New York. If it is the same Lavrov, which indeed seems likely, then he would many years later publicly describe me as a "charlatan."

This was mainstream debate material of the era, but one debate I organized at the time was highly controversial and broke new ground—a precursor, perhaps, to my later professional modus operandi at Orbis. This was to invite the London representative of the Palestine Liberation Organization (PLO) to speak at a Union debate for the first time, on the Middle East. Knowing the impact this would have, I kept the PLO invite secret until two weeks beforehand. Although it was a few years before the Oslo Accords between Israel and the PLO were signed, we suspected (and hoped) that such dialogue was going on in secret and that a high-profile Union debate might help push this process along. The debate was well-attended and fiery, though some of my Jewish friends and associates never spoke to me again on account of my giving a platform to what they saw as a terrorist organization. I still believe it was the right thing to have done, and it seems as pertinent as ever given what has been going on recently in Israel and Gaza. You cannot defeat terrorism by pure, and in the current Gaza case, disproportionate, use of military force. As our own experience in Northern Ireland has shown, you have to talk with such people to achieve durable results, however extreme and unpleasant you may regard them as being.

My focus on the Union in my final year at university did not leave a lot of time for lining up a job. I thought that journalism might be my future, and I went for an interview at the *Western Mail* newspaper in Cardiff. I didn't get it. I tried the Civil Service entrance exam, and I did not get through that the first time either.

My parents were still living in Cyprus, and so I did not have a solid home base either. After graduation, I went to live with my uncle, aunt, and grandmother in Horley, near Gatwick Airport. With university over and no job to go on to, I felt a little bit washed-up.

I also stayed for a while at the family home of a friend of

mine in Wokingham, where my parents' house—which was rented out—was located. His parents read the London *Times*. I was paging through it one morning when a job ad caught my attention. It was from a headhunter who was looking to interview people who were interested in careers involving travel and foreign languages. I posted in my CV to the headhunter and got on with my rather aimless summer.

Chapter 2

THE RECRUITMENT LIAISON OFFICE

A LETTER ARRIVED at my grandmother's house. It was from the headhunter, inviting me to attend an interview at the Great Western Hotel in Paddington. It was late summer 1986. I dressed smartly and took the train into London. There the mysterious headhunter asked me general questions about my ambitions, interests, and achievements so far. He said he was recruiting for, among other roles, international executives for Mars, the American multinational.

Soon after my interview in Paddington I flew back to Cyprus to spend the rest of the summer at my parents' home on the base at RAF Akrotiri. I passed much of my time at the beach, with friends, lazing around and doing various sports in the summer heat.

A few days after I returned to Cyprus, a brown, official-looking envelope arrived for me in the post. I opened it. "We are a government department, the Recruitment Liaison Office, and we understand you're interested in a career abroad," it read. "If you remain interested, would you please fill out these application forms?"

Neither I nor my parents had ever heard of a government
department called the "Recruitment Liaison Office," but this
oddity only served to pique my interest further and make me
think perhaps all was not as it first had seemed with this employment opportunity. My family immediately suspected that it
was British intelligence. However, it was also exciting, though
the world of diplomatic and military secrets was not wholly
new to me. My father had been vetted—the process that tests
the trustworthiness of British government employees—and
because of his job he had been privy to sensitive secrets. There
were American U2 spy planes operating from the British base
in Akrotiri, where he worked in the 1970s and 1980s. He was
one of the few people there who knew where the US planes
were going before they took off; his job was to brief the pilots
on what the weather conditions would be like on their route.
We were also constantly aware of security threats. So I was
already conscious to an extent of the world of secrets.

I decided immediately that I liked the sound of the job, assuming it was what I thought it was. If I was accepted by the
department, I would be serving my country in a direct way.
It would, I assumed, be intellectually challenging and exciting work. The nature of the job appealed to my tendency to
be quite determined and mentally disciplined. And I knew it
would also be a sociable job—because to be successful at it, I
would have to be the outward-going and engaging diplomat at
drinks receptions and meetings.

I filled out the form and sent it back.

Soon afterward another letter arrived inviting me for an
interview. I booked a flight back to the UK. The interview was
to take place at 3 Carlton Gardens, an elegant Georgian mansion designed by the celebrated architect Decimus Burton. The
history books have recorded that after World War II, MI6 used

the house as a location for interviewing candidates. It was not exactly a discreet office on a London backstreet but rather an imposing building at a prestige address, halfway along the Mall between Buckingham Palace and Trafalgar Square. The foreign secretary's official residence is opposite. *You are at the heart of imperial power*, it silently communicated to young people like me who entered through its black door. (It is now apparently owned by an American hedge fund manager. Reportedly it cost him £95 million.)

At the beginning of the interview the officials who greeted me pulled out a piece of paper and explained it was the Official Secrets Act, the law that prevents anyone who signs it from revealing anything about their involvement with Crown Service.

After two initial interviews at Carlton Gardens, I did a two-day Civil Service fast stream assessment center that involved presentations, group exercises, and mental capacity testing.

I passed and, just before Christmas 1986, moved on to the final board review at Carlton Gardens. I sat alone in front of three experienced officers, one of them senior, and fielded challenging but courteous questions from them all. I had happened to study up on Afghanistan, where there had just been a change in political leadership, and I knew the names of the former and current presidents. The interview board seemed impressed with this, and in that moment I allowed myself to wonder whether I would now begin a life as a Crown servant.

They called me the following day, a Friday, at my uncle and aunt's house: "Subject to vetting, you've been accepted."

That weekend I went to stay with friends studying at Guildford's then College, now University of Law. An exciting thing had happened to me. "This is wild," I thought, "and I can't even tell them about it." I did divulge that I had been accepted by the Foreign Office to be a diplomat, subject to vetting—the official version of my employment and one that would remain in place for years to come. They asked what I would be doing and I told them I didn't know exactly but that I'd like to learn a difficult foreign language and get a policy job.

The vetting was, however, no formality. People did fall at that final hurdle. I had a dedicated vetting officer who asked me to nominate five people who would vouch for me and agree to be interviewed. The vetting officer then interviewed all of them at length. In the course of those conversations, he would aim to pick up a name of someone salient I had not nominated and he would go on to interview that person, always probing for anything I might have kept hidden or secret or had not been truthful about. Once he had completed all of these interviews, I had a final going-over by the vetting officer.

* * *

MY DAY-TO-DAY LIFE as a new recruit was far from glamorous. I was living with my elderly grandmother in my parents' house in the Berkshire town of Wokingham. The commuter train took an hour to get to London.

I had to wait three months to join one of the scheduled training courses for new recruits. Meanwhile I needed money to live on. My new employers told me that if I began language training I could get on the payroll and then join the next new entry course.

Every new recruit is assessed for language aptitude. Your choice of language would determine where you were sent and indeed the initial arc of your career. I was attracted to learning Mandarin. I could see that China was a rising power, and it was then a much more closed-off and mysterious country.

The Civil Service ascribes different levels of difficulty to each language. My aptitude test result placed me in the eighty-fifth percentile. I was told I had good potential, but the assessor's tone made it clear that I was not top of that year's incoming class. So the officials in charge advised me against Mandarin and suggested Russian or Arabic. I chose Russian. It was a decision that has shaped my professional life ever since.

Shortly after Easter 1987 I began studying Russian full-time. There was a space for me and two established Diplomatic Service officers on an intensive Russian course at the Polytechnic of Central London. I began reading and studying voraciously about Russia and the Soviet Union. But it would be in a small house in Pimlico where I was to receive my first real insight into the country that would come to dominate the rest of my professional life.

I spent two mornings a week with Lyudmila Matthews, née Bibikova, my Russian, native-speaking language instructor. The lessons were followed by a lunch of mashed potatoes and less formal instruction.

Lyudmila had been living in London with her British husband, Mervyn, for almost twenty years by that time, but she had retained her deeply Russian character and her classically Russian understanding of the world. Her lessons planted the seeds of my deep understanding about her native country that have proved invaluable to me.

I can remember her key learnings to this day as if they were bullet points: it's hard to win the trust of a Russian but once you did they would do anything for you; there is a big difference between the public face of a Russian and the domestic face; if you are invited to someone's home it is a huge honor and, no matter how awful the food is, you should be gracious and thankful; Russian sense of humor is dry and self-deprecating; and get used to a very different understanding of privacy because in Russia there is a much weaker sense that people are entitled to privacy or personal space or their own property.

Lyudmila and her sister had been sent to an orphanage when Lyudmila was just three years old. Her parents had been imprisoned for voicing political opposition to the then Soviet leader, Joseph Stalin. Her father, Boris Bibikov, had been a senior official of the Communist Party. He was executed in 1937. Her mother spent a further ten years in prison.

When she was a young woman Lyudmila fell in love with Mervyn, a Welsh academic who was visiting Russia. When Mervyn returned to Britain, the couple were separated for five years because the Soviet state would not permit her to emigrate. Her suffering made Lyudmila an outstanding guide to Russia and its ways, both good and bad. And she passed on those lessons to me.

Lyudmila was wise and passionate, with a brilliantly dry, almost harsh, sense of humor. One of her highest priorities was to ensure that I could swear authentically in Russian. She taught me idioms and colloquialisms, instilling an appreciation of the Russian language in all its power and coloration. Lyudmila essentially assured I could make Russians laugh, which turned out to be a rare and useful skill for a young diplomat— and intelligence professional—in Moscow. Toward the end of my subsequent Moscow posting, my embassy colleagues requested that I draft an informal Russian dictionary of swear words, for their understanding and use.

At Lyudmila's house in Pimlico I learned about Russia's values and identity, its deeply entrenched importance of communalism, the way political opposition had so readily been a death sentence for Lyudmila's father, and the state's lack of humanity in not allowing young people in love to be together. Whether she was intentionally passing on historical and cultural lessons to me or just telling me stories that were lessons in themselves, Lyudmila was building up in my mind a picture of the country that I would soon move to.

She taught me the importance of trying to think like a Russian, filling my head with stories and anecdotes and showing how and where to look for crucial signifiers of Russian culture and history. And she taught me an invaluable life lesson, no doubt borne of her own struggles. She called this her "theory of small pleasures." Even something terrible, she would assure me, can be made exponentially better by some minor treat. This lesson stuck with me, and it came in particularly handy in 2017. A bar of chocolate is still usually enough to cheer me up regardless of what is going on around me.

There's no quick path to become fluent and literate in a language like Russian, even if you are doing intensive studying with a wonderful teacher. In retrospect, I was fortunate to have as much time with Lyudmila as I did, for there was a delay in my posting to Moscow, which I knew would be my eventual destination. But I was impatient; the 1980s was a time of remarkable tension and change in the Soviet Union and in its relationship with the West. I wanted to get over there as soon as I could.

During this time I was also undergoing professional training. I am limited in what I can say about this. However, a former officer did reveal some of his entrance course content. Richard Tomlinson was a former SIS officer who in 2001 published a book that revealed what he claimed were many of the Service's secrets. (Earlier—in 1999—he had been accused of publishing the names of around one hundred alleged SIS officers on the internet, including my future business partner, Chris Burrows, and myself.)

One key exercise that Tomlinson describes involved a new entrant being told to enter a specific bar and to obtain a complete stranger's key biographical data. Top marks go to whoever ends up with the target person's passport number. It is all about how far you can take a stranger on the journey of imparting remarkable amounts of personal and sensitive information—their name, address, date of birth, and as much as you can elicit. And then you walk away from them. Afterward, the supervising staff check your notes with the actual information about the person, using government and public databases. You use anything you can. You tell any story and bend any truth in order to persuade the target to reveal things to you that they would never normally tell someone who has approached them cold in a pub.

It's all about not being threatening, particularly as a man, especially in a pub at night.

In one notorious case a new entrant trainee apparently struck up a conversation with an employee at Aldermaston, the UK's nuclear weapons research facility. The poor man began divulging classified information, presumably to impress his interlocutor. The trainee then was obligated to report this to his superiors and the man was referred to Ministry of Defense security. It was a pure coincidence, but the story shows just how persuasive a good intelligence officer can be—or how bad some human beings are at keeping secrets.

Apparently it is an immense adrenaline rush if you can pull it off. I've rarely laughed about anything I've done as much afterward.

We use a similar exercise with some of our staff as part of their training in the private intelligence company I now run, Orbis. It is about picking the right target in the most propitious environment. You can also bump into people on the street on purpose to start a conversation. You can even fly someone in from another country in order to effect a happy coincidence that leads to a revealing conversation.

Once my training was over, I began work.

* * *

SOON AFTER I started my new job I met a young woman named Laura Hunt one evening in 1988 at a party in a pub on Fleet Street, famous for being the place in London where newspapers traditionally were printed. I was twenty-four. She was twenty-two. She worked in human resources at KPMG, the large accountancy firm. She was beautiful and I instantly enjoyed her company. My friend Neil Sherlock, who worked then at KPMG and whose birthday party it had been, was quite keen on Laura's then boss. So six months later the four of us—Laura was by this time single—met up at the Old Cheshire Cheese pub on Fleet Street. Neil's romance fizzled. Laura and I ended up getting married.

Laura and I were quite different. She was quiet, very private, an atheist. I was relatively gregarious, liked meeting new people, and an Anglican Christian. But we somehow complemented each other.

I could not tell Laura for quite some time much about my job in government. But I felt honor bound to tell her quite early on in our relationship that I was almost certainly going to be posted to Moscow before too long. She did not need me to tell her that Moscow in the 1980s was a place of long queues for bread and other basics; we all saw that on the television news. It would not be an easy life if she chose to stay with me and join me in Moscow. But she did.

My posting in Moscow was delayed somewhat because

there was a round of tit-for-tat expulsions going on between the UK and the Soviet Union. The Soviet leader Mikhail Gorbachev, who had come to power in 1985, was navigating his way through a crumbling Communist state and its collapsing economy; this led to a certain degree of lashing out by the Kremlin. I was meant to go at the end of 1989 but that was delayed till April 1990.

But finally, I arrived in Moscow. I was twenty-five years old, and I was now a diplomat—*officially* living in the capital city of Britain and America's greatest adversary.

Chapter 3

MIDNIGHT IN MOSCOW

ON THE NIGHT of my arrival, I put the key in the door of my new home—in an apartment complex in Moscow named after Marshal Mikhail Kutuzov, who defeated Napoleon's army in 1812—and flicked on the light switch on the wall. Nothing. I tried again. Darkness. I carefully made my way into the flat and found another light. Dead. I found the phone and called the embassy maintenance officer. He directed me to a small structure outside the building that contained the fuse box. I flicked the fuses a bit, and then, much to my relief, the lights came on in my apartment.

I fell asleep, knowing that the following day would be my first day at the British embassy. I was about to begin a high-pressure job, elements of which were highly classified and potentially dangerous. I was only twenty-five years old. My fiancée was in England and would not be able to join me for three months. It suddenly felt like a lot to handle.

The following night, after my first day at the embassy with my new colleagues, I came home, let myself in, and flicked the light switch in the hallway of the apartment. Nothing. I went to the fuse box in the small structure outside, but this time no amount of fiddling with the switches made any difference. I spoke to the embassy maintenance officer again, and eventually an electrician came around and fixed the problem. I had to spend an hour and a half sitting in the dark.

Maybe it was a genuine electrical fault. But it is much more likely that the Russian authorities were trying to unsettle a newcomer, as they liked to do with many incoming diplomats. They were most likely curious to gauge the level of my language skills—as they listened in through the bugs they would have long since installed in my apartment—but the primary goal was probably to put me on edge. If so, they succeeded.

The Soviet Union that tormented newly arrived young diplomats was in turmoil in 1990. The hardliner Leonid Brezhnev, who had been general secretary of the Communist Party of the Soviet Union since 1964, had died in 1982. Two elderly, unwell men had followed him—first Yuri Andropov and then Konstantin Chernenko—with each dying after less than two years as Soviet leader. In 1985 the Politburo turned to the most prominent of the next generation of senior Soviet officials, Mikhail Gorbachev.

The Soviet Union's intrinsic weakness was evident even in its first years; it relied almost from the start on oppression and violence to keep itself together and its people obedient.

The October Revolution of 1917 brought Vladimir Lenin to power, and in 1922 he established the Soviet Union, a new state that effectively put many of Russia's neighboring countries under the control of the Russian Communist Party. The new superpower-to-be included the vast and strategically pivotal land mass of Ukraine, and Belarus, Georgia, Armenia, and Azerbaijan. More countries would soon fall under Soviet control.

The egalitarian idealism of Marxism soon gave way to mass

oppression and murder. Lenin died in 1924 and was succeeded by Stalin, who grew the Soviet economy rapidly through collectivization and industrialization. But that transition caused a three-year famine in the early 1930s that resulted in the deaths of millions of Soviet citizens, mostly Ukrainians. At the same time Stalin began to eliminate his perceived enemies. He established a network of forced labor camps called the Gulag, and in the late 1930s initiated what became known as the Great Purge, a systematic murder of his perceived enemies. Historians estimate that between 700,000 and 1.2 million people died in this extended massacre. It also established terror as the core means of control and stability in the Soviet state for the rest of its existence. And terror inevitably results in government officials not speaking truth to power, and that in turn leads to inefficiency, frustration, and economic decline.

After World War II Stalin's victorious Soviet Union took advantage of its defeat of Nazi Germany in 1945 to set up puppet communist regimes in the Eastern European states lying between the two countries. The Soviets retained control over Ukraine, Poland, Hungary, Czechoslovakia, and Bulgaria, and they divided Germany in two, keeping the eastern part within the Soviet sphere of influence. The economic structure that ruled this now-vast geographical space, with 285 million inhabitants in the USSR alone, was called Comecon; the military alliance that underpinned it, and combated NATO, was the Warsaw Pact.

But these were no consensual alliances and arrangements, rather really just an extension of the Russian land empire that was the foundation of the USSR. And when the Hungarians, Czechoslovaks, and Poles rebelled in 1956, 1967, and 1980 respectively, they were put down ruthlessly by the Red Army, which killed twenty thousand Hungarians alone.

By 1989, however, the Soviet economy was in serious trouble, due to the intensifying and exceedingly expensive nuclear arms race with the US under President Ronald Reagan. The Soviets could simply no longer afford simultaneously to outspend the Americans, feed their people, and keep the economy growing.

The comparatively young Gorbachev—he was fifty-three when he became leader—inherited a crushingly difficult portfolio. The economy was stagnating; the 1979 Soviet invasion of Afghanistan was unpopular and failing. The nuclear arms race was not only financially crippling; he believed it posed a genuine threat to humanity and he longed to end it. His problems soon worsened: in 1986, the year after he assumed power, the Chernobyl nuclear power station disaster happened, causing unprecedented international embarrassment and further eroding the Soviet people's trust in the state.

To his credit, Gorbachev understood the system he'd grown up in was broken and needed major reform. As soon as he became leader, he began talking of perestroika—restructuring—and soon spoke of glasnost, or openness. He opened new discussions with President Reagan to reduce nuclear weapons. When Britain's own staunch anticommunist "Iron Lady" prime minister, Margaret Thatcher, met Gorbachev, she described him, rather surprisingly at the time, as a man she "could do business with."

When I arrived in Moscow the Soviet Union had less than two years left to run. But none of us knew that, of course. Reform, not dissolution, seemed the most likely course for the Soviet monolith. What was clear to all foreign diplomats, myself included, was that the events of the coming months and years would likely shape global security for decades to come.

* * *

MY GOVERNMENT TOLD the Soviet authorities that I was a diplomat. Whether the Soviets believed this or not is another matter.

And indeed my diplomatic job in Moscow was a full-time, genuine Foreign Office job, which I had to perform with as much focus and commitment as possible.

As a diplomat, my job—formally second secretary Chancery—was to research the Soviet economy and file reports to London. I showed up each day at the embassy and worked in the same room as other diplomats. I went to press conferences, I talked to journalists, I transacted business with Soviet government officials who were not of any particular intelligence interest. I hosted visitors and VIPs, including former UK prime minister Jim Callaghan, and I traveled inside the country, researching how the economy was functioning. It was, I am sure, of use to the British government—hundreds of British government officials read my telegrams about the Soviet economy.

As for the KGB, the Soviet Union's lead security agency, they made me understand from day one—starting with my stubbornly unreliable electric supply in my apartment—that they were watching me and would make my life as uncomfortable as they could. The initial unease changed into a bearable but constant state of general alertness. It was never something I got completely used to. No normal person would.

My apartment, which I would live in with Laura when she joined me in Russia (after we got married back in the UK) three months after my arrival, was in a guarded block that was shared with numerous other diplomats and journalists. It was situated near the Belorussia Station in Moscow in what was then, by Russian standards, an upmarket neighborhood.

Embassy staff, whatever their role, faced "attention" from the Soviet authorities. The Soviet government—which was, when I first arrived, still largely synonymous with the Communist Party—completely controlled the environment in which foreigners lived. We were watched constantly—either by a surveillance team, or by cameras and bugs in our apartments. We didn't try to evade or sweep for bugs because we knew they would just be replaced.

The rules were clear and agreed upon between governments: We were not allowed to travel more than twenty-five miles out of the center of Moscow without prior written permission. Any journey beyond this, for work or pleasure, required two full days' notice, with tickets purchased by local embassy staff. There were also designated forbidden places—officially referred to as "red areas"—and specific buildings inside the twenty-five-mile perimeter that we were not allowed to venture near or into.

Our surveillants, we knew, would be filing reports on where we went, whom we spoke to, and what we were saying. When we arrived back at our housing compound, which was fenced off with a guard posted on the gate (allegedly for our own protection), the guard would immediately phone in to the KGB to let them know our latest movements.

Not all diplomats in Moscow spoke Russian. Fluent Russian-speaking officers like me worried them. They did not want local people opening up to diplomats or any foreigners about their way of life, their lack of access to basic goods, how they felt about the regime, and numerous other aspects of everyday life that were not exactly state secrets but were, in some respects, sensitive information the Kremlin least wanted foreigners to know. They did not want outsiders seeing for themselves, or hearing from Russians, that the system was creaking.

The KGB made it hard for us to anticipate and handle their different forms of intimidation because they treated everyone slightly differently. They had numerous ways of unsettling us. One colleague's car tires were let down when he was on a trip to the countryside. Others could tell that intruders had been in their flats, noticing that belongings had been moved around or were missing. We were never quite sure how much of this interference we were going to get or what forms it might take. And we rarely, if ever, had proof that it was the KGB letting our tires down or stealing our household items. Were we even imagining some of it? That was part of the mind games they played.

One New Year's Eve I had an old friend, Rob, and his wife, Emma, visit us from England. We all drank a lot of vodka and crashed out. In the morning Rob woke up, groggy, with a Brussels sprout in his mouth. We could only imagine that the KGB had entered our flat at night, gone to the fridge, and, perhaps thinking my friend Rob was me because he was sleeping in my bed, decided to play a bizarre trick by placing the sprout in his mouth.

But the games they played were more serious at times. One of my senior colleagues was out jogging when a KGB surveillance car drove straight at him. Fortunately, he had a range of training that went beyond the strictly diplomatic and was able to dive behind a wall so that the car missed him. The consensus back in the embassy was that his KGB surveillance team had been somewhat overzealous or lacking in experience—or were perhaps drunk—and that it was an isolated incident rather than an ongoing threat to life. Killing a Western diplomat, even an intelligence officer, was just not something the Soviets did. But the incident was, as these things always were, disconcerting.

Nearly everything in Moscow felt quite out of our control. The work environment was incredibly busy and could change at very short notice. Walking down the street would inevitably involve being followed and watched. Our privacy at home felt constantly violated. That created a high level of stress. The feeling when you arrive home after a long day at work, put your feet up, turn on the television, and have a glass of wine was just not something you could experience in Moscow. I only ever truly relaxed when I left Russia to go on holiday.

* * *

I CARRIED ALL the lessons I had learned at Lyudmila's flat in Pimlico with me to Moscow in 1990. But I realized quickly how much I still had to learn and how impenetrable Russia could be. "Kremlinology is like looking at bulldogs fighting under a rug," Winston Churchill once said. "You couldn't see what was going on, but you could hear the growling and the snarling."

The need to understand what was happening to us, and to understand Russia itself, was critical. We sought insight into what was going on in real time. But we also strove to understand the soul and history of the country in order to help steer it toward a peaceable, prosperous, and hopefully democratic future.

All diplomats in Soviet Moscow wrestled with a set of key questions: If the USSR came to a sudden end, what would follow after? Would the country disintegrate into dangerous chaos? Or would we see a peaceful transfer of power to a new generation of democrats as had very recently happened in former Soviet satellites including Hungary, Czechoslovakia, and even East Germany?

Russia, I knew, was different from all those countries in a few key respects: It had nuclear weapons and a vast military; the country itself was huge; and, crucially, Russia saw itself as a great power and would continue to do so regardless of what system of government it had. It was never going to accept being demoted to a second-tier player in global politics. I was not alone in quickly concluding that if the West talked down to a weakened Soviet Union or to a post-Soviet Russia then no good would come of it. It would not be wise to humiliate or disrespect a nuclear nation with a proud history.

I began to study the country—to peer under the rug that Churchill had described—by attempting to look beyond what was happening in the Kremlin or even in Moscow.

My diplomatic role—studying the Soviet economy—meant that I traveled widely throughout the Soviet Union. It did not take many trips to the Russian countryside and outlying regions to see that the Soviet Union was barely holding together, that its political system was the root cause of that slow disintegration, and that if the West mismanaged its relationship with the Soviet Union and whatever came after it, the consequences would be highly unpredictable and hazardous.

* * *

GOVERNMENTS ARE ARGUABLY quite adept at performing certain functions, like running armies and providing a social safety net. What they are not good at, however, contra Marx, is owning the means of production and effectively running an economy.

I saw signs of the Soviet economic death spiral intensifying everywhere I traveled. For consumers, everyday purchases—buying bread, putting gas in the car, purchasing a new pair of shoes—required research, analysis, and tactics. The fundamental problem was that supply could no longer meet demand; the back end of the economy had never worked efficiently and had atrophied over the decades, and the nuclear arms race with the United States had siphoned off immense amounts of money from the national budget.

Take bread, for example: A loaf would cost the equivalent of two cents, which was very affordable, and so anyone who wanted bread should have been able to buy it. But because bread was so cheap, there was no financial incentive for anyone actually to produce it. Nor was there adequate investment in farming, transportation, or storage, so half the cereals harvest rotted in the fields.

As I traveled throughout the country I noticed an emerging counterforce to the crippled state-run economy. The majority of the arable land in Russia was state-owned, and most of the agricultural processes had been collectivized. But the state did allow people who worked on collective farms to have private plots. These private plots, I learned, accounted for approximately 5 percent of the farmland but produced 40 percent of the food grown in the Soviet Union.

This food was sold to the public in collective farm markets, or *kolkhoznyye rynki*. It was comparatively expensive—but far better quality. At these markets Russians (and foreign diplomats like me) could buy chickens, fruit, and vegetables grown locally or in the Soviet Union's southern republics. Occasionally we would visit one of the farms and eat the freshly cooked food the farmers would serve, using their own produce. Those were probably the best meals available in all of Russia—and they were the result of private ownership and a semi-concealed market economy.

The existence of an alternative way of conducting commerce provided a painful contrast for Russian families who did not have enough money to shop in the collective farm markets, let alone take a trip to the countryside to eat at a farm. The amount, range, and quality of food available in the state-run shops was dire and a daily reminder to most Russians of the broken promise of communism to provide enough for all. The queues for basics that everyone in the West had heard about were not a myth. Shelves were frequently bare. People bartered with colleagues, grew vegetables wherever they could, and would take home food from their work canteens.

Do not for a minute think that Russians were somehow accepting of this. Russians are passionate about good food. And decades of deprivation did not weaken that passion. In many ways it sharpened the hunger and anger Russians increasingly felt. And the food supply chain vividly illustrated to them that produce grown privately was more plentiful, of better quality, and would generate more profit than food produced by the vast lumbering machine of the state.

As I learned more on my travels, I realized that the seeds of this shift to private ownership had, in fact, been planted years earlier and that Russians' understanding of the frailties of their economic system had been growing for at least two decades. After World War II the victorious Soviet state, run with great ruthlessness by Stalin, all but banned private ownership of anything. But that changed in the 1970s. The first significant item that people began to privately own were cars, mainly the ubiquitous Lada Zhiguli, which started appearing in the early 1970s. Russians could actually own these remarkable machines. That was a fundamental and very public shift. Prior to the arrival of the Fiat-based Lada, nearly everything a family needed would have been supplied directly by the state or by their employers. But from 1970 onward a Soviet family that was doing reasonably well could buy a relatively reliable car that would give them the freedom to travel widely, despite various internal travel restrictions—and was, to some extent, a statement of affluence.

The consequences were significant. One by one, Soviets experienced private ownership. Demand for the finer things in life began to wildly outstrip legitimate supply. And that quickly led to lawbreaking and corruption. A black market—or secondary underground economy—emerged and began to further undermine the Soviet "command" one. Economic historians have estimated that around 10 percent of the entire Soviet economy during the final years of the Soviet Union was made up of illegal trade. The system was known as *blat*, an informal exchanging of favors and bribes and consumer goods. Imagine the damage to a Western economy if 10 percent of economic activity and trade simply disappeared from its GDP. The shadow economy eroded the tax base, undermined the respect people had for the state and its laws, turned nearly every government employee into a target for bribery, and empowered and incentivized criminals. The term for a professional criminal in Russian: *blatnoy*.

The longer I lived and worked in Russia, the more I saw that not only was the economy rotten but it was creating increasing amounts of criminality—inside and outside government. Corruption, of course, did not die out with the Soviet Union. Indeed, the seeds of what would come in the decades after communism were being sown.

Russians could get virtually anything they wanted on the black market if they were prepared to pay for it with hard currency, including luxury goods like televisions, VCRs, CD players, and video-game consoles. When I visited Russians in their apartments, as we started to do from around 1991, the evidence of this would be sitting on shelves and side tables. It was considered impolite to ask where these items had come from. I certainly did not judge. But I did see how the system was turning respectable people into default criminals, and how they laughed at the idea of respecting the laws of the state. For nearly every Russian I met, the fundamental relationship with law and order amounted to what they could get away with. They were particularly averse to paying taxes because there was no accepted social contract with the state. That trait continues to this day.

Hard currency—the money of the American or European enemies of the state—was fundamental to the black market. The true value of the ruble was incredibly volatile and made peoples' lives a complicated misery. In late 1991, hyperinflation kicked in. A subway token, for example, officially cost five kopeks. But despite hyperinflation their role in ordinary peoples' lives remained unchanged and the tokens began only to be available on the black market for fifty kopeks each, ten times their nominal value.

Laura happened to like the rugs available in the Soviet Union, and we had bought several. But hyperinflation made buying more carpets difficult. Legally, we had to buy rugs with rubles. So, we had to find a carpet, agree on a price, and then rush to an exchange bureau and rush back with the right amount of rubles before the price shifted again.

It was difficult for anyone, diplomats included, to function in Russia without engaging with the black market. That theoretically made us criminals too. In 1991 the government imposed gas rationing—incredible in a country that was one of the largest oil-producing nations in the world. We needed gas to get around and to do our jobs. I knew a couple of gas stations in obscure suburban parts of Moscow that were meant to be supplying essential service vehicles like fire engines and ambulances. So for a period of about three months my colleagues and I went once a week to purchase, with hard currency, fuel for our own cars. There was no realistic alternative.

The signs of decay in Soviet society were evident in other rather shocking ways. One Friday night we came home after an evening out and noticed that a car had crashed into a lamp-post around the corner from our apartment block. The driver, clearly dead, was still in the car. I thought to myself that the emergency services were moving rather slowly because there was no ambulance there, no police. But on Monday morning, when Laura went to work, she saw that the dead man was still sitting in his crumpled-up car.

We shuddered at the callousness and inefficiency—and what this meant for the future of Russia. We were living in a country that was almost the opposite of everything it claimed to be. The communist system promised equality, justice, and security. Instead, the Soviet state offered no effective social safety net; its officials were mostly corrupt and barely competent; it was lacking in empathy and humanity. And it left its dead on the streets.

* * *

AND YET WE did not expect it to end so soon, or as rapidly.

In 1989 Gorbachev's liberalizations and the evident weakness of the Soviet Union rippled out to Eastern Europe. A series of uprisings and revolutions resulted in formerly communist regimes that had been puppet states of Moscow becoming democracies. The Berlin Wall was breached, and East and West Germany began to reunify. Lithuania declared independence from the Soviet Union in March 1990. Other Soviet states followed. The Soviet sphere of influence in Eastern Europe had shrunk: Poland, Hungary, East Germany, Czechoslovakia, Bulgaria, and Romania were already gone. But the Soviet Union itself, with Russia as its anchor, still stood—vast and, we assumed, permanent.

Gorbachev continued with his reforms and decided to hold

an election to establish the position of president of the USSR. He concluded that the Soviet Union was not able yet to put the vote to the people, and on March 14, 1990, the Congress of People's Deputies of the USSR voted to elect a president for the first time. The stated intention was that the people would vote in 1995, when the new president's five-year term was up. Gorbachev was the only candidate and received 1,329 of the 1,824 votes available.

The Soviet leader quickly concluded that the best way to hold together what was left of his state was to draft a new union treaty between the member countries and to put it to a popular vote. The referendum—held in nine countries— passed and the member states began ratifying the treaty, which granted much greater powers of self-determination to each republic.

At the same time Gorbachev was finalizing a historic arms control agreement with the United States. In July 1991 he signed the START I treaty with President George H. W. Bush, who had been elected president in 1988. The treaty limited each side to deploying no more than 6,000 nuclear warheads and 1,600 intercontinental missiles. It was not the leap toward total eradication of nuclear weapons that Gorbachev and Reagan had dreamed of, but it was a significant step toward further reductions of arms. The hardliners in Moscow hated it.

In August 1991, many diplomats—including most British embassy staff—went on holiday. Gorbachev's new union treaty seemed guaranteed to become law, and a revised version of the Soviet Union was about to be born. It had been an intense spring and summer politically and much of the Moscow diplomatic corps wanted to recuperate, heading home or overseas on long vacations. Laura and I remained in Moscow.

Like the foreign diplomatic corps, Gorbachev also retreated

to his luxury villa on the beach at Foros, near Yalta, in Crimea on the Black Sea.

His enemies seized their opportunity.

The hardliners in the Kremlin thought Gorbachev's reforms were hastening the end of the Soviet Union, not its reshaping— and that they would not permit. The *putschisti*, including then KGB chairman Vladimir Kryuchkov, struck.

On the afternoon and evening of Sunday, August 18, 1991, KGB surveillance vehicles deployed to follow embassy staff vanished. This was unheard-of, a clue we puzzled over. We went to bed that night with a sense that something had almost imperceptibly shifted.

Laura woke me up on the morning of August 19. She had her treasured short-wave radio tuned in to the BBC World Service news. It reported that hardline figures in the regime had conducted a coup, or putsch, against Gorbachev in the early hours.

I was assigned to a small crisis management group in the embassy. We huddled in the secure, safe speech room and decided who should go where in Moscow to observe events and report back to London.

We scattered onto the streets and observed troop movements, tanks churning up the tarmac around the Kremlin, and protests, and then we reported it back to London, often by phone, which was not our usual way of communicating. The urgency required it.

There was an unreal air about it all. We were watching events that had the world worried about nuclear conflagration, about the end of the reform movement, about a possible lurch back in time to the worst moments of the Cold War. We were witnessing it with our own eyes. And yet for all the vastness of the Soviet Union and of the far-reaching global implications of the coup, the events that unfolded happened within about three square miles around the Kremlin and in the central governmental complex in Leningrad (as it then was), which was even smaller. Everywhere else in Moscow life seemed to continue as normal. A colleague and I drove out to the air base at Tushino in the Moscow suburbs, where Soviet paratroopers were rumored to be landing to suppress the protests. Tumbleweed.

That night the new rulers of the Soviet Union put us and everyone else under curfew, and the KGB restricted Gorbachev and his wife, Raisa, to their villa. The plotters took control of the nuclear arsenal—and they ordered up 250,000 pairs of extra handcuffs to be shipped to Moscow. For some reason they neglected to cut the phone lines, however, and so we were able to continue our reporting to London. We also could communicate and obtain reporting from contacts in Leningrad and other important provincial Russian cities.

On the second day of the coup, I walked from our flat on Gruzinskiy Pereulok (Georgian Lane), past the sad, run-down Moscow Zoo and right to the Russian White House. This ship-like building was the seat of Boris Yeltsin's new reformist Russian Republic government and quickly became the center of opposition to the coup in the capital. Yeltsin, once a committed communist, had become a leading reformer and had been elected president of the Russian Republic, then still a constituent part of the Soviet Union, on June 12, 1991.

At the White House, a large crowd of Muscovites had gathered outside in order to protect the oppositional Russian government inside from the conspirators and their forces. The atmosphere was serious but unthreatening, and a series of Russian democratic politicians addressed those gathered to bolster the resistance to the coup. I realized this was where the coup was either going to succeed or fail. I spotted one of Yeltsin's close advisors in the crowd, and we discussed whether the elite Kantemirov Soviet army division near Moscow would intervene, as had been rumored.

I remained in the crowd when, about fifty feet away, Yeltsin emerged and was hauled onto a tank by his chief lieutenant, Alexander Korzhakov. The Russian leader, wearing a brown suit and tie, stood flanked by aides.

"Citizens of Russia," he began. "On the night of 18–19 August 1991, the legally elected president of the country was removed from power. Regardless of the reasons given for his removal, we are dealing with a rightist, reactionary, anti-constitutional coup. Despite all the difficulties and severe trials being experienced by the people, the democratic process in the country is acquiring an increasingly broad sweep and an irreversible character. The peoples of Russia are becoming masters of their destiny."

I could barely comprehend what I was seeing. More than seventy years of history was being overturned. And yet much around me seemed strangely normal. The British Airways office in the Mezhdunarodnaya Center—where Laura worked— was a stone's throw away, as was our gym and local video rental store. The crowd was large—but it was not a mass gathering of thousands.

The decisive moment soon came. The *putschisti*, in the form of Soviet Defense Minister Dmitriy Yazov, a thickset, weathered-looking man, ordered a crack armored division (the Taman) based just outside the capital to intervene. They refused. Another hardliner and coup plotter, Soviet Interior Minister Boris Pugo, then shot himself.

Gorbachev returned to Moscow, and the unraveling of the Soviet Union began in earnest. It was accelerated by Yeltsin, who, while a reformer like Gorbachev, disliked the Soviet president personally and harbored greater political ambitions for himself.

For a brief period, the question of who would lead the Soviet Union seemed a side issue. Ordinary Russians, like so many of their counterparts in Eastern Europe, had stood up to the might of their security services and military and had won a victory over the men who wanted to deprive citizens of their growing freedoms. It was thrilling. Surely now reforms would accelerate and the Soviet Union would evolve into a democracy.

Several days after the failed coup, the staff at the embassy were informed that British prime minister John Major and Foreign Secretary Douglas Hurd wished to stop off in Moscow en route to an official visit to China. They would be the first foreign leaders to embrace Gorbachev and his victorious reformers.

I was assigned the job of accompanying Major and Hurd into the Kremlin and then to a walkabout on the Noviy Arbat, where an ad hoc shrine had been set up for several protestors who had been shot and killed during the coup attempt. I accompanied the British leaders into their meeting in the sumptuous St. Catherine's Palace in the Kremlin. I lent John Major my comb to brush his hair while looking into one of the majestic Romanov mirrors on the wall, then I left them there with the Soviet president.

I then headed onto the knoll inside the Kremlin complex (outside St. Catherine's Palace) where the official cars were waiting to take us, though not Gorbachev, to the Arbat so that the prime minister and foreign secretary could lay wreaths and do their walkabout.

Suddenly, Gorbachev appeared a few meters away from me.

He had unexpectedly decided to take a special shortcut tunnel to the departure point, while Major and Hurd had walked back around the long way.

I stood there, alone with the Soviet president, then the most famous man in the world. There were no bodyguards or aides around him. The international press stood behind a cordon about thirty feet away. I couldn't help noticing that his Western-style suit looked more expensive than mine. To avoid awkwardness, I congratulated him on defeating the coup. He was gracious and asked me in his characteristically heavy southern Russian accent: "What do you do in the embassy?" I explained that I followed the Soviet economy for the British government. I was certainly not going to tell the Soviet president about any other role I might have had, but I added: "Я следую вас очень близко!" which translates to "I follow you very closely."

Gorbachev laughed. "We also study *you* closely," he said, in the Russian language "you," singular form, that is, addressing me as an individual.

Our VIP party appeared several minutes later, and we jumped into the various black Zils and other limousines that were taking us to the Arbat. As we approached the site, I saw my father in the front of the crowd, with his distinguished shock of thick silver hair. He and my mother had just arrived for a visit. Major and his wife, Norma, walked toward him, clearly hoping to interact with regular Russians for the cameras.

"Your English is excellent, sir," said Major to my father, after their initial greetings. "Where are you from?"

"Wokingham, Prime Minister," my father replied, poker-faced.

Inevitably, I got a lot of criticism for this from embassy colleagues. The ambassador, Sir Rodric Braithwaite, commented at his morning meeting the next day that when he had asked me to make the arrangements for the Arbat walkabout he had not expected me to provide the cast. The journalist Robert Hardman, whom I had known at Cambridge, wrote the story up in the *Daily Telegraph*. The anecdote emerged once more a year or so later in a television documentary about the Queen. Major can be heard recounting the story of meeting a Moscow man from Wokingham to Her Majesty, to both their amusement.

A more consequential result of the visit was that Gorbachev agreed to allow the wife of KGB defector Oleg Gordievsky to leave the Soviet Union so that she could join her husband, who was living in Surrey, outside London. Having been KGB "Rezidyent"—in other words, station chief—in London, Gordievsky had been perhaps the most valuable defector the West had welcomed in the latter years of the Cold War. He had been sentenced to death in absentia. We hoped the Soviet government's decision to allow his wife, Leyla, to join him in Britain was a sign of a democratic and civilized Russia emerging from the dying Soviet state.

Today, people like Gordievsky are hunted down and assassinated, not reunited with their wives.

* * *

AFTER THE PUTSCH Gorbachev tried to keep the Soviet Union together, but Yeltsin and his allies were determined to bring an end to the communist state. On December 25, 1991—during our Christmas lunch in our neighbor Tim, later Sir Tim and Ambassador to Moscow himself, Barrow's flat—Gorbachev resigned. Yeltsin became president. The Soviet Union was dissolved the following day and was largely replaced by a federation of nine independent countries, the Commonwealth of

Independent States, which still exists. Its members are bound by agreements to cooperate on economic, military, and political matters.

Russia finally had a chance to fulfill its enormous potential. Like all Western diplomats in Moscow I found this moment thrilling. We had an unprecedented opportunity to help the West's greatest adversary become a representative democracy, a functioning capitalist state, and, crucially, an ally.

Chapter 4

WINDOWS ON THE WEST

AS RUSSIA EXPERIENCED its first weeks and months as a fledgling democracy, I made a study of its history as much as I reported on the remarkable events unfurling in front of me. I knew that history would help me—and the British government—better understand in what direction this unstable nuclear superpower might be going. Up until the end of my posting in Moscow in 1993, I read deeply, traveled around the country, and constantly quizzed Russians on their understanding of their own past. And the more I learned the more I found myself coming back, again and again, to two key questions whose answers might help the West understand what lay ahead for Russia and for our relations with it: Why had such a sophisticated, cultured, resource-rich, and huge country been politically benighted for so long? And what were the chances that centuries of oppressive forms of government might finally—and permanently—end?

These questions are as relevant today as they were in the early 1990s. I found Russian history to be revealing—but not reassuring.

Besides the period that began in 1991, Russia arguably has had five other clear windows of opportunity in its modern history to approach pluralism and democracy, to become a country where the rule of law could have taken root and in which autocracy could have begun giving way. Each of these firmly and rather quickly closed windows helps explain to us why Russia has never become a modern-day Germany or Japan, ex-authoritarian states where democracy has firmly taken root.

The first window of opportunity—and to be clear, none of these openings witnessed anything close to a sudden burst of actual democracy—closed with the death of Peter the Great in 1725. Peter was an autocrat and a man who could be savagely violent. But his desire to transform Russia into a modern, Enlightenment state—with much improved education, and systems of government and industry—did help establish Russia as a great and largely unified nation. No democrat, to be sure, but Peter was certainly inspired by the Enlightenment. He talked about opening a "window on the West." His heirs did not have the confidence to build on his program of reform and instead dialed them back, fearful that they would empower the populace beyond the point where it would be safe for the tsar.

The second reformist moment came after the Napoleonic wars, which lasted from 1805 to 1815. Russian troops had pursued the Grande Armée all the way back to France in 1812 and there tasted Western sophistication, culture, and politics. The relatively young tsar, Alexander I, allowed various reforms to proceed. But in 1825 his son and successor, Nicholas I, brutally repressed a rebellion by liberal young army officers, killing many and exiling their leaders, the Decembrists, to Siberia.

We need to leap forward half a century to see the next window open and close. It did so in 1881 when Tsar Alexander II was assassinated. Alexander was a genuine reformer. After

Russia's defeat by Britain, France, and Turkey in the Crimean War in 1856, he emancipated Russia's serfs, he made military service mandatory for the sons of the privileged as well as the peasants, he reformed the judiciary and local government, and he began the process of establishing a constitution for Russia.

This was, arguably, the closest Russia has come to embracing liberalism.

On account of my stern criticism of the current government of Russia, I have been accused by my critics and regime apologists of being Russophobic. This is simply not true. One of the reasons why I am so critical of what the country has become is precisely because I believe it should be a civilized European state and natural ally of ours, as it has been in the past. But sadly, it is a country that has been badly led and thus let down by most of its political leaders.

There have been many great Russians who had a different vision and led by example. In our own era the chess master, Garry Kasparov, would fit this bill. But in my opinion the greatest of them all was Lev Nikolaevich Tolstoy. For Russians and those of us foreigners who love the country, Tolstoy embodies what Russia could have become, if the cards had fallen differently. Aside from being arguably the greatest novelist not only in Russian, but also in all world literature, Tolstoy was a soldier and an enlightened thinker and radical social reformer, leading by example.

The apex of my Russian-language achievements, such as they are, came when I was able to pick up a copy of *Anna Karenina* and read it in its original, which I did in two volumes from cover to cover. The Russian language employed by Tolstoy was both beautiful and surprisingly simple, unlike the prose of the other great Russian novelist of the nineteenth century, Fedor Dostoyevskiy, who nonetheless offered the greatest depiction of the dark side of Russia—something I have had to grapple with for most of my professional life but have never accepted as Russia's inevitable destiny.

Everywhere in Russia the very different worlds represented by Tolstoy and Dostoyevskiy still collide and play out. Tolstoy had fought in the Crimean War and aided the Russian empire's attempts to subjugate the North Caucasus. But as an aristocrat on his estates at Yasnaya Polyana near the city of Tula, Tolstoy emancipated his serfs, educated and housed them properly, and introduced new technologies and enlightened means of production. He was shunned by many conservatives among his aristocratic peer group for doing this in the late 1800s and early 1900s. He led a comparatively modest life that was reflected in the management of his estates, which still survive to this day.

A visit to Yasnaya Polyana was a must for anyone on a posting in Moscow, even though it entailed a full day's round trip from the embassy requiring prior travel permission from the Russian government and navigating severely potholed roads. I took my visiting, Tolstoy-loving parents there in the late summer of 1992. En route we passed the heavily polluted city of Tula, famous for its metal industries. Under communism Tolstoy had been reviled as a liberal aristocrat with delusions about peaceful social reform. However, in the darkest moments of 1941, when the Germans were at the gates of Moscow, extracts from *War and Peace* (which centers on the story of heroic Russian resistance to the Napoleonic invasion in 1812) started being posted all over the city on Stalin's orders to whip up patriotic spirits and resistance.

It seemed fitting, as another element of such political contradictions surrounding Tolstoy, that a surveillance team of officers from the KGB's successor agency, the FSB, trailed us on the road to Yasnaya Polyana—whose name means "clear" or perhaps "bright clearing" in the woods in Russian—and followed us around the estate all day. We were the only other visitors there, and even my parents could not help noticing them.

It was a beautiful early autumn day and the simplicity of Tolstoy's grounds was striking, compared with the opulence of the contemporary tsarist palaces like Pushkin and Peterhof near St. Petersburg. The original house and icehouse were still there, not far from Tolstoy's own modest grave, located in a clearing in the birch woods nearby. Someone was clearly still tilling the fields on the estate. It was an uplifting vision of what Russia might have become. Even the FSB surveillants appeared interested in the guided tour, which they sheepishly joined. We later bought a large painting of Yasnaya Polyana at Moscow's Izmailovo art market. Capturing the green beauty and tranquility of the place, it still hangs on our staircase wall at home in Farnham. Though humble, it's one of my favorite Russian paintings.

The liberalism of Tolstoy and the reforms of Alexander II were not to last. Alexander II's vision for a new Russia was too much for Russia's reactionaries. The tsar's son, the soon-to-be Alexander III, witnessed the bombing that killed his father in March 1881 and decided that his father had made naïve errors, perhaps well-intended but ultimately fatal. Alexander III abandoned many of his father's reforms, clamped down on the new freedoms, ramped up violence by the police, and introduced anti-Semitic regulations that oppressed Jews in Russia. In the process he made Jews a convenient scapegoat for disaffected Russians, embodied by the Black Hundreds, an ultranationalist and anti-Semitic movement that emerged in the early twentieth century.

In 1914 the outbreak of World War I put an end to the fourth window. Tsar Nicholas II had tempered the autocratic rule of his father, Alexander III. After Russia's surprise defeat by Japan in 1905, he was forced to concede real influence in the country to political parties and their leaders. Russia was becoming more of a European nation. But the country's involvement in the war—and the Russian Revolution in 1917—brought an end to this brief, forced trend toward liberalization. Nicholas and his family were shot dead and a new form of dictatorship began.

The darkest period of Soviet rule—the Stalin era of 1922 to 1952, which I have already touched on—was followed by the eventual ascension to power of the Ukrainian Nikita Khrushchev in 1956. Once he had wrested control of the Politburo, the so-called Khrushchev "thaw" began. The new Communist Party general secretary ousted Stalin loyalists from the Kremlin, visited rivals China and the United States, and allowed more free expression than had ever been experienced in the Soviet Union. The thaw sadly didn't last. The hardliners scorned Khrushchev's changes, and after the setback of the Cuban missile crisis, another Ukrainian, Leonid Brezhnev, led a bloodless coup in 1964 that ousted Khrushchev and returned the Soviet Union to another long period of political oppression and economic stagnation. The ice had returned.

* * *

STUDYING THIS HISTORY in Moscow, during a fresh time of upheaval and reform, I asked myself: What do those five missed windows of opportunity have in common? Why did Russia not flourish for more than those brief moments in time and bring centuries of autocratic rule to a close?

I had already sensed the beginnings of an answer in Russia's language as well as its history. I remember asking a question, early in my Moscow posting, what the Russian for "private property" was. There really isn't a term in the Russian language that matches it. The closest is *chastnaya sobstvennost*, whose literal translation is "personal substance," which is a sort of abstract hint at ownership but lacks the unambiguous declaration of ownership that "private property" connotes in English. This inflection of language is indicative of the fact that even during those five windows of opportunity the rule of law never fully established the right of every Russian to own property. For most of Russian history the term "private property" would not have made much sense. And that is more broadly indicative of the fact that Russia had repeatedly failed to establish a strong and independent rule of law.

I realized that it's hard for any society to emerge with a representative form of government without first establishing an agreed-upon set of legal rights and wrongs, of crimes and punishments. There's no great point in holding elections before you have an acceptance by the authorities and by most of a country's citizens that everyone will respect and obey the laws. And those laws must be more or less fair, and justice, for the most part, must be administered evenly, without fear or favor. Russia had simply never reached that sort of consensus. There had never been a social contract between all parts of Russian society that knitted the country together in even an imperfect, begrudging agreement that everyone should play by the same rules.

Even the most fundamental elements of law had remained elusive in Russia. This was partly because a pivotal set of laws introduced in 1649, after a period of great instability in Russia, that precisely restricted individual freedoms and property rights for nearly every layer of society. In other words, there was law—but it was imposed, not agreed upon.

Those laws, the Sobornoe Ulozhenie, or Council Code, made it illegal for Russians to travel between towns without a passport, froze every citizen in place wherever they happened to be in the Russian class system, and restricted the powers of the clergy and the nobles. *Everyone*, wherever they stood in society, was either owned or controlled by someone above them or had their fundamental rights, including the right to own property, greatly restricted. Ultimately, only one person in all of Russia had full rights to own property, say what he wanted, go where he wanted, and do what he wanted: the tsar (a Russian diminutive of "Caesar" in Western European languages).

The Council Code was not a blip. It remained largely unchanged until 1832. One hundred and eighty-three years of codified, universal disempowerment is not an experience a nation shakes off easily.

Nor was there some magical flourishing of personal freedoms in 1833 and beyond. Millions of Russians were not just restricted in what they could own but were themselves owned by others. Serfdom, a system that effectively gave ownership of rural workers to their aristocratic landlords, was not abolished until 1861. Russia banned the buying and selling of African slaves in 1842 but it was almost another two decades before it would end the enslavement of 30 to 40 percent of its own people.

In the latter half of the nineteenth century and the beginning of the twentieth, the reforms of Alexander II and the lukewarm liberalization of Nicholas II certainly chipped away at some of the Council Code and Russia's other autocratic ways, but there was no leap toward American-, British-, or French-style democracy, imperfect as those were.

Instead, there was a leap into the communism that was still holding on when I arrived in Moscow. The Russian Revolution was meant to sweep away these ancient, embedded injustices with a new rule of law that would benefit all equally. Communism was, its adherents evangelized, the solution to inequality. But while the state certainly enacted laws based on Marxist ideas of fairness, the shape and enforcement of those laws were far from impartial and fair. They benefited one entity above all—the Communist Party. They might as well have been called the Communist Council Code.

Besides the lack of a rule of law, there had always been—and continues to be, to this day—another gaping hole in the political and social structure of Russia. The country lacked any other strong independent institutions or civil society. These are another important and almost universal characteristic of countries that enjoy long periods of stability, harmony, economic growth, and peaceful relations with neighbors. The legal and judicial system is, of course, one of these crucial independent institutions. But often a powerful church or other religious body can also provide an essential counterbalance to a leader or regime inclined toward absolute power, with all the dysfunction, corruption, economic fragility, oppression, and violence that nearly always accompanies autocracy. The Catholic Church in communist Poland after World War II is an excellent example of this dynamic.

There is no such countervailing religious force in Russia. The Russian Orthodox Church has always been controlled by the tsar or by the regime of the day. It has never had the political influence that the Vatican has so often wielded in the face of authoritarian governments. On the contrary, the Russian Orthodox Church has either been cowed and complicit, or riddled with informants—as it was in the communist era—or it has fully embraced and legitimized the country's leader, becoming interwoven with and benefiting from the governing autocrat, whether tsar or president.

Without the support of an independent church, or other

institutions, and without reliable recourse to a fair legal system, Russians for centuries have had little protection from the whims of the powerful. And that means fear and distrust run through the country's whole history. I came to the conclusion in Moscow that trust is the rarest commodity in Russia. As elsewhere, it arrives slowly on foot and leaves in a Ferrari.

* * *

INITIALLY YELTSIN APPEARED to be the transformative democrat and free market advocate the West dreamed of seeing in the Kremlin. But he managed the transition from dictatorship at best clumsily and, at worst, with criminality, cynicism, and corruption. His economic shock therapy and privatization of state assets spurred economic growth—and wild inequality. The poor suffered while a small group of Russians—who came to be known as oligarchs—became richer and arguably more powerful than any private Russian citizen in its long, tortured history.

The opportunity seized upon by these men was presented by the so-called voucher privatization of the Russian economy. This was a scheme conceived of to redistribute Soviet state-owned assets and property to the general population as part of the effort to privatize the economy and kick-start a market-based one. The problem was that there was high inflation—and at times hyperinflation—raging, which meant the average Russian could not afford to meet their basic needs and were therefore willing to sell their privatized voucher assets to unscrupulous, emergent businessmen who vacuumed them up at greatly discounted prices. The assets became concentrated in fewer and fewer hands.

The increasingly powerful oligarchs allied themselves with

organized crime groups, especially in Moscow and St. Petersburg, which had fed like parasites on the shortages and deficiencies of the previous Soviet command economy. The new private banking system sprung up and, poorly regulated, enabled large-scale fraud and money laundering. Each oligarch or organized crime group controlled or owned their own bank and were able to use these further to increase and launder their wealth.

By 1996 the relatively small number of oligarchs who had come out on top also had become politically powerful by buying up newly independent media outlets and donating money to politicians and their election campaigns, with almost no constraints.

Yeltsin, seeking reelection that year, famously turned to the so-called Big Seven to fund his campaign. After that, these oligarchs effectively controlled the government.

When I returned to Europe in 1993 from my three years in a Russia that had transformed so radically on so many levels, I brought back with me a sense of excitement and optimism about the country I had just left. The newly independent Russian news media were dynamic and confident. Elections were contested. Investment was pouring in. People could speak openly about politics. And Yeltsin seemed like a genuine democrat—and a sufficiently powerful, bullheaded figure to guide his country to becoming a capitalist liberal democracy. Even Queen Elizabeth II made a state visit, the first ever by a British monarch, in 1994. Besides, that economic and political model was assumed by so many in the proglobalization West as the ideology that recently autocratic countries would inevitably adopt.

But I also had a strong sense of the unique fragility of this changed superpower.

There were evident problems. The level of surveillance

in Russia had not eased after communism ended. The intelligence services had never been dismantled and rebuilt. The judiciary was corrupt and had not become truly independent of the Kremlin. And, unlike in the former communist Eastern European countries, the truth about the past had not been uncovered, investigated, and acknowledged by the state. Nor had the people who had been responsible for the crimes of the past ever been held accountable.

Many of the Soviet Union's most bloodstained butchers were walking the streets as free men. This is not a unique problem in postdictatorship, postconflict societies. But the most successful transformations occur alongside a parallel program of accountability. A new government can hold war crimes trials, as West Germany did in Nuremberg, or Rwanda did after the genocide there. Or it can take the approach of postapartheid South Africa, with the establishment of a Truth and Reconciliation Commission. None of this happened in post-1991 Russia. And that allowed for some of the worst criminals of the Soviet era, for example, the KGB's chief political assassin, Pavel Sudoplatov, to end up becoming heroes and enjoying a long and peaceful retirement. Many of these mistakes—the brushing of history dangerously under the carpet—took place during Gorbachev's period in power. Gorbachev certainly had to manage many competing interests and forces as he eased the Soviet Union toward liberalization; overall, he was unquestionably a force for good.

But his cautiousness meant that when the Soviet Union did cease to exist in 1991, it had not faced up to its past. Nor, crucially for the future, had it removed from its body politic and its business elite the bad actors who had spent the previous decades sucking the economy dry and eliminating their rivals. Gorbachev took until 1990 to acknowledge formally the

Soviet Union's guilt in murdering nearly five thousand Polish military officers in the Katyn Massacre in 1940. He allowed the KGB to execute—without trial—CIA assets identified by the KGB-controlled CIA officer Aldrich Ames. He lied to the West about the extensive secret and illegal biological weapons program and, initially at least, about Chernobyl. Over and over, the leader who could have transformed Russia let too many secrets, lies, and crimes continue.

His successor, Yeltsin, cemented that failure. And he did it in ways that now seem almost preordained. I've talked above about the rule of law; under Yeltsin, the judiciary became ever more compromised and the rich flouted the law. Without that foundation of law, and without strong and independent institutions, Russia's democratic experiment quickly began to fail. Like so many Russian rulers before him, Yeltsin's main priority as he came to the end of his time in power—by then an unpopular drunk—was survival. So he struck a deal that would keep him and his family safe—and would seal Russia's fate for years, and arguably decades, to come.

The sixth window had closed.

Chapter 5

THE FRENCH DIRECTION

AFTER A FIVE-YEAR period back in London, I moved to Paris in 1998 with the title of first secretary Chancery at the British embassy. I'm limited in what I can share about my work during those five years in London or during my posting in Paris, but it is safe to say that I kept my eye firmly on Russia throughout—and what I saw gave me a growing sense of unease, particularly during my time in Paris.

In July 1998 the intelligence services of the West all rushed to find what they could about a hitherto midranking Russian official. His name was Vladimir Putin and Yeltsin had just appointed him head of the Federal Security Service (FSB), which was the main successor agency of the KGB. That made this former KGB officer from St. Petersburg—someone we did not know much about—one of the most powerful people in Russia. Putin was unsmiling, his slightly drooped eyelids giving him a sense of holding back, of not showing too much of himself. He appeared at first to be a largely apolitical Yeltsin yes-man, but his KGB background and his almost studied blandness concerned me from the start. I had encountered his sort numerous times in Moscow and there was always menace to such cold-eyed KGB men.

One year later, in August 1999, Yeltsin appointed Putin prime minister and declared publicly that he wanted Putin to succeed him as president. Putin immediately agreed to run. That same month rebels from the restless region of Chechnya pushed into neighboring Dagestan. In September there were bombing attacks at four apartment complexes in Russia, resulting in 307 deaths. Putin and Yeltsin blamed Chechen rebels for the bombings and unleashed a second full-scale war in Chechnya. Putin projected an image as the new protector of the Russian nation and people. (We had suspicions from the start that the FSB had planted the bombs themselves, to give Putin and Yeltsin cover for launching the second brutal war in Chechnya. I remain convinced that was exactly what happened.)

Yeltsin unexpectedly resigned on December 31, 1999, and, as prime minister, Putin automatically ascended to the role of acting president. In June 2000 he won 53 percent of the vote in the presidential election.

In less than two years, this barely known former agent of the KGB had raced through the senior ranks of government in a frictionless ride to the top and was now in charge of the world's largest nuclear arsenal. Western leaders began a period of collective wishful thinking about Putin, yearning for him to be a partner for their hoped-for vision of a more peaceful, unified world. Closely watching and analyzing events from Paris, I understood their optimism—and I shared none of it. And on my doorstep in Paris I was seeing signs of a new sort of politics emerging in Europe that I sensed posed a threat that could one day dovetail with what I saw as ominous signs from Moscow.

* * *

I ARRIVED IN Paris during the aftermath of the sad death of
Princess Diana in a car crash and France's first-ever home victory in the soccer World Cup. My daughter, Georgina, was born
there in August 2000, after her brothers, Matthew and Henry,
in London in 1996 and 1998 respectively. Laura, in the first
sign of her serious impending medical problems, needed a hip
replacement operation at the age of only thirty-five a year later.

We began our posting living in central Paris, in an apartment owned by the pop star Annie Lennox and rented by the
embassy, but we later moved to a large house ten miles up
the Seine on an island in the river near Bougival, the former
nineteenth-century home of the French impressionist painter
Auguste Renoir and the exiled Russian writer Ivan Turgenev.

The final year of my four-year posting—2002—saw two
events whose significance would only later become fully clear.
That year the majority of countries in the European Union
adopted the Euro as their currency, which most saw as a positive but a significant majority of Europeans—particularly in
the UK—perceived as an encroachment on individual national
sovereignty.

More significant yet was the shock result of the first round
of the French presidential election, which saw the then Socialist Party prime minister, Lionel Jospin, defeated in the first
round by the leader of the extreme right, Front National leader
Jean Marie Le Pen, who progressed to the second-round runoff
against the sitting center-right president, Jacques Chirac.

The three leading candidates had received a similar number
of votes in the initial round (19.8 percent for Chirac, 16.8 percent for Le Pen, and 16.1 percent for Jospin), though Chirac
went on easily to win the runoff (by 82 to 18 percent). But Le

Pen's success was a warning. It marked the beginning of the contagion in some of the more civilized and traditionally stable countries in Europe of the sort of populist authoritarianism that has since come to dominate and threaten the established postwar world order.

Le Pen's Front National was overtly xenophobic, clearly racist, protectionist, and anti-EU. It was, as I understood it, a resurfacing of France's periodic tendency to embrace the far right. During World War II the Vichy government collaborated with the Nazis. In the 1950s die-hard nationalists militated against French withdrawal from Algeria and plotted to overthrow and even assassinate Charles de Gaulle. Le Pen's party was also heir, further back, to the horrible anti-Semitism of the Dreyfus case in the late nineteenth century. The party subsequently changed its name to the Rassemblement National (RN) and it chose a new leader—Le Pen's daughter Marine—in the attempt to shed its racist past and present itself as more mainstream.

But its ties to authoritarianism were and remain deep—and transnational: it was caught accepting clandestine, illegal loans from Putin's Russia prior to the 2017 presidential election.

The headquarters of the Front National was located in Saint-Cloud, a wealthy suburb to the west of Paris, not far from where we lived. The building was nicknamed "Le Paquebot" on account of its resemblance to an ocean liner.

An embassy colleague and I decided to take a look at this epicenter of political disruption one evening between the two rounds of the presidential vote in spring 2002. It was not easy to find, and when we did locate the building we found it a rather unimpressive sight. It was a two-story gray construct surrounded by high barbed-wire fences and guarded by loud Alsatian dogs. There was little sign of life. It seemed squalid and slightly sinister.

Front National was a trailblazer for similar extreme right parties in Germany (the Alternative für Deutschland), Italy (Giorgia Meloni's Fratelli d'Italia), and Spain (Vox), as well as in Austria, Poland, Hungary, Slovakia, and nearly everywhere in Europe. Most observers, myself included, had assumed that the Eastern European countries would follow a politically liberal and free market evolutionary course in the period after the fall of the Berlin Wall in 1989. In many cases we were mistaken.

How far has Le Pen's 2002 revolution spread exactly? Consider this: people now take it for granted that the extreme right party in France will make it through to the runoff for the presidency in 2027, as it did again in 2022 (with 41.5 percent of the vote). That means it is now conceivable Marine Le Pen's RN actually could win power at the highest level, as well as entrench itself in the main legislature, the Assemblee Nationale, where it now has 89 seats out of 577 in total, which was an increase of 81 seats compared to the previous elections in 2017. It easily could end up holding the balance of power in a future coalition government. Its stance remains fundamentally pro-Russia and pro-Putin, and some of its leaders have even gone so far as to visit Russian illegally occupied Crimea in the years after Moscow's invasion of the peninsula in 2014. Ten years on, in June 2024, the RN won the most votes in the French elections to the European parliament, and Macron's decision to call a general election in response, raised the frightening prospect of their entering government at the national level for the first time.

The RN now represents a serious threat to liberal and tolerant republicanism in France and could even threaten the future of the EU. It is anti-NATO. Its clones in other European countries pose a similar threat. Putin has supported them in any way he can. And he will continue to do so. They are his proxy armies and fifth columns in the halls of power all over the continent.

Chapter 6

THE BEATING OF WINGS

DURING MY TIME in Paris, Putin was consolidating his power.

In the early 2000s he neutralized a potential threat—the oligarchs—and made them his loyal servants, primarily by having the richest and most powerful of them—Mikhail Khodorkovsky—arrested on charges of fraud and tax evasion, stripped of most of his assets, tried, convicted, sentenced, and sent to a brutal prison. The rest of the politically powerful, criminally connected billionaires all got the message and fell into line. Putin permitted them to continue to do business, to live overseas—many of them in London—and to become politically and socially powerful at home and abroad. In return, they knew never to challenge him politically.

Putin's corruption, antidemocratic impulses, and intolerance for dissent seemed to be growing rapidly. His critics increasingly met early and violent deaths. On October 7, 2006, a well-known journalist named Anna Politkovskaya, who had written about Russian human rights abuses and corruption in Chechnya, was shot dead in the lobby of her apartment building. October 7 happens to be Putin's birthday.

Earlier that year I had been appointed to lead the Russia

(reporting) desk in London. British intelligence, even more so than our Diplomatic Service, has always been focused on Russia and the Soviet Union as a priority. Working to recruit sources and produce intelligence on Russia, and to influence British government policy accordingly, has always been a great challenge and opportunity for them. It is effectively the professional equivalent of playing in the English (soccer) Premier League or, in US terms, the Super Bowl. Historically and culturally it has almost been a service within the Service. An elite service. The fact that I held this position has been previously widely reported in the media and US government investigative reports, so I feel able to acknowledge it here, but I am limited in what else I can say about my work at that time. But one incident, for me and for many, felt like the confirmation of all my fellow Russia hawks and I had been fearing.

* * *

ON FRIDAY NOVEMBER 3, 2006, I heard a rumor that a Russian defector in London named Sasha was claiming he had been poisoned.

"Sasha" was Alexander Litvinenko, a former KGB and FSB officer who had defected to the UK and was an important counterintelligence asset of the British government. While back in Russia and still an officer of the FSB, Litvinenko had publicly accused his FSB bosses—and by implication Putin—of ordering them to conduct assassinations and a kidnapping. Litvinenko had previously told Putin about corruption inside the FSB, news that Putin clearly did not want to hear, Litvinenko later said. He and his family had subsequently fled Russia, fearing for their lives.

Sasha's British intelligence case officer had visited him in the hospital. He had been admitted to Barnet General Hospital earlier that day after having fallen sick the previous Wednesday. He was vomiting and was already in agonizing pain.

Initially I thought the poisoning claims were far-fetched, as did many of my peers in government. When it came to Putin and his willingness to violate international norms, I was probably among the most hawkish people working on Russia in the British government at that point, but surely even Putin would not order the killing of his enemies on British soil. The Bulgarian secret service had famously murdered dissident Georgi Markov in 1978 on Waterloo Bridge by jabbing him with poison via a specially modified umbrella. But the Soviets themselves had never, as far as we knew, assassinated anyone in the UK. Putin wouldn't cross that line—would he?

However, it became clear within days that Litvinenko had indeed been poisoned—and almost certainly by Russian agents who had since returned to Moscow. I was one of the first to draw that conclusion.

Litvinenko was transferred from Barnet to University College Hospital's intensive care unit. Doctors and government scientists raced to identify the type of poison in his system so that they could know how best to treat him. His internal organs were shutting down, one after another. The incident had quickly become a national crisis as news leaked that a KGB defector was saying he had been poisoned and was getting sicker by the day.

My new role drew me into the investigation into his death— and the policy implications arising from it.

The security and intelligence services worked quietly while the Metropolitan Police conducted a more public investigation into what had happened. We learned quickly that Litvinenko had met two other former Russian security officials, Andrei

Lugovoi and Dmitry Kovtun, for tea in the bar at the Millennium Hotel in Grosvenor Square, very near the American embassy in central London. Litvinenko considered the men to be potentially useful business contacts, and he had judged them to be friendly. But he was now convinced that they had poisoned him. Both men had returned to Russia soon after meeting with Litvinenko.

During this time I attended the emergency Cabinet Office Briefing Rooms meetings—the forum for the UK government's crisis management—and dealt with the then Labour home secretary, John Reid, and other senior officials. "Chris, I know for you and your colleagues that this is personal, this is human, this is not just a policy issue and I understand," Reid told me after one such COBR meeting. Reid was not just thoughtful in his comment to me—he was right. This did feel personal. We had to figure out what had happened to Litvinenko and bring those responsible to justice.

The British government began to get intelligence that suggested the operation indeed had been ordered by the Kremlin. As always with intelligence, this was information that was steered first and foremost to ministers and policymakers. The police continued on with the forensic work.

Meanwhile Sasha was clearly dying and no one knew what was killing him. Eventually blood and urine samples were sent to Aldermaston, Britain's secret nuclear research facility in Berkshire, where, as it happened, my then father-in-law had worked throughout his career. Scientists there detected a small spike in the very unusual radiation when they analyzed the samples. One of the most experienced scientists immediately realized what was causing the spike: it was polonium-210. If you ingested it, he explained, you would die. This insight was the key to unlocking the case.

Soon after, investigators found traces of polonium-210 in the Millennium Hotel bar and in more than forty other locations. Litvinenko's wife, Marina, had to leave her home immediately. The trail of polonium-210 matched exactly locations visited by Lugovoi and Kovtun.

There is only one source for polonium-210 in Russia—the Avangard nuclear plant. It is tightly controlled by the Russian state.

The pieces had come together—and they were shocking. Russian agents had traveled on commercial flights, stayed in hotels in Germany and Britain, and had visited numerous other public places while carrying a radioactive poison produced in a secret Russian nuclear facility, a poison that would kill anyone who ingested it. They had come to the UK and had poisoned an enemy of the Russian president. Litvinenko had four months earlier written online that Putin was a pedophile, after the Russian president was pictured kissing the belly of a young boy. Litvinenko had also been investigating if the Kremlin was behind the bombings in 1999 of apartment buildings in Moscow and two other cities, another taboo subject and a red line for the regime. It seemed that Lugovoi and Kovtun had been operating under the orders of senior Russian officials and that they had come to London to silence a critic and take revenge on a traitor.

Understandably, our politicians did not initially know how to react. I remember sitting in a meeting with Margaret Beckett, then the foreign secretary. "I just can't believe that a member of the UN Security Council P5 is going to come to London and use radioactive poisons on people," she said.

She was told by us officials in the room that she needed to believe it.

I could see that ministers were struggling with the news

conceptually. I had sympathy for their shock—I had also initially dismissed the idea.

Putin, after all, had been on a state visit to the UK three years earlier, in June 2003. He was the first Russian leader to visit the UK in this capacity in more than 125 years. Prince Charles welcomed him at Heathrow Airport. During the trip Putin and the Queen rode together in a horse-drawn carriage. He slept at Buckingham Palace as her guest. She threw him a state banquet at Buckingham Palace. "We support your efforts to create a modern, prosperous and dynamic state, and we look forward to working with you on this and on many international questions on the basis of our shared values," the Queen told her guest.

Knowing what we did about Putin, the visit was hard to stomach, but the government considered it essential for the successful prosecution of the "war on terror" after 9/11. The United States and the United Kingdom wanted to create as broad an international coalition as possible in the pursuit of Islamist terrorists.

Three years later we were telling the foreign secretary that the Russians had done something they had never done before—attempt an assassination in the UK.

That attempt succeeded. On November 22 the scientists told Litvinenko's doctors what was poisoning their patient. Litvinenko died the following day.

* * *

THE BRITISH SECURITY and intelligence services continued to gather intelligence. Eventually it was overwhelming. The evidence was submitted to Ken Macdonald, then the director of public prosecutions. In 2007 he announced that the British government would try to extradite Lugovoi from Russia. We all knew that attempt would fail.

Lugovoi is currently a deputy in the Duma, the lower house of the Russian legislature. Kovtun, Lugovoi's childhood friend and suspected co-assassin, died of Covid-19 in 2022. No one in Britain mourned him, for sure.

The day after Litvinenko died, a nationalist member of the Duma said: "Last night Alexander Litvinenko died in a London hospital. The deserved punishment reached the traitor. I am confident that this terrible death will be a serious warning to traitors of all colors wherever they are located. In Russia, they do not pardon treachery." Later the same day Putin cryptically commented: "The people that have done this are not God, and Mr. Litvinenko is, unfortunately, not Lazarus."

Revenge had been duly taken. But why did the Russians kill Litvinenko in this elaborate way rather than just, say, shooting him?

I have two answers to offer. They are somewhat contradictory. One, both, or neither might be true. My first is that the killers were trying to silence an enemy and were trying to do it without being detected. It was a mixture of luck and genius that led to the scientist at Aldermaston identifying the poison as polonium-210. Radioactive traces of polonium-210 decay rapidly. They almost got away with what would have been a mystery killing.

But there's another answer: the planners of the operation knew that Lugovoi and Kovtun would quickly be identified as the chief suspects in the poisoning and that the news would ripple around the world. They wanted investigators to figure out that polonium-210 was the poison, precisely because it is produced in only one Russian facility and therefore the death of Litvinenko must have been a state-organized killing. And the message to all of Putin's foes would be clear: we will stop at nothing; we will hunt you wherever you are hiding; and we will use the might of the state to kill you, and in the most agonizing way possible.

If you shoot someone it doesn't send quite the same message.

* * *

FROM HIS DEATHBED Litvinenko delivered and signed a message of his own. It ends:

As I lie here I can distinctly hear the beating of wings of the angel of death. I may be able to give him the slip but I have to say my legs do not run as fast as I would like. I think, therefore, that this may be the time to say one or two things to the person responsible for my present condition.

You may succeed in silencing me but that silence comes at a price. You have shown yourself to be as barbaric and ruthless as your most hostile critics have claimed.

You have shown yourself to have no respect for life, liberty or any civilized value.

You have shown yourself to be unworthy of your office, to be unworthy of the trust of civilized men and women.

You may succeed in silencing one man but the howl of protest from around the world will reverberate, Mr. Putin, in your ears for the rest of your life. May God forgive you for what you have done, not only to me but to beloved Russia and its people.

Alexander Litvinenko
November 21, 2006

Those were strong, prophetic words. But to my mind, even Sasha Litvinenko on his deathbed understated the level of threat that Vladimir Putin posed to the West and to global stability.

And yet his warning was largely ignored by Western policymakers and business leaders. They should have distanced themselves from Russia and Putin. They did not. And that helps explain why we find ourselves where we are nearly two decades later.

Chapter 7

PASTURES NEW

THE CHIEF EXECUTIVE of the bank where I had just given a Russia briefing pulled me aside. "You do realize," he said quietly, "we can't task you, but if you set up in business with your skill set you would make a big success out of it."

The bank CEO was suggesting, it seemed to me, that I consider quitting my government job to set up in business.

It was 2007, and I had just given one of the many presentations to major British companies that the government often provides. These briefings serve an important national security purpose, helping significant pillars of the British economy to anticipate threats and understand global security concerns. The flow of information, data, and intelligence is two-way; business leaders pass on information they have gleaned that could be important for national security reasons. It benefits the government greatly; and it also means that individual intelligence officers and other officials see the inner workings of the private sector and form relationships with senior business executives.

The CEO's comment was not the first time I had thought

about starting my own company. As early as 2003 my friend and colleague Chris Burrows had raised the prospect with me and we had discussed it, on and off, thereafter. At that point we both worked in staff recruitment and training, and so our somewhat idle musings focused on starting a personnel management firm. Chris, who was then my boss, and I had worked hard to improve the screening and vetting processes so that the government would hire the people most suitable for the job. We introduced more psychological profiling so that our recruiters would, as soon as an interview with a candidate was over, immediately give the candidate marks for personality traits. This instant screening was designed to filter out people who evidenced, for example, too much self-regard, brittleness, or a thin skin. Chris and I thought we could apply these learnings to the broader corporate recruitment world.

Those conversations came to an end when Chris took a foreign posting in India in 2005. But they had resumed when he returned to the UK in 2007. This time we began kicking around the idea of leaving to start a business intelligence firm. Some of our colleagues had left to join large British energy companies and banks as their in-house intelligence heads. Their role: to do due diligence on potential business partners; to assess the risk of doing business in certain jurisdictions; to help unblock channels of communication overseas; to try to discover, legally, secrets about governments, rivals, competitors. And they were, we knew, getting paid much more than we were.

The British bank executive's comment stayed with me for weeks afterward. The clients are out there, I told Chris, and we might do better if we formed our own company and worked with multiple clients rather than get hired by a single multinational, as some of our colleagues had. He agreed.

I had worked for twenty-two years as a government servant.

It's probably no great secret that government can be incredibly bureaucratic, slow, overlegalistic, and underresourced. As head of the Russia desk, I was running a team that was tasked with giving the government—the prime minister included—the best insight into our longest-standing rival, and often adversary, on the world stage. And yet I was often told who could be on my team, what they were and were not permitted to do, and what we should be doing and focusing on, by people in government who knew nothing about intelligence or even, frankly, much about Russia. Intelligence officers traditionally had been—and certainly had seen themselves—as rule-breakers and even pirates. They were the maverick fighter pilots who had to make life-and-death decisions in real time, and if that meant occasionally ignoring regulations, then that was just how it had to be. Their bosses had been like tolerant air marshals, letting their pilots lead from the front. That era had come to an end in recent years. The head counts that seemed regularly to grow were in the legal and human resources departments. The organization seemed to have plenty of tinkers, tailors, and soldiers— but the others felt they had been pushed to one side.

That change was, in part, a result of the shameful role in the Iraq War debacle. And that was another factor pushing me away from government service.

The Labour government of Tony Blair had exploited the British intelligence community in its attempt to make the case for invading Iraq. The political neutrality of the Service should be unimpeachable and must be respected by whichever party is in power in Britain. Blair and his aides demanded that British intelligence find evidence to support their political case. And senior figures at the Service obliged. During the buildup to it, an old friend of mine was on the receiving end of orders from above to make sure the intelligence backed up the case for war in Iraq. My friend was arguably the best-informed person within the Service about what was really going on there and whether or not Saddam Hussein had in fact managed to continue producing weapons of mass destruction. Two months before the war a well-placed friend told me that the case for war was "a crock of shit." He and his deputy resigned from their positions, although they would remain within government service.

Somewhat ironically given my strongly negative views on the Iraq War, a few years later Chris Burrows and I were invited to a reception at Tony Blair's London house to mark the launch of his wife Cherie's new consultancy practice. Given my political curiosity, this was too good an opportunity to miss. I had voted for Blair in 1997 and 2001 and, although maybe unfashionable nowadays, thought and still believe he was right about the earlier military interventions in the former Yugoslavia and Sierra Leone and the importance of Britain's relationship with Europe. During the reception, Blair and I had an interesting conversation about the emerging cyber threat and whether the West should be prepared to develop and threaten to use its cyber capabilities offensively to protect us from being attacked by Russia and China in what has been termed "the gray zone" of conflict. Given what has transpired since, Blair's interest and concern about this was prescient and, like me, he was hawkish on the issue. Many in Britain who remember it now long for the days of optimism and change that characterized Tony Blair's early period in office. I know I do.

But given the Iraq weapons of mass destruction intelligence debacle in 2003, the Service was forced to change after the war. The exposure of its involvement in supporting the government in justifying the calamitous Iraq War tragedy led to a new era of oversight, hierarchy, systems, and caution. Those changes were entirely understandable given how the Service had allowed itself to be politicized by the Blair government, but for many still working there it was no longer the organization that they had fallen in love with. It was now becoming a risk-averse bureaucracy where everyone seemed to be looking over their shoulder the whole time.

Added to which, the organization was focused on counter-terrorism, given the salience and threat of Islamist extremism at the time. I did some work on Iraq for several months in 2005; we were engaged in promoting Sunni political integration, trying to bring that community back into the process, through election participation.

I watched during those years as resources were taken away from our diplomatic and intelligence operations on Russia. And then I experienced this firsthand from 2006 to 2009.

Putin's power had grown in the six years since he had become Russia's president and his behavior continually worsened. The public furor around the Litvinenko assassination did not seem to have chastened him at all. On the contrary, he seemed emboldened by it. Putin had sent killers carrying a radioactive poison to the heart of London; the assassins had escaped; the target had died an agonizing and public death, sending a message to the world about what happened if you dared to betray Putin; and Putin and Russia had shrugged and essentially gotten through it without any meaningful consequences. It was a major win for Putin, at least in his eyes. He increasingly felt that he could strike blows at the West, and at his enemies, without paying any meaningful price.

It was little surprise to me then when Russia invaded Georgia in 2008.

I received a call from an official named Katherine, who

worked in the private office of a top-level policymaker, asking me to brief him on the Russian invasion. I knew Katherine by sight and by her good reputation, but we had not spoken before. I knew her boss well, however, from my Moscow posting. He was a Russianist like myself, and we should have had a meeting of minds. At the appointed time I went up to his office and was met in the anteroom by Katherine. She showed me straight in to the boss.

Unfortunately, Katherine's boss and I did not agree on Russia. He believed that Putin could still be reasoned with. I saw Putin as an enemy of the UK and the West—and I was convinced his policies and behavior would worsen. I was not sure how much more evidence we needed of this after the apartment bombings of 1999, which we firmly believed were ordered by the then prime minister Putin, a man prepared to kill 307 of his own citizens in order to secure his control over the country; after Putin described, in 2005, the end of the Soviet Union as the "greatest geopolitical catastrophe of the twentieth century"; after the prosecution of the dissenting oligarch Mikhail Khodorkovsky and the seizure of his oil and gas company by the state; after the shooting and killing of Anna Politkovskaya and other journalists and critics of Putin; after the Litvinenko assassination; after Putin brought his black Labrador to a public meeting in 2007 with then German chancellor Angela Merkel, who he knew had a phobia of dogs, at a time when Germany and Russia were in dispute about energy supplies; and now after the attack on the pro-West state of Georgia. I felt the West, and certainly the British government, should have long since moved on from President George W. Bush's assessment of Putin in 2001: "I looked the man in the eye. I found him to be very straightforward and trustworthy . . . I was able to get a sense of his soul."

The judgment of this and other top British officials on Russia, however, worried me and felt stuck in the era of Bill Clinton's and George Bush's naïve, wishful thinking; Clinton had also hoped Putin would become a partner rather than an adversary. As head of the Russia (reporting) desk I felt that I was increasingly unable to do my duty as I interpreted it. Putin was a generational threat, and an ever-worsening one, and we needed to treat him as such.

All of this further nudged me toward a future where I would be my own boss.

I had known Chris Burrows for many years. He was a talented professional—a skilled linguist, an instinctive reader of human beings, and highly emotionally intelligent. I do not think the latter is my strong suit. I can be a bit literal sometimes; I take people at face value; I can misread them. One example that pains and confuses me: there are friendships in my life that have come to a sudden end and to this day I feel utterly baffled as to why this happened. Saddened, certainly, but also mystified. Chris, I suspect, would fully understand what feelings and dynamics were in play during such situations.

Chris was a great networker, and that would prove invaluable when we came to look for clients. And he had webs of very well-placed and reliable contacts.

What I brought to the table, I suppose, was my own network of contacts, my deep experience of Russia, and a bit of a relentless, determined streak. I have run six marathons and twenty half marathons, and I have completed sixteen triathlons; the repetitive, focused, somewhat spartan nature of hard tasks appeals to me. I like challenges, even when I know they will cause discomfort.

I also found myself drawn to business development—the

craft of finding and bringing in new clients. Part of that interest came from meeting and interacting with the sort of people
intelligence professionals naturally encounter in the course of
their work. Many of those encounters were with people like the
British bank CEO mentioned above. Potential clients like
that were relatively mainstream. Others were, let us say, less
orthodox.

* * *

I MET ONE such prospective client at a dinner in London in
June 2007. The encounter did not ever lead to new business
once we had started our private company, but it was an odd
foreshadowing of events to come in my life.

The investor Nat Rothschild—the scion of the British
banking family and recently ennobled after his father Jacob's
death—invited me that summer to a dinner he was throwing
at Annabel's, the private members club in Berkeley Square in
London. He was an active investor with a keen financial and
political interest in the former Soviet Union; he and I had had
lunch in Farnham in April that year, and we had discussed the
economic and political situation in Russia and its neighbors. As
I have said, it was part of the job of intelligence professionals
and diplomats to meet with senior business leaders. This fell
into that category.

The dinner at Annabel's did too—although it was somewhat more glamorous. At our first meal in Farnham, Nat and
I had dined in a modest restaurant, surrounded by quiet suburban residents of Surrey. The Annabel's dinner took place in
a basement dining room whose walls were lined with some
of the most expensive bottles of wine in the world, and the
guests included David Cameron, then the Conservative Party

leader and soon to be prime minister. Other guests around the table included Strobe Talbott, a former US deputy secretary of state. Billionaires and former government figures made up the rest of the guest list. The declared purpose of the dinner was for American players in the academic think tank sector, both executives and donors, to impart their knowledge of the private funding of political research to their counterparts in Europe, which lacked such a tradition of private academic philanthropy.

At dinner I was seated between James Wolfensohn, former director of the World Bank, and a twenty-five-year-old Ivanka Trump, daughter of the American reality TV star and business-man. Up until that point I knew very little about the Trump family, other than that Trump was a rather brash and outspoken New York property developer whom my American relatives had talked about in the past from time to time.

I assumed that Nat seated me next to her because, as she explained over dinner, she and her family were interested in doing business in Russia. She asked me about how best to sell her jewelry line there. She was keen to identify potential business partners in Moscow. She also said that she and her family were exploring real estate investments and partnerships in Russia and she was eager to know if I could suggest potential partners. In 2007, this was a perfectly legitimate line of inquiry—Russia was a market for nearly every international business—and so I said I would be happy to help. I was not, to be clear, scouting for possible business for my future venture while taking a government salary; I was simply doing what government professionals often did—helping Western businesses in Russia. And at that time Orbis was only a vague notion.

We exchanged business cards and kept in touch via email.

"Let me know if you meet anyone that would be a good

prospective partner for us," she emailed me in the summer of 2008.

I said I would. In the months and years to come I made some suggestions of potential business partners for her and the Trump Organization in Russia and the other countries of the Commonwealth of Independent States (CIS). After I left government service and started Orbis my goal in keeping in touch with Ivanka was indeed to turn the Trump Organization into a paying client. The company clearly had deep pockets and a desire to work in Russia—and that combination made it a clear prospect for Orbis.

Nothing ever came of it—and indeed the Trump Organization, as I would find out some years later, mysteriously never found a business partner in Russia for a real estate project, in spite of Donald Trump's numerous visits to the country. Ivanka and I kept in touch. I saw her a couple of times in New York. On November 3, 2010, I met with her for an hour in her office in Trump Tower. As I did with all meetings that could lead to business, I wrote it up directly afterward. She is identified in my memo, which is dated November 8, as "IT":

> After a discussion of our respective life and career trajectories in the last 18 months IT asked about Orbis. I explained our business model; our niche areas of work and expertise; our wish to expand our US private sector client base.
>
> IT responded positively. We had a long chat about Russia, including the demise of LUZHKOV and the climax to the KHODORKOVSKY trial, on which she was impressively up to speed. She mentioned her interest in PROKHOROV, the rather feckless oligarch who has bought a US basketball team. However she said her

appetite for (investment) risk did not extend as far as Russia on account of the adverse political and legal environment there. China was different . . . She said [the Trump Organization] were looking for reliable local Chinese partners with whom to do hotel and other real estate projects.

I write in the report that Ivanka brought in Serena Rakhlin, her new VP for strategic planning and hotel business development, and said that Serena would be our point of contact going forward if there was to be any business between Orbis and the Trump Organization. I told them that we had a good associate in Hong Kong who could help them with due diligence.

I also noted that halfway through the meeting Donald Trump Jr. came in with his wife and baby son. I held the baby for a moment or two.

My report concludes:

Disregarding the depressing tendency of mega-rich contacts to expect Orbis favors and briefing free of charge, I do think this one has legs. The Trump projects in China and elsewhere will be big and prestigious and the potential for spin-off elsewhere and recommendations to other wealthy US clients and corporations should be good. We shall need to work this one very carefully with [the Orbis Hong Kong associate] and ensure his commitment to it and us in the process. A promising development.

By that stage Chris and I would have been pleased at the time if the Trump Organization had joined our roster of clients.

That didn't happen, and eventually Ivanka and I lost contact.

None of this is of much significance in and of itself. But, as I mentioned, Trump's allies would later claim that I had a vendetta against him. The truth is much less interesting: I had barely heard of him—and his daughter and I saw each other as potentially helpful on a business level and were friends for a while. The rather more interesting interactions with Trump and his family were to come later.

* * *

THROUGHOUT 2008 CHRIS and I talked about our possible private business plans almost constantly. We felt we had served our country and done our duty. I sensed that I probably had some promotions ahead of me if I stayed in the Service, but I also knew I was unlikely to get the top job. Chris is six years older than I am, and he felt that he had perhaps gone as far as he was going to go in the government.

And frankly, we wanted to seize a business opportunity and build more comfortable lives for our families. Chris's partner was pregnant. I had three school-age children. Laura had developed health problems, and I was the sole breadwinner.

There was a question that ricocheted around the government in those days: do you think you would be able to make it in the private sector? Some people asked that question in quiet, curious inquiry. Others weighed it as a mixture of a goad and a dare. That got under Chris's skin. I was feeling impatient. We began seriously to explore our options.

My then brother-in-law, Nick, was a successful entrepreneur. He helped Chris and me with the business plan and a start-up loan. Nick became a director in the new company and was always there whenever Chris and I needed help in how to do the basics.

By the end of 2008 we felt we were ready. Chris and I said to each other: Let's do this. We handed in our resignations in 2009 and then spent several months haggling with the Cabinet Office about what we would and would not be permitted to do once we'd left. They did not want to make it easy for people like us to leave, otherwise a brain drain might have followed. And, I suspect, they did not yearn for us to succeed once we had left—for the same reason. The last piece of the jigsaw to fall into place, surprisingly perhaps, was the name of our new company. It took several months to choose "Orbis," partly because it meant "the World," and we were striving for as wide a geographical reach as possible, but also because it was easy to pronounce and memorize in the majority of the world's leading languages, something which is important commercially and more difficult to achieve than you might think.

Chris and I decided to keep the firm's early focus, however, on Russia and the former Soviet states, many of which were now part of the CIS. I had expertise in that area. Russia also presented more business opportunities in London at that time than any other part of the world; every major British company wanted help navigating the baffling, treacherous Russian business world. And London was already full of wealthy Russians who battled each other in the marketplace, in the courts, and in the gossip pages of British newspapers. There would be clients among this pool, we felt, who would want our expertise and help.

Like many middle-aged parents, Chris and I, and our wives, had decided to raise our families outside the expensive, intense bustle of London. I lived in Farnham, in Surrey. Chris lived thirty miles away in Winchester. We wanted to keep costs down, and neither of us liked commuting to London every day. So the original Orbis Business Intelligence office was not in a glamorous central London town house but rather was located in a low-ceilinged rented office in the village-like center of Farnham.

If you'd happened across our original office, you would have probably thought that Chris and I were a couple of local insurance brokers rather than former senior intelligence professionals who had collectively spent more than four decades working in the heart of government.

We knew we had taken a huge risk. And we knew we had to make it work right from the start. We only had a few months' runway of cash. We had no margin for error or delay.

* * *

ON SEPTEMBER 8, 2009, two weeks into our new lives as business owners, I came home midafternoon from a trip to Oxford, where I had had a meeting. I opened the front door. The house was unusually quiet. Laura would normally have been at home. There was not even a note on the kitchen counter. I tried to call her and then, when there was no answer, I texted. She did not respond, and I started to feel anxious.

Eventually one of Laura's friends called me. She had become sick at lunch, at a friend's house, and was now in the hospital, at Frimley Park. Her friends had driven her there.

I raced to the hospital. The doctor there explained that she had septicemia—blood poisoning.

In the mid-2000s Laura had somehow contracted hepatitis. After that her health was never the same. The previous week Laura had had what we suspected was swine flu, but we thought she had recovered.

I do not know what caused the septicemia, but her body's defenses must have been depleted over the years and perhaps by her recent bout of illness.

Her condition deteriorated rapidly. Initially Laura was in a normal hospital bed. Soon after that, however, she had a fall and was moved to intensive care. Then she was in an induced coma. By Monday morning of the following week—September 14—a doctor was explaining to me that my wife had only a 50 percent chance of surviving. And then the following day the odds changed again; they said she was now unlikely to survive this illness.

It is a terrible shock to lose your partner, especially so young. But I knew that losing your mother at a young age would be exponentially worse. I had three young children who were about to experience that impossible grief. I tried to imagine the pain they would soon feel—the immediate sharp stab and then the sadness that would be with them for the rest of their lives. I found it hard to grasp, and, in truth, I will never be able fully to understand what my beloved children have been through.

I had a decision to make. Should I bring them in to say goodbye to their mother or were they too young? Would it scar them not to see her? I don't know to this day if I did the best thing for them all, but I decided that the two youngest should not—my elder son, Matthew, though, then thirteen, would want to say goodbye. I don't know what he said to Laura and I have never asked him; it was a private moment between a son and his mother.

I was holding Laura's hand as she passed away. It was around 3 p.m. on Tuesday, September 15, 2009. She was forty-three.

The children were at school. Matthew had known that Laura might die. The other two had no idea. The rain was falling heavily that afternoon, ensnarling traffic. It should have been a twenty-minute drive home from the hospital, but I got back about an hour later. I sat in the car, crawling along the familiar road to Farnham, staring through the windshield wipers, knowing what lay ahead.

Telling them their mother had died was the worst thing I have ever had to do.

Chapter 8

FOUL PLAY

I COULD NOT afford to go to pieces after Laura's death.

I was now a single father to three small children. Making a success of the business suddenly felt like something I had to achieve for their sake. It needed to be the bedrock for their future. If I had gone under then, the business would have failed, Chris would have struggled, and I would have had no way of supporting my family. It was like we were all rock climbers roped together on a cliff face.

At one point during my time visiting the hospital, and as Laura's condition had worsened, I had spoken to Chris on the phone. He too was in a hospital. His partner, Claire, had gone into premature labor. "What the hell have we done?" we said to each other, referring to the fact that we had just left salaried jobs with guaranteed pensions due within a few years.

I had to be organized and focused. We held Laura's funeral in early October. After that I felt winter begin to close in, and there were days when I was pretty low. My focus was on the children—but I also had to develop the business.

Orbis Business Intelligence had three clients from the outset.

I needed to make them feel they were getting their money's worth.

One of those clients was a British confectionary company. Shortly before I left Crown Service I gave a talk, as is common for senior officials, to a new entry class. In the bar after, one of the new recruits asked me what I was planning to do when I left Crown Service. I mentioned Chris's and my plans to start Orbis. The recruit said that his uncle was head of security at the confectionery company and that I should talk to him.

I met with his uncle, and it quickly transpired that the company had a problem in Russia. It owned and ran two factories there, and the company had fallen out with the governor of a region where one of the factories was located. This was proving to be profoundly unhelpful for their business in Russia overall. They wanted to understand why the governor was angry with them and how they might solve whatever problem it was that had turned the governor against them. I told the young official's uncle that we could help him. We engaged our contacts in Russia, interceded with people close to the governor, and made their situation more tolerable than it was before.

The second client—who came to us through a reputable law firm—was someone whom my critics and enemies now like to wheel out at every opportunity by way of illustrating that Orbis allegedly has no principles and will take money from the very people whose interests we claim to be working against. This was Oleg Deripaska, a Russian oligarch who was at one point the richest person in his country. He has now been sanctioned by the American and British governments for his role in supporting Putin's invasion of Ukraine. For many years Deripaska was one of the oligarchs closest to the Kremlin, although he has publicly criticized the war in Ukraine and our sources have always told us he is part of the Yeltsin family group, not Putin's St. Petersburg–based inner circle.

We were introduced to Deripaska-related work by another ex-colleague who was working with a British client who knew one of the oligarch's lawyers. Deripaska was in a commercial dispute with another Russian, Mikhail Cherney, over owner-ship of his aluminum business, RUSAL, and his lawyer wanted intelligence. The lawyer needed someone—us—to do some digging to help support Deripaska's legal arguments. Cherney claimed Deripaska had stolen the business from him, but on all counts Cherney was a more brutal and dubious operator than Deripaska. He also had an Interpol Red Notice over his head, which spoke volumes and meant he could no longer enter Britain. He holed up in Israel, which was effectively protecting him. (He is now an Israeli citizen.)

Times were different then. Deripaska was planning to float his company on the London Stock Exchange before doing so in 2010 on the Hong Kong exchange. He was controversial even then—he had, after all, won the so-called aluminum wars in post-Soviet Russia, a violent struggle for control of that vast industry. But that did not stop powerful and influential people in the West from doing business with him. Most famously, in the summer of 2008 Deripaska and Nat Rothschild, whom we have encountered earlier in this story, hosted the then shadow chancellor of the Exchequer George Osborne and EU Trade Commissioner Peter Mandelson on Deripaska's yacht in Corfu. The optics were not great, but tellingly, Mandelson kept his job and Osborne became chancellor in 2010. At the time, the world showed little concern for how Russia's oligarchs had come by their wealth, nor was there much concern about the degree of political influence they enjoyed in Western countries like Britain.

I met Deripaska only once, in New York in 2015. Chris and I had been keen to deal with Deripaska's lawyers rather than the oligarch himself, as far as it was possible. But in 2015 I was asked to meet him directly by America's Federal Bureau of Investigation, with whom by that stage we had a long-standing and close commercial relationship. The FBI wanted to engage Deripaska as an informant, and they wanted my help in that effort. The oligarch had been refused entry to the United States for several years because the American government suspected him of having links to organized crime. This restriction had been hurting his attempts to secure financial support from leading American banks. On this occasion he was traveling to New York for the UN General Assembly on a Russian diplomatic visa. The Americans wanted a chat.

We met in the Manhattan offices of EN+, Deripaska's holding company. In private, we knew Deripaska was contemptuous of Putin. One trusted contact reported that in a private conversation Deripaska's views on Putin and Russia and my own views had been only "a cigarette paper's width apart."

Deripaska was primarily a businessman and was uninterested in the sort of aggressive Russian nationalism that drove Putin, who he knew was leading his country into trouble. He shared these thoughts with me and the FBI, and he was happy to maintain a dialogue with the Americans, though declined to become any kind of controlled asset of the FBI. (It is entirely possible, of course, that Deripaska was playing to the audience when he was critical of Putin to the FBI, me, and others, but I doubt it.)

I did not know at the outset that Deripaska had, in 2005, hired an American political consultant named Paul Manafort, who entered into a contract to help the pro-Russian Ukrainian regime of Viktor Yanukovych improve its international standing. The partnership continued for years, with Manafort working to help elect Yanukovych to the Ukrainian presidency in 2010. Deripaska and Manafort later fell out, and in 2014 Deripaska sued Manafort and his partner, Rick Gates, claiming they had defrauded him of millions of dollars. Two years later, with Deripaska still pursuing him in court, Manafort most unexpectedly became the chair of the Trump presidential campaign. The person now running the Trump campaign had deep ties to Putin's Russia.

* * *

OUR THIRD INITIAL client was also Russia-related. My old friend Neil Sherlock was a partner at the Big Four accounting firm KPMG. His former assistant was married to a man named Andy Anson, who was the chief executive of the company formed to pursue the English Football Association's bid to land the 2018 FIFA World Cup. Neil had met Andy at a party, and they had discussed how the England campaign to host the tournament was going. We're doing well, Andy had told Neil, but we can't get any sense of what is going on with the competing Russia bid. I know whom you should be talking to, Neil told him—Chris Steele.

There was much at stake. The English bid had the backing of the UK government, Prince William, David Beckham, and many other prominent figures. Winning the World Cup would be a huge boost to British prestige. At the same time, the United States was competing to secure the rights to host the 2022 World Cup; its main rival was the Gulf state of Qatar. Both campaigns were conducted simultaneously, and the voting would take place on the same day in December 2010.

We began looking into what the Russians were doing behind the scenes to help secure a majority of the votes of the twenty-two members of the FIFA committee that would make the decisions about who would host the 2018 and 2022 tournaments.

We hired what's known as a collector, or "head agent," to obtain the required reporting. A collector is a subcontractor who will have relevant sources in a country and who will likely travel to the target country, or countries, to meet with those sources and potentially recruit new ones. The subsources and the collector form what is called a source network. These networks can be deployed repeatedly for different assignments, and very often the more you use a source network, the better it performs. But they do not last forever. I've found that primary sources—the collectors—tend to have a shelf life of about ten years. After that their lives move on, their sources dry up, they find something else to do, or they simply become less reliable or effective at getting you the intelligence you want. But for this particular job we had an excellent collector—a Russian.

This individual and his subsources began to report that Russia was bribing officials, doing whatever it took to win. Putin's oligarchs were suborning FIFA executive committee members, our sources reported. Then deputy prime minister Igor Sechin, they said, was believed to have traveled to the Gulf state of Qatar to agree that the two countries would vote for the other's respective and successive World Cup bids. Sechin, to this day one of Putin's closest aides, was closely involved in the campaign, as was then deputy Russian premier Igor Shuvalov and also the well-known soccer-loving oligarch Roman Abramovich.

On December 2, 2010, the FIFA executive committee met in Zurich to vote. In the first round of the 2018 voting Russia won nine votes. England won two and was eliminated. In the second round Russia secured a majority, with thirteen votes, and had the prize that the Kremlin badly wanted. In the 2022 voting, Qatar prevailed, beating the United States 14 to 8 in the final round of voting. Two autocratic petrostates had prevailed over Western democracies, a sign of the new world disorder to come.

When news of the voting broke, I felt surprisingly angry. This was not just a matter of which country got to host sporting events; it was an international conspiracy at the heart of one of the most high-profile, feel-good sectors of the economy. It was epic cheating before a ball had even been kicked.

I had met an FBI agent named Mike Gaeta at a conference in Oxford in 2009. Mike, whom I liked, was still based in the FBI's New York Office as head of their Eurasian Joint Organized Crime Squad. We were no longer working for Andy Anson and the Football Association—the bid was now lost, so the contract ended—but I did not feel like letting the matter rest. And we had retained all the reports and intelligence we had collected for the FA 2018 bid.

We also were in touch with the great campaigning sports journalist Andrew Jennings, who wrote books on the subject and pursued FIFA corruption like a terrier. He subsequently helped the FBI after we had introduced them. Nicknamed "Dirty Raincoat" by his detractors, on account of his rather disheveled appearance, Jennings was a brave and dogged huntsman in pursuit of his corrupt prey. He used to surprise then FIFA president Sepp Blatter by lying in wait for him and literally jumping out of the bushes to ask him difficult questions.

As a private citizen I no longer had direct access to the British security services, but to be honest, the British do not have the same resources, legal reach, and desire that the Americans do when it comes to investigating complicated international criminal enterprises. The FBI has a long history of taking on such cases in part because of the global dominance of the

American banking and financial systems and in part because of the Bureau's legal remit over any transactions in US dollars worldwide. If you are doing business, or committing financial crimes, anywhere in the world you are almost inevitably going to pass money through the American banking system. If you are breaking the law when you do that, then you are almost certainly breaking American federal law, and that makes you a legitimate target for the FBI, wherever in the world you are based. So, with client approval, I reached out to Mike and asked him if he would like to discuss specific reporting Orbis had collected on possible illegal activity surrounding the World Cup bids.

Before long we were having regular meetings with the FBI on FIFA corruption and the World Cup. I shared with them numerous reports that our collector had delivered. The reporting we provided was from sensitive Russian and other sources; they included top Russian leadership figures discussing state-sponsored corruption to win the 2018 bid and a lot else, including details of some of the specific bribes paid.

This might be a good moment at which to make a pivotal point about intelligence reporting. The purpose of intelligence gathering is to collect as much information as possible and to present it to political or business decision-makers—always with caveats and a discussion about how reliable the information likely is, and where it came from. It is not—and is never presented as—always 100 percent accurate. No one with any experience who produces or consumes intelligence reports expects the information to be much more than about 70 percent accurate—and that is on a good day. Intelligence reports are not usually evidence to be used in court. They contain credible information that either is true or might be true; and in all instances it is information that the gatherers feel ought to be passed on to what are essentially the policymakers or decision takers.

This is especially true when it comes to Russia. To prove that Vladimir Putin ordered the 2023 murder of mercenary leader Yevgeny Prigozhin, for example, would be almost impossible. There is no piece of paper ordering the murder (which was, of course, at the very least approved by Putin). There was probably not an explicit conversation. It would have been informal. It would have been in a sauna perhaps. That is how these people work. Years ago Lyudmila Matthews taught me a phrase in Russian that means "it all ends in water." In other words, everything dissolves without trace and is deniable.

No one in Russia knows all of what is going on, even Putin. If you were a foreign intelligence service and you wanted to find out all the government secrets in Britain you would aim to recruit a key person like the cabinet secretary or national security advisor, and if you were successful, you would have nearly all of what you needed. You cannot do that in Russia. Senior officials and political and military leaders do not trust each other. They are all consistently lying to each other. It is impossible to get universal or holistic (as opposed to high-quality fragmented) intelligence penetration in Russia. So you collect widely and relentlessly and you provide context and leads to the decision-makers who are the ultimate audience for the intelligence.

Those decision-makers are usually in one of three categories.

The first is the entity that has commissioned the reporting—in other words, a government agency or a private client. These are the people paying for the intelligence to be collected.

The second is law enforcement. Private intelligence gatherers will sometimes pass on reporting to law enforcement agencies, often free of charge. But at that point it becomes incumbent upon those investigators to do their own research and to firm up the facts, because ultimately their information needs to be 99 percent solid in order to persuade juries and judges of the truth of a case.

The third destination for intelligence reporting is a less official one—journalists, activists, and politicians who are not in government but who can apply pressure and influence, and generate publicity. This passing on of what is generally secret information can happen for numerous reasons—manipulation, a crisis of conscience, political animus—but it should always come with a health warning: the information is not 100 percent solid so please take it, build on it, confirm it, and live with the consequences of publishing it. Where we think it is necessary, we apply caveats. For example, we shall tell a client when we believe a source is trying to "influence as well as inform."

In the case of the FIFA intelligence, the professionals at the FBI understood perfectly well that they fell into the second category and that they would have to confirm the information themselves if they were going to indict anyone. You cannot base criminal indictments on the work of others—on what is essentially hearsay.

We helped them more than private intelligence professionals usually do: I introduced them to some of our sources. But then we stepped back. We had done what we felt was our moral duty. We had helped the FBI and now it was up to them to pursue criminal investigations if they felt our leads and their ensuing work would be solid enough to obtain convictions.

They were relentless. In May 2015 the FBI indicted fourteen FIFA officials and associates on charges of racketeering, wire fraud, and money laundering. The alleged crimes extended far beyond Russia, and in fact most of the targets of the investigation were from Latin America. Other countries subsequently initiated investigations into corruption in football in their own jurisdictions. The scandal spread to the Middle East, Africa, the United States, and Europe. The Swiss authorities began an investigation into the 2018 and 2022 bids (FIFA is based in Zurich).

Noticeably missing from the people who were indicted were any Russian officials. They had all returned to Russia and remain there today. The Kremlin claimed all the computer data from their 2018 bid team had been destroyed after they had won the competition. This is unlikely, to say the least. The Russian officials involved know that if they venture abroad they would almost certainly be arrested and brought to justice.

The US federal investigation was one of the most broad-ranging and successful conducted by the Obama administration's Department of Justice. And it cemented my faith in the FBI and, evidently, theirs in me.

The FBI had become a significant client for Orbis. In the years after Mike Gaeta and I had our first conversation about corruption in world soccer, Orbis had provided many dozens of reports for the FBI. Those reports had been passed on under the table, free of charge. But in 2013 we decided to formalize the arrangement, getting approval from the British government. Our work for the FBI after that was paid.

It's not broadly known that the FBI often hires outside contractors to augment its work. The Bureau has limitations as an intelligence-gathering agency, especially overseas. In many respects it is a slow, lumbering, bureaucratic, and rule-bound organization—and like all government agencies it does not pay very well. It is also simply not an intelligence service, but rather primarily a law enforcement agency. There are limits on what it is permitted to do, and to its foreign experience, capabilities, and resources. So the Bureau hired Orbis repeatedly over the next several years to work on multiple projects. We had sources where they had few, if any—particularly in Russia.

Most of our communication was with Mike Gaeta, but we had occasional contact with other FBI agents. The Bureau's London-based agents used to come and pay us in cash. It was a curious arrangement: the agents often did not know what they were paying for, and they would always come in pairs, presumably because they were not permitted to handle such large amounts of money on their own.

To us, the FBI was a good source of business and one that was aligned with our values. Even though we were now in business for ourselves, Chris and I were united on a key point: if, during the course of our work for private clients, we came across evidence of wrongdoing or criminal activity we would always try to pass that information on—usually sanitized for source protection—to agencies or relevant Western governments, including the UK, the US, France, and Germany. This does not make us unusually ethical. Most of us, if we witness a crime, feel duty bound to share that information with the police. It is not much different, in my opinion, with intelligence leads.

And so during those years we also passed on numerous reports to the State Department about Russia's actions in Ukraine, which it first invaded in 2014. We sent these in pro bono through my friend and close associate Jon Winer, who was working for the State Department at the time. He passed them on to Victoria Nuland, who was then the assistant secretary of state for Russia and Central Eurasia.

These reports were paid for by a private client who wanted regular updates on and insights into the conflict for commercial reasons. The client used the information to make investment decisions. The client agreed with us that the reports should be provided to the US government because they might be helpful. It would not be right for Orbis and the client to keep them to ourselves, we felt. So we sent the US dozens of reports on the evolving conflict in Ukraine, and we continued passing this intelligence to them until 2016. All through this period we had great feedback on the value and reliability of our Russia-Ukraine reporting from the officials in the State Department who had access to it. That feedback was a form of validation of our capabilities—and of the veracity of our sources.

* * *

AS I HAVE said, I enjoyed the business development part of being an entrepreneur and that was what led me, in 2010, to meet with a man named Glenn Simpson, a former investigative reporter at the *Wall Street Journal*. Like Chris and me, Glenn had recently left his steady job to cofound a private investigative firm in Washington, DC, called SNS Global, which later became Fusion GPS. We had friends in common who had suggested we meet, knowing that we had both spent much of our careers—in our different ways—looking into Russian organized crime and its links with the Russian state.

Glenn and I met at an Italian restaurant named Franco's in the upmarket St. James's neighborhood of London. We exchanged stories about Putin, corrupt oligarchs, and Russian organized crime figures. I instantly liked him. We were fishing in the same waters, but our services were not competitive. Fusion GPS, founded and staffed by former journalists, relied mainly on open-source material for its work for corporate clients. They knew how to comb through vast amounts of documents and paperwork, especially US legal filings. Orbis was an intelligence firm; we sought out people who knew secrets and we persuaded them to share those secrets with us. Fusion GPS was in the United States. We were in London.

Glenn and I agreed to explore ways to work together in the future.

* * *

THE FIRST YEAR starting up Orbis had been challenging. Laura's death was—and will always be—desperately hard for the children. But by the autumn of 2010 I was beginning to feel that my children and I had all to some extent shown our resilience, and I also took heart from the growth of Orbis. I had started to believe that I could now look forward in life with hope once more. I was able to meet up with friends socially, both my long-standing university pals and supportive ex-colleagues from government service. One of these was Katherine, whom, as mentioned earlier, I had first come across in government service a couple of years previously.

She and I began to meet for the occasional postwork drink and catchup in London. This progressed to pizzas and over time developed into romance. We were both single parents— Katherine had a daughter from her first marriage—so we took things slowly at first. But in October 2011 we went on a short holiday to Cyprus together, a place that had always been close to my heart and spiritually my second home. I chose this moment, much to Katherine's evident surprise, to propose to her. Much to *my* surprise and elation, she said yes. Maybe this was a bit impulsive of me, as there were obviously family circumstances and sensitivities to be factored in, but I knew in my heart that it was right, and I was so happy to have such feelings again and the prospect of a loving family life going forward.

And so, on a beautiful late summer's day in September

2012 we got married in the local parish church of St. Andrew's in Farnham, with a reception afterward in a country manor house on the nearby North Downs. We honeymooned in Mauritius and then settled in Farnham with our four children and began to build what we expected would be a quiet life together.

Part Two

THE DOSSIER

Chapter 9

PROJECT SNAKE

SEVERAL YEARS LATER, on a weekend in late May 2016, I received a phone call from Glenn Simpson. We had kept in touch. I had met with him regularly when I passed through Washington, DC. Now, he said, he was going to be transiting through Heathrow Airport the following Monday, on his way south from Edinburgh en route back to the United States.

"What are you doing here?" I asked him.

"I'm looking at Trump's golf courses," he explained. "The client is a political one linked to the election. Can we have a chat before I go back as to what you might be able to do on this subject?"

It was a holiday weekend. Katherine had just come back from two temporary overseas assignments in Hong Kong and Australia, and we were just spending time at home, catching up after more than six months apart. So it was not great timing for me to head over to Heathrow. But I was intrigued—Glenn was not the type to waste my or anyone else's time.

In the run-up to this meeting Orbis had been doing investigative work on Paul Manafort, focused on his lavish lifestyle and expenditure, for a private legal client. Glenn was aware of this.

"Let's meet at Carluccio's at Terminal 5," I said.

In the seven years since Chris and I had started Orbis, we had concluded, over and over again, that business and politics were nearly always inseparable, especially in the so-called emerging markets—of which Russia was one. Our clients tended to be companies or wealthy individuals who would hire us to find out information that would give them an advantage in legal or commercial disputes or competitive situations. In most such cases, sooner or later, we would discover that politicians were taking bribes, or were blocking our clients' operations for other reasons. We would help our clients to understand the internal workings of governments, especially Russia's. But our work was rarely, if ever, overtly political. No politician or party had ever hired us previously.

We happened to be particularly busy at this time. Orbis was working on a series of reports for Bilfinger, a German engineering company. This was an extremely complicated client project and involved work in multiple jurisdictions, and it was a sizable contract. We were under pressure to deliver good work. At the same time we had another client that represented a leading candidate for the vacant role of secretary general of the United Nations. They had hired us through their PR company to gather intelligence on what the Russians and other member states were doing in the background before the election and what their voting intentions were. They wanted an inside track that would help their client get elected to this important international position.

After arriving at Heathrow, I parked at Terminal 5 and made my way to Carluccio's, an Italian chain restaurant. I got there before Glenn.

Glenn's outbound flight to the US was from another terminal, so he was a bit pushed for time.

After we ordered food, Glenn told me that Fusion had been looking into Donald Trump's business dealings for eight months. The original client for this work had recently been replaced by a new one with a substantial budget. He didn't tell me who either the previous or present clients were—other than that the current client was a law firm—and I didn't ask. But it seemed to me that they were obviously something to do with the Democratic Party and the 2016 US presidential campaign. I did not follow American politics in granular detail, but I knew that Trump was now almost certain to become the Republican Party nominee for president. His rivals had been, up to this point, fellow Republicans. Now he would face off against a Democrat.

Glenn said that Fusion's work so far had unearthed numerous connections between Trump and Russia, including his links with alleged Russian organized crime figures. And he said that Trump had made many trips to Russia, starting during the Soviet era, in apparent attempts to build or open or license hotels there. None of these projects had materialized. That was a lot of work, and a lot of travel to Russia over a period of about two decades, for apparently nothing—for a man whose own bestselling book was called *The Art of the Deal*.

Just days earlier—on May 19—Paul Manafort had been appointed chairman of the Trump presidential campaign. Glenn knew that we had been reporting on Manafort for a private client. This had led Fusion to conclude that we might be the right people to do some digging on Manafort and on Trump's connections to Russia.

I was stunned when Manafort was appointed to head up Trump's presidential campaign. He had been missing in action for two years and then suddenly he popped up as head of a campaign whose candidate had a genuine shot at the White House. I had to clarify the potential ramifications of this in my own head: the person running one of the two political campaigns for the most powerful job in the world had made millions in Ukraine by helping a Kremlin acolyte, Viktor Yanukovych, get elected president.

Glenn's initial interest was more on Manafort's possible ties to Russia than Trump's, given how well-documented it was that Manafort had worked for pro-Russian figures, including Yanukovych, in Ukraine. The rest of the evidence about Trump's connections to the Russian regime was a little less direct at that stage, although there was one clear lead to an American, David Geovanis, to whom we shall return later.

Fusion needed someone who could make general inquiries in Russia about both Manafort and Trump's business dealings there. Glenn asked me if we would be interested. He said it would initially be for a month's worth of research. It might come to nothing. After all, Glenn said, Trump could just be visiting Russia for pleasure, and if that were the case, no one would really care.

That's not right, I said. The FSB would almost certainly have bugged Trump's hotel room and that could open him up to blackmail. That could be a serious concern to American national security. Once each major party chooses its candidate that person receives top-level security briefings. I could see immediately that if the Russians had any leverage over Trump— for any reason—it would be important for that to be known by the relevant authorities before he received a security briefing rather than after. The American primaries were coming to a close in a matter of days.

* * *

BY CHANCE ORBIS had been working on a separate project for two years—from 2014 to 2016—for another private client that somewhat dovetailed with Glenn's work. Project CHARLE-MAGNE, as we called it, had focused on allegations that Russia was increasingly attempting to interfere in European elections, coming to the aide of politically extreme politicians and trying to sow political divisions in Europe.

Putin hated and feared the European Union and NATO, the two bodies that united Europe and largely held together the continent's disparate, disputatious nations politically and militarily. We had come across evidence that the Kremlin had a large budget—tens of millions of dollars—that it devoted to supporting populists, of both the extreme left and the hard right, as disrupters of the established order. Those populists included nationalists and anti-EU politicians and parties in Western Europe. Moscow spent some of that money on social media disinformation, whose goal was to create division in Europe; and it had loaned serious money to extreme right-wing parties in Europe, especially Le Pen's Front National in France. The goal was clear: destroy the EU and thereby bring an end to this unified, consensual political bloc that sat on the same landmass as Russia, and at the same time bring an end to the sanctions on Russia that the EU had imposed after Moscow's illegal seizure of Ukrainian territory in 2014. The first Project CHARLEMAGNE report, which was dated April 7, 2016, had concluded:

Our overall assessment is that the tactical necessity for Russia to oppose the EU over Ukraine, sanctions and energy market liberalization has led to the formulation of a more strategic effort by the Kremlin and the Russian Intelligence Services to undermine and even seek to destroy the EU. Within the KGB modus operandi this involves influence operations using "agents of influence" . . . and opaque financial support for anti-establishment / anti-EU political parties and figures. In our judgement this process is likely to grow in size and reach over time if, as seems likely, the various EU crises worsen.

Our client asked us to pursue our reporting, so we produced a second CHARLEMAGNE report in late June 2016. The executive summary of this second CHARLEMAGNE report reads:

- Evolving Russian leadership program to undermine the EU. Secret budget allocation to fund associated subversion in Europe, with MFA [Ministry of Foreign Affairs] having won lead role in competition with SVR [Foreign Intelligence Service]. Deputy premier SHUVALOV responsible for wider Russian government input

- Program includes offering bribes and favors to anti-EU politicians and parties/movements, both with their knowledge and indirectly. Notable successes in Czech Republic, Slovakia and Romania with current efforts concentrated in Germany, Italy and Austria, as well as France. Russian "International Investment Bank" the main, but not only, financial conduit

- Setbacks for Kremlin in Bulgaria and recent narrow defeat of HOFER, whom they had [supported] for Austrian presidency. Brexit on Kremlin

agenda too but thinking/planning surrounding
this less advanced

- Principal aim remains to create divisions within
  EU with view to lifting of organization's sanctions
  on Russia. However PUTIN and PA [Presidential
  Administration] Head IVANOV beginning to think
  they can hasten demise of the EU itself

We completed work on Project CHARLEMAGNE and with
the client's permission we had passed copies of the reports to
the US government. It was important that our American allies
understood the extent of Russia's attempt to undermine the
United States' allies in Europe. And, as I have said, we had
become comfortable with sharing intelligence with the FBI
and the State Department that private clients had funded and
where they had given us permission.

Despite having touched on this in Project CHARLEMAGNE,
we did not have a paying client tasking us specifically on Brexit
in the run-up to the June 2016 vote. But after setting up Walsingham Partners—an offshoot of Orbis that focuses on political
research—in 2017 and attracting substantial donor money to
collect intelligence on Russian interference in Western democracies, a picture of Russian operations on Brexit started to emerge.

Although the Russian leadership was not united on the issue back in 2016, some arguing that the UK inside the EU was
a break on German dominance of the continent, our intelligence indicated that Russian military intelligence (the GRU)
and especially its former director, Gen. Igor Sergun, had led
the charge to influence the British electorate to favor the UK
leaving the EU. Substantial money, reportedly £2–3 million
per year, had been clandestinely funneled into activities supporting the pro-Brexit campaign. One source reported that

this money had been injected into the British political system using leading Russian banks, exploiting a loophole in the rules requiring declaration of origin for political donations that then existed in Northern Ireland. But after Sergun's suspicious death in early 2016 these financial transfers had ceased.

After the Brexit referendum result, however, the Kremlin became more interested in how this toxic issue could be exploited to create divisions within the UK itself to paralyze and deflect British foreign policy attention away from Russia and to encourage nationalism and separatism in Scotland, where, most significantly for Moscow, the British (submarine) strategic nuclear capability was based.

The Russians also realized how useful the opportunist Boris Johnson was in this respect, with his faux hostility to France, in addition to the fact that he constituted the greatest recruitment asset for the separatist Scottish National Party, many of whose compatriots loathed him.

We shared much of this intelligence with the British Parliament's Intelligence and Security Committee when they were working on their Russia report in 2018–19, and the then chairman formally expressed his gratitude.

Neither Orbis nor its sister company, Walsingham, took an ideological position on Brexit itself. We were simply focused on Russian interference in it. Orbis staff, and members of our families, had voted on both sides in the referendum. But my position was that Brexit was the greatest self-inflicted wound in British peacetime history and that Russia was literally invested in bringing it about. This remains my view today.

* * *

"I CAN'T TRAVEL to Russia myself," I told Glenn in May 2016. "But we have good sources there. The Russian diaspora in the

West also gives us pretty good opportunities to develop relevant assets."

Glenn's requirement for new intelligence on Russian interference in the American election appealed to me as an extension of CHARLEMAGNE. And also because it seemed clear from the beginning that the stakes were potentially quite high for the United States, given Glenn's description of the ties Fusion had found between Trump and Russia. At that point it seemed unlikely that Trump could win the election against Hillary Clinton, but given the evenly divided nature of US politics, both leading candidates had a clear chance. If the Kremlin was spending tens of millions of dollars to influence elections in France, Italy, Britain, and Germany—as well as Turkey, which had long sought membership of the EU and is a key NATO member—then Putin must at the very least have considered trying to meddle in the US election.

We paid the lunch bill and shook hands, and Glenn walked off to catch his flight back to Washington.

* * *

ON THE DRIVE home from Heathrow, I began formulating an initial approach to the project. To me, it was really just a modest business opportunity. I thought that we would maybe get some intelligence on a few dubious business deals Trump had been engaged in with Russians and that would be the end of it. Besides, the focus of the project was as much on Paul Manafort as it was on Trump himself. None of us at Orbis had ever heard of many of the people we—and the rest of the world—would soon become familiar with. The likes of Carter Page, Michael Cohen, and Michael Flynn.

When I got back home to Farnham I discussed the project with Katherine. I do not tell her about every inquiry that comes in, but I did share this one. There was a very good reason for this caution: she was a Crown servant working in the British government. And her role at the time happened to be particularly relevant to the matter Glenn had asked me to look into; she had close working relations with the US embassy and government.

To protect her sensitive position, Katherine never saw the detail of the Orbis projects. But she expected me to warn her if I was working on anything that might blow up in her face. This one certainly fell into that category. And it would come to have a huge impact on Katherine's life and career.

* * *

THE DAY AFTER my lunch with Glenn we held our weekly team meeting at the Orbis office in London. I told my colleagues that we had a potential new project. It was what we call a sampling operation. We would propose to Fusion GPS—and its still-anonymous client—an initial round of intelligence reporting. If we turned up nothing, then we would recommend that they called it a day. If we found something interesting, however, we would see if they had the appetite and budget for more work.

Orbis works project by project. We go from initial conversation to proposal to acceptance, and then delivery. Sometimes a job and a client will be a one-off; other times we will agree on a retainer for a project that is likely to take several months, especially in our litigation support work with law firms.

In this case we did not do a detailed proposal because the client's request was quite simple. I sent an email to Glenn saying we would be happy to look into this matter and that it would take about a month. The initial fee would be $30,000, fairly standard in our industry at the time and certainly not inflated, as was later falsely claimed.

Glenn confirmed the terms with his client and by the end of that week we had the green light.

Almost as soon as Glenn floated the idea of the project past me, I knew who I was going to use as our lead collector: Igor Danchenko.

* * *

IGOR DANCHENKO WAS a Russian lawyer and an academic researcher who lived in the United States. An expert on Russian energy issues, he was also a prolific intelligence collector. I had met him in 2010 when Fiona Hill, an Anglo-American former Russia advisor to George W. Bush and Barack Obama (and later Donald Trump), introduced us. Fiona, who was then working at the influential Brookings Institution, a Washington, DC, think tank, sang Igor's praises and suggested he might be a good person for Orbis to consider working with. I had known Fiona for several years, and in fact she and Katherine had met each other earlier in life when they were both studying at St. Andrew's University in Scotland in the 1980s.

Igor was good at what he did. In 2006 he and another Brookings researcher, Clifford Gaddy, had demonstrated that Putin's doctoral thesis on Russian energy had been heavily plagiarized. This had not endeared him to the Kremlin, but their anger at him had passed with time. Fiona had included Igor in the acknowledgments of her 2013 book, *Mr. Putin*. She described him as someone who had a "remarkable ability to locate sources and material that other researchers considered totally inaccessible" and that he had "provided us with a wealth of insights into and information about Vladimir Putin's life, career and connections in St. Petersburg." That was quite a reference.

To be clear then, Igor was not an undercover agent who would slip into Russia under a false name. He was a Russian citizen who, like many Russians, lived overseas and regularly returned home. He owned an apartment in St. Petersburg, had family in Russia, and traveled freely and openly around the country. And most of what he did for us, and for other clients, was entirely routine and required little or no secrecy or deception: conducting due diligence about potential business partners or rivals; asking around his network of friends and associates for inside information about a particular company, executive, or politician; obtaining documents that would shed light on the inner workings of the person or entity the client wanted to know more about. If ever he was stopped by the police or the FSB or at passport control he could, in all honesty, tell them what he was doing. I'm conducting some research for a respected Western client who might want to start a joint venture or buy a business here, he would say, hand on heart. He was hiding in plain sight and had even been invited to give seminars at the Kremlin. He was, as far as anyone in power knew, simply a respected academic and researcher who knew a lot about business, energy, and politics in Russia.

Besides, for all that Putin's Russia in the 2010s was an increasingly authoritarian state, it was a lot less restrictive and paranoid than it is now.

When we gave him the Fusion GPS task, Igor was working on four other projects for Orbis. We had him on a retainer because he was reliable; his reporting in other areas had checked out.

Igor was also working for other clients at this time, not just Orbis. He was a freelancer who could consult for whomever he wanted, and he juggled the competing demands and interests of his clients efficiently.

I briefed Igor about the Fusion project, which we had named Project SNAKE. (All projects at Orbis, as is common practice in the intelligence world, get a code name that is capitalized when written down.) SNAKE, in this case, was a lighthearted code name that seemed fitting for Trump. Like many, we did not take Trump very seriously. He seemed like a semi-comic historical blip that the world would puzzle over once Hillary Clinton had roundly defeated him in the election.

Igor and I agreed that his retainer would extend to the new project. I did not tell him who the client was. I rarely did, if ever. And in fact one of his other projects—gathering intelligence about suspected Russian doping efforts in sports—had another client he did not need to know about: the FBI. That is standard practice for intelligence collectors. And in turn, it meant that Igor's subsources would also not know. Even I did not know at that point—although, as I say, l suspected—who the ultimate client was.

* * *

AS ALWAYS, THERE would be radio silence when Igor was working in Russia. He would not call or email us; we would not call or email him. Because while most of his work was low-risk, this more politically charged assignment—Project SNAKE—had the potential to be more sensitive, more problematic. If Manafort and Trump had powerful friends in Russia, then it would be best not to attract too much attention. Igor would meet his regular subsources, and eventually—after warming them up—he would cleverly ask them if they had heard anything about Manafort or Trump.

Igor told me he would be in London around June 18 or 19. I said, "Fine, just get in touch with us when you arrive here." Soon after, he left the United States for Russia and went silent.

When a collector is in a hostile country like Russia you must be patient. Now and then I wondered how he was getting along, but we had a lot of work to juggle and so I did not give it a large amount of thought. Sure enough, toward the end of June he called and said he was back in town.

"I've got some stuff," he said. "Can I come into the office?"

Igor arrived at our office in Victoria in the late morning. We had two rooms in that office; Igor and I were in the smaller one, which was regularly swept for eavesdropping devices. It was our secure room. We sat around the board table. I took out my notebook. And then he began, in his usual calm and deliberate manner.

"There's some pretty hot stuff here, Chris."

Chapter 10

COMPANY INTELLIGENCE REPORT 2016 / 080

"WELL, THIS IS pretty shocking stuff, isn't it?" I said.

Igor agreed.

I took detailed notes from what he was telling me. Igor's practice was to write cryptic notes to himself as memory prompts; he would record initials, dates, places, and dollar signs, and he would draw arrows between some of his written notes. It was a code only he would understand. He also sometimes recorded memos on his phone and audiotaped conversations with sources, often in Russian.

His reporting was unsettling. The Kremlin, his sources said, had been cultivating and supporting Trump for years in the hope that Trump's increasing influence would help create divisions in the Western alliance and foment civil and political discord within the United States. Furthermore, Trump had been offered favorable real estate deals in Moscow, which for some reason he had not taken advantage of. The Trump team, Igor's sources said, had accepted intelligence from the Kremlin about Trump's political rivals. The sources also said that the Russian intelligence services (RIS) had bugged and recorded

Hillary Clinton's private conversations when she had previously visited Russia and that the Kremlin could use these to undermine her—although there was nothing apparently that embarrassing about the contents.

There was no question, however, that Igor's most important intelligence focused on the possibility that the Kremlin held deeply compromising material about Trump.

The debriefing took about half the day. We discussed, as we always did, who his subsources were. Many of them were familiar to me from earlier projects, when he had worked indirectly for our clients like one of the world's largest oil and gas companies. We would always do secondary research on his sources, trying to confirm that they existed and that they were who he said they were. This was not because we didn't trust Igor: it is simply standard procedure in intelligence gathering, and it is what we were trained to do. We still operate this way with all our collectors and their subsources. One of Igor's subsources, for example, had met with one of my colleagues at Orbis for advice on getting his son into a language school in the UK, so we had direct knowledge of that person.

I got on the phone to Glenn soon after Igor had left the Orbis office. I didn't tell him over the phone what was in the reporting. "You're going to want to see this ASAP," I told him. "It's big. And it's controversial. How should we get this to you?"

We agreed that I would send it to Washington on a USB stick by courier. Email, even of the encrypted variety, did not feel secure enough. We didn't discuss the contents on the phone. FedEx seemed, rather counterintuitively, secure because it was so mundane and not potentially vulnerable to cyberattack.

That evening I went home and told Katherine what Igor had returned from Russia with.

Katherine listened before sharing her thoughts. Her advice was clear: do not include the most embarrassing bits. Chris

Burrows said the same thing when I told him. "I would leave it out if I were you," he said.

I disagreed. I felt and still do that if you get into the business of smoothing off the sharp corners of intelligence, leaving out elements that are embarrassing or a bit difficult or are even contradictory—facts that jar with some of the other intelligence you have—then you are not doing the job properly or with integrity. As I have said, an intelligence report is potentially valuable if it is only 70 percent accurate. It is not intended for public consumption; it is not normally meant to become evidence in court, not least because that can lead to the exposure of confidential sources—people who either do not know they have been used for intelligence gathering or individuals who have passed on information only on a promise of anonymity. Often the best use of intelligence is prophylactic. Rather than using it to prosecute someone, you might ask the target if they would like to have a chat, you lay out what you know about what they have been up to, and you suggest that it would be in their best interests to cease immediately. Or you can whisper in their boss's ear and suggest that they reconsider employing this person. There are concerns, you might explain, and if you continue employing them you might have a serious problem on your hands—not least because you now know that the government has concerns, and if you knew and did nothing, then that could make things all the worse for you. Intelligence is, fundamentally, confidential information that is meant to be seen by select people to help them make good decisions, business or political.

And then there was the question of how reliable Igor's information was and whether it was strong enough to pass on to Fusion in its entirety. As I have said, Igor had been one of Orbis's most reliable and productive collectors in Russia for years. He had obtained intelligence for the consumption of some of the world's top corporations. Furthermore, I knew

who Igor's subsources were. Despite all the difficulties of independent verification I could not discount the possibility that
what he was telling me was right.

And there was another reason I felt I had to be comprehensive
in what I passed on to Glenn and his client: the minute Igor began sharing his findings, I realized the stakes were suddenly—
and unexpectedly—very high. In June 2016 few people thought
Trump had a chance against Hillary Clinton, who was comfort-
ably ahead in the opinion polls. But in any US presidential election
it is impossible to write off any Democratic or Republican candidate, no matter how unlikely a win seems to be for the underdog.
(Opinion polling showed its sometimes shocking unreliability
that same month. Few people in Britain thought there was any
real chance that a majority of voters would opt to leave the European Union. The polls were showing a clear lead for the Remain
campaign, but Brexit ended up carrying the day 52 to 48 percent.)

In other words, Igor's intelligence raised a possibility that
the West's most dangerous and most determined adversary,
Vladimir Putin, might have the ability to blackmail one or both
of the main candidates for president.

If true, something Trump has vehemently denied, the intelligence pointed at the following possible outcome: if elected
president, Trump might one day be faced with Putin using the
threat, or implied threat, of releasing compromising material
on him unless Trump agreed to do something at Putin's behest.
I felt, and still do, passionately that it would have been morally
wrong of me to keep that information to ourselves. What Igor
was telling us deserved to be investigated.

But I also felt that the kompromat—the Russian term for
compromising information used to blackmail people—was but
one detail in a much larger story: Russia was trying to influence the US presidential election against Hillary Clinton and

in favor of Donald Trump, and Trump's camp was reportedly colluding with Moscow.

I wrote it up in the form of a report, or memo, which later became known—and read by millions—as Company Intelligence Report 2016 / 080. It was the first report of Project SNAKE.

* * *

BEFORE WE PROCEED further, I would like to make clear that Donald Trump has strongly and repeatedly denied the allegations against him contained in the abovementioned report—commonly referred to as the "Steele Dossier"—and now in this book. Perhaps Trump's most explicit denials are contained in a sworn witness statement he made as part of his legal action against Orbis and myself over the contents of the dossier:

> It has consistently been repeated by Mr Steele on behalf of the Defendant [Orbis Business Intelligence Limited] that none of the allegations about me which are contained in the Dossier have been "disproven". The allegations are wholly untrue. I can confirm that I did not, at any time:
>
> (a) Engage in perverted sexual behaviour including the hiring of prostitutes to engage in "golden showers" in the presidential suite of a hotel in Moscow.
>
> (b) Provide the Russian authorities with sufficient material to blackmail me.
>
> (c) Pay bribes to Russian officials in order to further my business interests.
>
> (d) Take part in "sex parties" when in St Petersburg.
>
> (e) Arrange for or connive in the silencing of any witnesses by coercion or bribery.

These broad denials are echoed in other public statements Trump has made, attacking the source of the allegations: "[A] group of opponents . . . put that crap together." And in a January 2017 news conference he made even broader denials: "It's all fake news. It's phony stuff. It didn't happen."

Moreover, I must reemphasize the inherently uncertain nature of much of the sourcing used in this book, especially with regard to events in Russia. As is typically the case in assessing intelligence materials—as I have done for decades as an intelligence professional—I must make reasoned judgments on the credibility of the sources, knowing that many of them are unverified, secondhand, and potentially motivated to reveal something less than the full truth. To be clear, I have not and cannot be certain of each reports' accuracy.

However, I would never issue or share human intelligence source reporting with clients, Western governments, or regulators unless I was satisfied as to the access, motivation, and contextual/ background consistency of the information provided. Particularly important in this regard is how well we know the source/ subsources and how long, good, and reliable their reporting track record on other issues has been. In cases where we are dealing with a new source/subsource or one who we suspect may be trying to "influence as well as inform," we make this clear to the client/ consumer, either at the end of the written report or in oral briefing. In the case of the Trump-Russia dossier, the main source (collector) and most of the subsources were assessed as established and with a good reporting track record. Where we were dealing with a new subsource, this was made clear to the readers at the time.

* * *

IN TERMS OF the broader counterintelligence context, several relevant matters have emerged subsequently. The first came independently from an unexpected source, one of Orbis's British business clients. He told us that he used to stay at the Ritz Carlton hotel in Moscow on business trips there but had ceased doing so and advised his staff and colleagues not to after several incidents in the hotel, including one where a fully leather-clad woman with a whip had gotten into the lift with him. He assumed she was en route to a client's hotel room. That was not the sort of situation a senior Western business leader wants to be photographed in, and he was concerned that it could be a setup.

Some of our sources also had highlighted the importance of the Russian-Azeri magnate Aras Agalarov when it came to Trump's relationship with Russia and his visits there.

Agalarov, whom we had never heard of previously, hosted the Miss Universe contest in Moscow in 2013, paying the future US president $14 million for the rights to do so.

Trump's then head of security, Keith Schiller, testified to Congress under oath that a Russian participant in a meeting in Moscow about the Miss Universe pageant had told Trump just after the meeting that he could "send five women" to Trump's hotel room. Both Agalarovs had been at the meeting, Schiller said.

As later chronicled in a much-overlooked part of the Mueller Report, a Russian-Georgian associate of Agalarov called Giorgi Rtskhiladze had had a text exchange in October 2016 with Trump's then lawyer and associate Michael Cohen. The report reads:

> On October 30, 2016, Michael Cohen received a text from Russian businessman Giorgi Rtskhiladze that said, "Stopped flow of tapes from Russia but not sure if there's anything else. Just so you know...." ... Rtskhiladze said "tapes" referred to compromising tapes of Trump rumored to be held by persons associated with the Russian real estate conglomerate

Crocus Group, which had helped host the 2013 Miss Universe Pageant in Russia.... Cohen said he spoke to Trump about the issue after receiving the texts from Rtskhiladze.... Rtskhiladze said he was told the tapes were fake, but he did not communicate that to Cohen.

In addition, Trump later tried to claim—falsely—to then FBI director James Comey that he had not stayed overnight at the Ritz Carlton, Moscow, in 2013 for the Miss Universe contest. But others testified under oath that he did.

One further data point emerged in July 2021 in the *Guardian* newspaper. Three experienced journalists—Luke Harding, Julian Borger, and Dan Sabbagh—reported the existence of an apparently leaked Kremlin document describing a meeting of the Russian National Security Council in January 2016 at which Putin authorizes "a secret spy agency operation to support a 'mentally unstable' Donald Trump in the 2016 presidential election." The *Guardian* story goes on to say:

There is also apparent confirmation that the Kremlin possesses *kompromat*, or potentially compromising material, on the future president, collected—the document says—from Trump's earlier "non-official visits to Russian Federation territory."

The paper refers to "certain events" that happened during Trump's trips to Moscow. [Russian] Security Council members are invited to find details in appendix five, at paragraph five, the document states. It is unclear what the appendix contains.

I don't know where the *Guardian* journalists got their information. But I do know Luke Harding well and, like many, I respect him as one of the most reliable and authoritative reporters on Putin's Russia. I have seen the documents in question, though I have never possessed them.

Trump not only denies this, but sued Orbis in the UK claiming that he could prove it was false. His claim was never tested in court, because it was out of time. Does what we know now add up to a smoking gun? No, it does not. But nor does it undermine our original view that our sources were telling us enough to require proper investigation.

* * *

WE SENT THE USB stick to Glenn by courier on June 20, 2016.

Britain was in a state of political turmoil and tension at the time. The country was about to vote on whether to leave the European Union or to remain a member. And there were reports that Russia was interfering and doing all it could to nudge a major Western democracy to vote in a way that would be potentially helpful to the Kremlin. Britain leaving the EU would weaken an alliance on Putin's doorstep that helped keep sometimes fractious European partners generally pulling in the same direction. We had not been contracted to do any reporting on whether the Kremlin was interfering in the referendum, but I heard things from Russian contacts and sensed it at the time. And what I had just learned from Igor about the Kremlin's determination to sow division in American politics and society made me hope that my former British government colleagues working in the intelligence agencies were investigating and acting on any threats they uncovered about Moscow's attempts to interfere with the Brexit vote. And also to investigate any use of disinformation to create division in Britain in the run-up to that vote.

On June 23 our FedEx package was crossing the Atlantic as the British people went to the polls. The result came in the early hours of June 24. A slim majority of voters had chosen to leave the EU. There were cheers in the Russian Duma.

June 24, 2016, also happened to be my fifty-second birthday. I felt deflated by the referendum result. I passionately believed—and believe—that Britain would be more secure and prosperous in the EU, and that Putin would see the departure of one of Europe's biggest and most powerful countries from the union of European nations as a great victory.

Katherine had booked us a table at the restaurant at the Royal Horticultural Society Wisley, a beautiful manicured 240-acre public garden in Surrey. As we drove the twenty-five minutes there from our house, we had the radio on and listened as British prime minister David Cameron's resignation speech from a podium outside his official residence at Number 10 Downing Street was played over and over. It was a dramatic—borderline traumatic—day. A lunch at a lovely restaurant, looking out across Wisley, would hopefully be somewhat soothing.

But my surprise birthday lunch was not entirely relaxing. My phone kept ringing. Glenn was on the line, unsettled by the fact that the package had failed to show up at the Fusion office in Washington. The FedEx delivery driver could not find the right address. Could I help track down the package? Eventually they managed to retrieve it from the local post office on K Street.

Glenn called again. We were still eating. He had received the package and had read the contents. I had to get up and go outside to avoid being overheard, leaving Katherine alone in the middle of the lunch she had so thoughtfully planned. I found a quiet spot outside.

"Jesus, what are we going to do about this?" Glenn said.

"Do more work is what we're going to do, or should do," I said. "You have to show it to your client, see what they say."

Glenn needed time to digest what I had sent. We agreed to talk soon.

* * *

AFTER LUNCH, KATHERINE and I went for a walk around the gardens. We discussed the report. I do not think either of us realized the full impact it would have. But we did understand this: there was someone else besides Glenn and his client who I felt needed to see the report. Even as I was debriefing Igor in my office, I knew that this was information I already felt duty bound to share with the FBI. If Vladimir Putin had any kind of leverage he could use to blackmail one of the two people who could be the next American president, then US law enforcement authorities needed to know about it. Sure, Glenn and his client had ownership of the information, but that was politics. This was now a question of US—and by extension UK—national security.

The logic seemed inescapable to me. If you saw your neighbor's house being burgled, would you speak up or mind your own business? I think most of us would speak up. We would all agree that we certainly ought to. Then let us say you learned about something that had potentially far-reaching implications for the future of democracy, what would you do? Most of us would, of course, speak up. At least, I hope so.

* * *

IT IS PERHAPS worth recapping here just how long it seemed to take for the various parts of the US government to catch up to the fundamental realization that Russia was attempting to interfere in US democracy and was trying to help Donald Trump get elected. Although Barack Obama claims to have told Putin in person in September 2016 to stop interfering in the US election and "cut it out," it was only *after* Trump won the November general election, and a few days before the inauguration, that all of the main agencies in the US Intelligence Community signed up to the collective view that the Kremlin had tried to influence the election *in favor of Trump*. And it wasn't until April 18, 2019—almost three years after our first report—that the redacted version of the Mueller Report was made public. The first sentence of its second paragraph reads: "The Russian government interfered in the 2016 presidential election in sweeping and systematic fashion." I could not possibly have known how slow the US government would be to respond to the Russian threat to American democracy, but in the summer of 2016, I felt great urgency to alert the FBI.

Before I could pass on the intelligence Igor had gathered to the FBI, I needed Glenn's approval. The reporting Igor had done was not my intellectual property. It belonged to Fusion's client, whoever that was.

A couple days later I called Glenn. He knew we had a relationship with the FBI. "We can't be working with the FBI as a client and then sit on this and not tell them about it," I told him.

"Maybe, maybe not," Glenn said.

"We've got to do it, Glenn."

We discussed it more the next day, and eventually he gave his assent.

So much, then, for what would become a right-wing conspiracy theory peddled by Trump acolytes that the Clinton campaign wanted or even directed me to pass our intelligence on Trump to the FBI, thus to stir up trouble and gain a political advantage in the campaign. It was entirely our independent decision to do so, based on loyalty to an ally. It was simply best practice; something I had done countless times before. For us, as intelligence professionals and with the FBI as our longstanding paying clients, however, it was an easy call.

I already knew who at the FBI I would contact: Mike Gaeta.

Chapter 11

RAISING THE ALARM

I SENT MIKE GAETA a text. "Something important has come up. I think you should come over to London as soon as possible." He was by this time working as a legal attaché on a posting to the US embassy in Rome.

Soon after that I spoke to him on the phone. I didn't tell him what we had collected. He knew I would not waste his and the FBI's time and resources if it was not potentially significant. As a Rome-based agent he needed approval from Washington to travel to the UK, but on the strength of our long-standing and ongoing work with the FBI, he received the green light and flew over to London.

Mike arrived in London in July. He came to the Orbis office and met with Chris Burrows and me. We shared the SNAKE reporting with him.

He was stunned. We said we knew it would present him with political and other handling problems, but given the Russia counterintelligence thrust of the report, we judged that he should have it immediately.

Mike confirmed that he would circulate the reports to

a small group of senior managers and analysts at FBI head-quarters. He said he would do whatever he could to protect our sources and operations. We told him that Glenn, at Fusion GPS, was the person who had commissioned the work and that we believed our ultimate client was linked to the Clinton campaign.

I printed out a copy for him. "Take it with you," I said. He put the printout in his briefcase and left.

* * *

IN JULY 2016, as we later learned, the FBI received two other concerning reports. On July 5, a Trump foreign policy advisor named Carter Page delivered a speech at the New Economic School in Moscow that deviated greatly from the orthodox policy position of the Republican and Democratic parties, and from the US government. Page criticized the West for harboring what he called "unnecessarily perpetuated Cold War tendencies." The whole speech was peppered with what seemed to be warm gestures to Putin's Russia; he appeared to be signaling to the Kremlin that a President Trump would be very much more accommodating than a President Clinton. The FBI took note.

Also that month, the Australian government reported to the FBI that in May the Australian ambassador to the UK, Alexander Downer, had had drinks in London with another Trump foreign policy advisor named George Papadopoulos, during which Papadopoulos had claimed that Russia was in secret possession of compromising information about Hillary Clinton. (Russia did, in fact, have thousands of her stolen emails at that time.)

Meanwhile, we carried on our Trump-Russia election reporting. Fusion had contracted Orbis for an initial six-week period and we had some time left on the term. Igor returned to the United States. He had subsources there—Russians based in America who knew more. He set up meetings with them in person to elicit more relevant intelligence.

We felt an increasing urgency to keep working. The Democratic Convention was scheduled to start on July 25. On July 22, WikiLeaks published thousands of emails that Russian hackers linked to the Kremlin had stolen from the Democratic National Committee (DNC) and then passed on to them. The emails were embarrassing to Clinton and her campaign.

It was now clear to us, to Fusion, and to many journalists that Russia was trying to tip the election in favor of Trump. The DNC hack turned what was a strong suspicion into an evident fact. Even Trump seemed to accept—if briefly—that Russia was behind the hack. On July 27 he did something no other candidate for the American presidency had ever done: he publicly called for an adversary of the United States to conduct a further cyberattack on his political opponent.

"Russia, if you're listening, I hope you're able to find the thirty thousand emails that are missing," Trump said at a press conference, referring to emails that the FBI had not been able to find on Clinton's private server. "I think you will probably be rewarded mightily by our press." I could barely believe this when I heard it; it was collusion in plain sight.

Glenn and I spoke later that day. We were just over three months away from the US election. I had heard nothing from the FBI after passing our first report to Mike Gaeta three weeks previously. Little did we know at the time that Gaeta, not knowing where to send our reporting in FBI headquarters, had dispatched it to the New York Office, where it languished in a security cupboard for six crucial weeks during August and September. (It is also possible that an FBI officer named Charles McGonigal had access to the report when he transferred in early October 2016 to the New York Office to be the chief of counterintelligence there for the Bureau. McGonigal was convicted in 2023 of money laundering, violating US sanctions, and lying to the FBI; he had taken money from none other than Oleg Deripaska to investigate an oligarch rival of his and, separately, from a former Albanian intelligence officer. He was not the sort of person you would want seeing sensitive documents like our reporting on Russia. It would be valuable—and instructive historically—to know whether or not he did.)

Glenn and I felt increasingly anxious as the news about links between the Trump campaign and Moscow cascaded. Surely the FBI would do something? I decided that I could not just sit and cross my fingers. As the new Republican Party nominee for president, Trump was due to receive the traditional classified briefing from the US security and intelligence services that all nominees from both parties do in the run-up to the election. While Igor continued his work in Russia, I went to the US. I felt I had to go to Washington to make sure the message had been received and understood. And if necessary, we would share it elsewhere.

* * *

SO IN LATE July 2016 I traveled to Washington with an Orbis colleague. We arrived there early in the afternoon and checked into our hotel in central Washington. It was to be a quick two-day trip.

Igor was reporting that the Kremlin and Trump's associates had become spooked by the accelerating exposure of Moscow's attempts to influence the election. The Russians were, I wrote in a report for Fusion, dated July 30, "keen to cool situation and maintain 'plausible deniability' of existing/ongoing pro-TRUMP and anti-CLINTON operations. Therefore unlikely to be any ratcheting up of offensive plays in immediate future." In spite of that, I remained extremely concerned that the FBI and the American government did not fully understand the extent of the Russian attempts to undermine the election. Putin had merely pressed the pause button.

On the Saturday morning we had breakfast with Bruce Ohr, an old friend and government liaison partner who worked at the Department of Justice. Bruce was a senior official in the DOJ's Criminal Division. He had been part of the earlier efforts to cultivate Deripaska and to establish a confidential US government relationship with him and other Russian oligarchs. We had known each other for years, and I was confident he was a person of integrity.

I had not given Bruce a heads-up about what I wanted to discuss with him. Over breakfast with him and his wife, Nellie, a Russia expert who had worked for the US Intelligence Community—and who, unbeknownst to me, was also coincidentally doing consultancy work for Fusion—I shared the highlights of what Igor had so far uncovered, which Bruce would later famously summarize in congressional testimony as the Kremlin having "Trump over a barrel." I told them that I had shared the first two reports with Mike Gaeta, whom Bruce knew.

Bruce seemed shocked. He did not say what he would do with what I had shared with him. But I had now alerted the FBI and a senior DOJ official to the possibility that the Russians were trying to get Trump elected. Surely now the message would filter up.

We later learned that within days of having breakfast with me, Bruce passed on the intelligence to senior FBI officials, including Andrew McCabe, the then deputy director of the FBI.

* * *

IN THE EVENING, at about 6 p.m., We took a taxi to a church in downtown Washington. Glenn had told me that his client wanted to meet with me. As instructed, We met Glenn at the church before he, my Orbis colleague, and I accessed a building through the back door. This was the offices, I now saw, of a law firm named Perkins Coie.

In the office we met with a lawyer named Mike Sussmann and sat with him in a boardroom. Sussmann was probing and cautious, and he asked numerous questions about Orbis's reporting and our working methods. He would periodically get up and leave the room. He was, Glenn and I believed, consulting with his boss, a lawyer named Marc Elias, who I would later learn was the general counsel to the Hillary for America campaign and was Fusion's ultimate point of contact. My strong sense was that Perkins Coie wanted to get a feel for me for themselves, to see whether I came across as reliable and professional. Interestingly, Sussmann did not ask about the substance of the reports.

* * *

THE FBI NOW had multiple reasons to worry about Russia's possible ties to Trump and its attempts to interfere in the American democratic process. It knew about Page's trip to Moscow; it had Downer's report about Papadopoulos; the hack of the DNC was now public; Manafort and Michael Flynn, a

former general and another Trump advisor, were also on the
FBI's radar for suspected links to Russia; and Mike Gaeta at
the FBI had our first two reports and some of the most senior
officials at the Bureau now knew their contents.

Quietly—and unbeknownst to me and Fusion—FBI Director James Comey had initiated a top secret investigation into
the reported Trump-Russia links. On July 31 an FBI agent
gave the investigation a code name: Crossfire Hurricane.

* * *

OUR SIXTH REPORT, dated August 5, described a split among
Putin's top officials. The Russian president's chief of staff, Sergei Ivanov, was reportedly furious about the exposure of the
campaign to swing the US election and believed it had gone
too far. Putin's spokesman, Dmitry Peskov, was the leading figure behind the campaign, we reported, and was now "scared
shitless" of being made the scapegoat for what had become a
public relations problem for Russia. Our subsource predicted
that Peskov would now "lie low."

Peskov need not have feared. Our subsource was right about
the split. But on August 12 it was Ivanov who got demoted by
Putin. The lesson seemed clear to me: Putin's aides might have
been unsettled by the media revelations about Russia's interference in the US election but Putin did not care very much.
Peskov, the architect of the campaign, kept his job. Ivanov, the
critic, was now demoted to special envoy for transportation
and the environment. He had been sidelined. We're sticking
with the plan, Putin had clearly decided.

Igor kept collecting intelligence.

* * *

OUR SOURCES CONTINUED to report that the Kremlin was pushing ahead with its campaign. Ivanov had told a close colleague in early August, I wrote in a report dated August 10, "that the audience to be targeted by such operations [the spreading of rumors and misinformation] was the educated youth in America as [Ivanov] assessed that there was still a chance that they could be persuaded to vote for Republican candidate Donald TRUMP as a protest against the Washington establishment (in the form of Democratic candidate Hillary CLINTON). The hope was that even if she won, as a result of this CLINTON in power would be bogged down in working for internal reconciliation in the US, rather than being able to focus on foreign policy that would damage Russia's interests."

In other words, Ivanov—and presumably his boss, Putin— believed that they had a lot to gain in the remaining weeks of the campaign no matter who won.

As our intelligence reporting continued to flow in, I became increasingly concerned that my attempts to alert the American law enforcement authorities and the country's political leaders to what we were finding—through Mike Gaeta, Bruce Ohr, and even through Perkins Coie—had failed. Was someone sitting on our intelligence on purpose? Had it simply not made it up the food chain? Neither Fusion nor Orbis wanted anything in return; we just sought to make sure that the US government had the reporting and understood what its significance was.

* * *

ON A SECOND visit to Washington in September I met Bruce Ohr again for breakfast, this time alone.

I updated Bruce on the latest developments. He was in listening mode and made no mention of the FBI investigation. By then, we would later learn, most of the top officials in the Obama White House had been told about the intelligence community's concerns about Russia's interference campaign and about Crossfire Hurricane. Obama was weighing his options.

Glenn and I agreed we needed to redouble our efforts to get the Trump-Russia issues properly investigated. He proposed that we should brief a select group of journalists, off the record, about the main thrust of what Orbis had uncovered.

Glenn booked a room at the Tabard Inn, a charming colonial-style hotel in downtown Washington, discreetly located away from the main lobbyist haunts of K Street. He made calls to some of the best-connected national security and political reporters in the United States, and we agreed on times for each one to meet with us in the hotel.

We did not meet them with the intention that they would see or publish the dossier memos. It was too close to the election, and they would likely not have had time to do their own digging or come up with reporting of their own that was sufficiently watertight before November 8. But what they almost certainly would not do, Glenn and I agreed, was to sit on the information we would share with them for four years—as the FBI might—in the event that Trump pulled off an unlikely win. We needed to plant a seed.

Those reporters included Michael Isikoff of *Yahoo News*, Jane Mayer of *The New Yorker* (who later wrote a profile of me for the magazine), David Sanger and Eric Lichtblau from the *New York Times*, Tom Hamburger of the *Washington Post*, and Matt Mosk of ABC News. In one-hour sessions, spaced apart so that none of them would run into any of the others, we briefed them in general terms about our election reporting.

All of the journalists agreed to keep my identity secret. I could only be described as a "former senior Western intelligence official" in any story that emerged from the meeting. We did not show them or give them any of the reports. The goal was clear and understood: we will alert you to what we are finding out and we will wish you all the best in confirming it yourselves, but we cannot tell you who our sources are and you cannot have our written reports.

Yahoo News was the only outlet to publish a story after these meetings. Appearing on September 23, the story focused on Carter Page: "U.S. intelligence officials are seeking to determine whether an American businessman identified by Donald Trump as one of his foreign policy advisers has opened up private communications with senior Russian officials—including talks about the possible lifting of economic sanctions if the Republican nominee becomes president, according to multiple sources who have been briefed on the issue," the story, by Michael Isikoff, began. I was cited in the story as a "well-placed Western intelligence source." The piece caused minor ripples and was quickly forgotten amid the deluge of late-stage campaign reporting. The election was only six weeks away.

In addition to those briefings and just before the November 8 election I sought advice from a mentor of mine, Sir Andrew Wood, who had been Britain's ambassador to Russia from 1995 to 2000. I wanted his wisdom, and I shared with him what we had uncovered. Andrew took the reporting seriously and suggested we share it with former US deputy secretary of state and my old Russianist US colleague Strobe Talbott. In early November we did as Andrew suggested. Strobe then discussed it with Secretary of State John Kerry and Assistant Secretary Victoria Nuland.

But these senior US officials, whose primary duty supposedly was to protect American democracy, showed little sign, as far as I could tell, of taking action.

Chapter 12

THE FBI WILL SEE YOU NOW

IN LATE SEPTEMBER, Mike Gaeta called me. The FBI wanted to talk. And this time it would not just be him in the room. Something had clearly shifted.

Could I travel to Rome?

Mike explained it would be quicker and easier than all of us meeting in Washington or in London. I agreed, booked a flight for October 2, and was soon in central Rome. I had wanted Chris Burrows to come with me for support, but he could not make it due to another work commitment. The result was that I was rather outnumbered in Rome and had no witness to the conversation.

I was instructed to come to a location close to the Colosseum, to what is called, in intelligence parlance, an OCP, or Operational Clandestine Premises. "I was asked to make my own way there (by taxi from my hotel) and was escorted in and upstairs by a young man (seemingly not part of the team) without any questions being asked," I wrote in a memo of the meeting, which is dated October 5.

The young man showed me to a boardroom with no

windows. I assumed it was a secure room that could not be penetrated with listening devices.

Three senior FBI Russia counterintelligence officials had flown in from Washington for the meeting. We sat down and began what would be a three-and-a-half-hour conversation.

Two of them asked most of the questions. The others were listening, watching, writing notes. In my memo I wrote:

————

> FBI clearly took our (Trump-Russia) reporting very seriously; were now investigating it and other relevant intelligence with vigor. This left them in a hugely difficult situation.

To be clear, the FBI had shared with me in Rome that they had, in fact, begun their own investigation. This was a positive.

They confided to me the lead they had on the Trump advisor George Papadopoulos, and they outlined their investigative tactics in determining whether there were further links between the Trump campaign and Russia, and to what extent Russia was interfering in the election. They said that they wanted to compile enough evidence against Carter Page so that he would then cooperate with their attempts to build a case against a more significant target, Paul Manafort.

I was relieved. The FBI clearly was now taking this seriously and, to its credit, was already on the case and was pursuing its own leads. The agents were, I thought, moving in many of the right directions—particularly on Manafort. From the moment Igor had first shared his findings with me, I had wanted the FBI to understand what was happening and to investigate. We did not need validation for our own work—we had been collecting secret intelligence in and on Russia for

years and knew it was generally reliable—but it was neverthe-
less encouraging to know that Orbis and the FBI were separately uncovering elements of the same larger story: Russia
was trying to swing a US presidential election. In my memo
I wrote:

The key operational request coming out of the meeting was that [Danchenko] be asked to get chapter
and verse on Carter PAGE's alleged secret meetings
in Moscow last July from the two sub-sources. I underlined how difficult and potentially dangerous it
would be to get this request to him/her and for him/
her to follow up on the ground but we said we would
discuss it. . . .

A good enough meeting with the FBI team, if a little
spooky. The key was FBI's avowal that they have intel from other sources, particularly from a London-
based source quoting (Trump) FP [foreign policy]
adviser POPADOPALOUS [sic], which tallied closely
with ours. They want to nail Carter PAGE as the
weakest link in the chain by turning him under in-
terrogation in due course. They are also interested
in prosecuting MANAFORT but admitted they were
a way off any criminal indictments yet. Their problem will be that time is short before the election and
if (Trump) wins, they will be forced to back off. If
he loses, I suspect they will go for the jugular.

Another positive to come out of the meeting was that we
had nothing to be concerned about when it came to the safety
and anonymity of us and our sources:

━━━━

They sought to give us security guarantees that our
reporting, sources and role would be protected by
them in the event that (Trump) were elected president. The FBI director was in office for a 10-year term
and could not be removed by presidential directive.

That, of course, turned out to be, at best, naïve of the FBI
agents I met with. If one were being uncharitable, one might
say that these were deliberate untruths. Comey would last only
a few months into the Trump presidency—the president *is* empowered to fire the FBI director—and the anonymity of our
sources and of Orbis would last only about three more months.
At the time, though, these promises felt reassuring. In the end
I was the naïve party in this arrangement, not the FBI agents.

I was relieved that the FBI was on the case, but the tone of
the conversation rather dampened my sense of relief. I had, the
FBI agents clearly felt, stumbled into *their* investigation—and
so now it was time for *them* to take over and for us to not just
step aside but to hand over our sources so that the FBI could
manage and direct the investigation from this point forward.
This was unrealistic.

I explained that we had shared our intelligence with the
Bureau out of goodwill, but we were not going to jettison our
client and suddenly work for them instead. The FBI agents told
me that they did not want me to discuss "our interaction with
them with our other client." In my memo I wrote:

━━━━

I identified this up front as a potential conflict of
interest and difficult to manage. They accepted this
but insisted that we tried, the case and associated
issues being too important for anyone to walk away.

And whilst they accepted that we should remain loyal and working under contract for our other client, they were keen we should not share the intelligence elsewhere in the USG [government] system (especially with State Department of CIA) or any new client. . . . FBI asked if we had shared it with our old Service or anyone else in HMG [Her Majesty's Government]. I replied that we had not but given our residual CI [counterintelligence] information commitment to SIS, that would change were (Trump) to be elected. In that event we would go to the Prime Minister, through Charles FARR at the JIC [Joint Intelligence Committee], both of whom we knew. We did not trust Foreign Secretary Boris JOHNSON who had poor judgement, was highly indiscreet and had what we regarded as dodgy Russian émigré contacts.

This did not go down well. But we were professionals, and we were all pulling in the same direction, so I told them I was happy to keep helping. Putting our differences aside, I discussed our subsources, although I did not identify either them or the main collector by name.

The FBI agents asked if our collector could pursue specific avenues of inquiry the next time he was in Russia. I told them I could not ask him, I said, because he was there right now on an operational visit—and we had a rule of never trying to contact him when he was in-country. The agents pushed me to get more reporting from Russia:

FBI were quite aggressive on the operational front, unlike our other client who has urged caution re

[Danchenko's] activities in the RF [Russian Federation] at present, demanding that we should continue actively pursing [sic] more detailed intel there even though, like we, they had noticed that the hatches had been battened down in Moscow on this issue since the Democratic Convention and the email hacks release.

Neither Fusion nor Perkins Coie knew Igor's identity at this point. But I realized that the FBI would work out who he was eventually; travel records would lead them to him. And I had once asked Mike about whether the US government could help someone who worked with us obtain his green card, which had alerted the FBI to the fact that our collector was probably based in the United States but was not a citizen or a green card holder.

I told them that we did not normally communicate with our sources when they were in-country, for obvious security reasons, but that there was one form of communication we could try. I made the attempt, but Igor did not pick up the message while he was in Russia on this trip.

The visiting FBI agents, toward the end of our conversation, posed another key question: Would our subsources be prepared to leave Russia and testify in the US? "We've got a budget in excess of a million dollars," one of the agents said.

"No, frankly," I said. "First of all, they would be leaving their families behind. Second, they're all very successful people—that's why they're good sources. They're not dissidents or oppositionists. They're embedded in the system, they make a good living, they're successful professionals. The last thing they're going to want to do is throw that all in and appear in front of Congress or whatever. I can ask but the answer is almost certainly going to be no."

And the truth is that a million dollars, even to resettle two people in the United States, was insufficient. They would have burned through that amount in two or three years. Trump and his MAGA acolytes later made much of what they portrayed as the "one-million-dollar offer" supposedly to validate the dossier. They claimed I had refused this because, they said, I knew I could not validate our information. That is entirely wrong. The offer of the money was made to our subsources, not to me.

I felt that it was a bit crass of the FBI to try to get people to defect on limited budgets but, again, what mattered here was the work. The stakes were too high to get bent out of shape on details. So I let it slide. I ended my October 5 report with this:

> Their initial offer to pay large sums of money to [Danchenko's] sub-sources in Russia to go on the record about (Trump)-Kremlin etc. was naïve and unrealistic and I told them so. They were able to change track thereafter and look at making recruitments among key figures based outside the country, including within Russian operation network in the US. This was much more realistic, sensible and secure.

In other words, I had suggested to the FBI that they might want to go and develop their own sources.

* * *

ONE POINT THE FBI agents made chilled me inside: they said they would probably have to back off this whole investigation if Trump were elected. And that was why it was important to get this work done as quickly as possible. "We can't do a CI [counterintelligence] investigation on a sitting president," they said. They were prepared for the possibility that Trump would be elected, and that they would have to sit there for at least four years knowing what they knew.

And it is important for me to be clear that at no point did they ask me if I had discussed our Trump-Russia reporting with journalists as Republican senators Charles Grassley and Lindsey Graham later suggested they had—and that I had lied in response. Grassley and Graham would cite this in a criminal referral of me to the Department of Justice in 2018, which of course was a disgraceful political stunt and went nowhere.

And if the FBI's insistence that they would not be able to investigate a sitting president Trump was chilling, one further point they made was equally disturbing: they said that whatever they uncovered before the election, they would have great difficulty making it public because the Hatch Act prevented employees of the federal government from acting in ways that could influence the outcome of elections in the ninety days preceding them.

"But this is hardly normal fare, is it?" I said. "This is a potential CI issue involving a hostile foreign power."

At the end they offered me $15,000 plus travel expenses for that meeting. In my memo I wrote:

The FBI team, led by an officer who had investigated the Bureau's Russian traitor [Robert] HANSSEN, were willing to pay us whatever it took to meet their objectives. They would be paying $15,000 for the (Trump-Russia) reporting to date and this meeting, plus my expenses. This would be in cash in London, where they preferred not to meet us because of the required clearances and intelligence bureaucracy.

Someone else from the FBI, they were saying, would swing by our office at some point soon with a bag full of cash, as had happened many times in the past.

I accepted, and noted that they also owed us $30,000 for other project work.

We never saw another cent. The FBI still owes us the money. Collectors and subsources had taken serious risks to obtain the intelligence involved, for work that was entirely separate from the Trump-Russia issue. The relationship between Orbis and the FBI was soon to become very complicated, and not in a good way.

Chapter 13

COMEY AGONISTES

I FELT UNEASY on the flight back to London. The FBI had made it clear to me that no matter what they uncovered between now and November 8, they would not make it public. And if Trump won, they might sit on their findings for years, letting a man who—the evidence suggested—might be vulnerable to blackmail by America's most powerful adversary continue unabated.

I decided to return to Washington one more time before the election. In mid-October I flew there with an Orbis colleague and we met with Isikoff, Tom Hamburger from the *Washington Post*, and Steven Lee Myers of the *New York Times*. I wanted them to intensify their Russia investigative work with the help of our leads. I had a growing sense of alarm that we were days from the election and American voters were about to enter the polling stations not knowing the truth about the Republican candidate for president.

* * *

THEN ON A Friday afternoon in late October 2016, as I drove home from an errand, I heard the news on the radio: James

Comey had publicly announced that the FBI was reopening its investigation into Hillary Clinton's missing emails.

"In connection with an unrelated case," Comey wrote to congressional leaders on that day, October 28, "the FBI has learned of the existence of emails that appear to be pertinent to the investigation. I am writing to inform you that the investigative team briefed me on this yesterday, and I agreed that the FBI should take appropriate investigative steps designed to allow investigators to review these emails to determine whether they contain classified information, as well as to assess their importance to our investigation."

In his final paragraph Comey noted: "I cannot predict how long it would take to complete this additional work." In only eleven days, the American people would choose their next president.

I was astonished. What about the Hatch Act? The FBI had told me in Rome that they could say nothing in public about the fact that they were investigating ties between the Trump campaign and Moscow because it might be perceived as influencing the outcome of the election. But here was the director of the FBI, days before the election, announcing a revamped investigation into Hillary Clinton. I simply could not understand what Comey had done. He was a registered Republican. Was he actively trying to swing the election in Trump's favor?

I was furious. I spoke to Glenn and Chris Burrows over the next few days about what we should do. We had trusted the FBI. We now felt we had misplaced our trust. They knew all that we knew, and more, about Trump—and still the FBI director had taken a decision that seemingly would only make it more likely that Trump would get elected. He had said nothing publicly about Crossfire Hurricane. Why the double standard?

Comey would later defend his decision. He had agonized

over it, he said. He assumed Clinton would win, and if it had emerged after the election that he had not made public the fact that he had reopened the investigation into her emails, then he would be accused of doing so to help Clinton get elected.

Whatever Comey's motivations, he had made a terrible mistake. Orbis and Fusion GPS understood the significance of that immediately. And so Glenn and his business partner, Peter Fritsch, asked if I would join them in making one last attempt to get the issues raised by our intelligence reporting aired before the election. Glenn reached out to a journalist named David Corn, who was an experienced intelligence reporter for the left-leaning *Mother Jones* magazine.

And so, on October 31 Glenn, David Corn, and I spoke via Skype. Later that day *Mother Jones* published a story under the headline: "A Veteran Spy Has Given the FBI Information Alleging a Russian Operation to Cultivate Donald Trump."

Mike Gaeta called me the following day. It was not an easy conversation. He was vexed at me for disclosing that we had passed on information to the FBI about possible connections between Trump and Russia; that was meant to be confidential, Mike said. Your boss, I countered, just did something much worse—he breached the Hatch Act.

The relationship between Orbis and the FBI seemed to be over. As I found out later, the FBI officially crossed me off their list as a CHS—confidential human source. Not that, as far as we were concerned, I had ever been one. It was Orbis that had the relationship with the FBI, not me as an individual. Chris Burrows and other Orbis staff had regular working contacts with Mike and his FBI colleagues over the years, separately from me.

The rift with the FBI was a price worth paying, I thought. But once more, nothing much happened. The *Mother Jones*

story made a minor dent in the news cycle. A *Slate* article raising the possibility that a computer server in Trump Tower was
configured to be in constant communication with a server at
the Putin-linked Alfa Bank made a bigger stir. But soon after, an FBI-sourced story in the *New York Times* dismissed the
Slate and *Mother Jones* stories with the headline: "Investigating Donald Trump, FBI Sees No Clear Link to Russia."

This became known among us, pejoratively, as the "Hallow-
een Special" and seemed to be based on misinformation fed
to the *New York Times*, possibly by senior FBI officials. Other
news outlets followed the *New York Times*' example and dialed down plans to follow the fresh leads. Someone seemed to
be intervening to tip the scales in Trump's favor—again.

Meanwhile, time had run out. November 8 had arrived.
There was nothing more we could do. Besides, surely Hillary
Clinton would still win.

Chapter 14

GOING BADLY

I STAYED UP late to watch the US presidential election results come in. Glenn called me at about four in the morning. "It's going badly—we might have to get out of here," he said. He meant that he and Peter and their colleagues and their families might have to leave the United States. This was not the calm Glenn Simpson I had known for six years. He sounded deeply worried.

Once it became clear that Trump had prevailed, I slept in a spare bedroom because I was so disturbed by what had just happened and didn't want to wake up Katherine. And, truth be told, I was afraid—for democracy, for the United States, for the world at large, but also for friends in the US and even for Orbis. We were no longer even on good terms with the FBI. We had tried to warn them, and the public, about Trump and Russia and we had failed. How long would it be before Trump himself found out about our reporting—and about us? How would he respond?

"Chaos is about to break out," I thought.

Chris Burrows and I told the Orbis staff to take the day off.

The whole team—all of them having worked on Russia—needed a day to recover from the shock. More than most, they understood what Trump's victory meant for the global balance of power. Autocracy—Putin's brand of it in particular—had scored a huge win.

"Hillary Clinton has admitted defeat in the US presidential election, and a second ago Trump began his speech as president-elect of the United States of America, and I congratulate you all," Vyacheslav Nikonov, a pro-Putin member of the Duma, the lower house of the Russian legislature, said that day on the floor of the chamber to his colleagues, who burst into applause.

* * *

THE FOLLOWING DAY I spoke with Chris to discuss what we should do now. We both felt we had a fresh duty: we needed to tell the British government because Trump's election could pose a direct threat to UK national interests. The US is the UK's most important ally, and there is a vast amount of coordination and sharing of intelligence that happens between the security agencies of the two countries. If Trump were compromised, the British government needed to know.

I reached out to Charles Farr—later Sir Charles—an old colleague of mine and Chris's in government service, who was then working as chair of the Joint Intelligence Committee, the government body that tasks the relevant UK agencies and coordinates the intelligence they generate.

Charles asked me to visit him at his home in Wimbledon, south London. On November 15 I took the train and a taxi to his house and over a beer gave him an oral summary of the intelligence we had collected. Charles then wrote an executive summary that combined what I later told him and what I had passed on to him on paper. He circulated it among the key people in government including senior British officials and ministers.

The British government essentially were faced with two possible ways forward: it could act on the information and ask questions in Washington and initiate its own investigation, pursuing the leads I had given Charles; or it could sit on that information and avoid alienating the incoming American president. The British prime minister, Theresa May, evidently chose the second option, even though she knew us and had been directly briefed by me on Russia in the past.

She was clearly worried about alienating Britain's most powerful ally. It was cowardly behavior, in my opinion, and wrong. There is being close to the United States, and then there is being close to the United States to the extent that one's own national security is jeopardized. Trump himself could not keep secrets from the Russians. In May 2017 he would go on to share top secret intelligence reportedly given to the US by an allied intelligence agency with the Russian ambassador, Sergei Kislyak, and the visiting Russian foreign minister, Sergei Lavrov. The information allegedly was about a person working as an asset inside the terrorist group ISIS for the Israeli government. Our sources believe the Russians then informed Iran, and they in turn tipped off ISIS and the Israeli asset was killed.

And more recently, just to underline the point, I was reliably informed by impeccable sources that among the classified documents which Trump, apparently unauthorizedly, took with him to Mar-a-Lago at the end of his presidency were British naval secrets, some of the most sensitive ones in our governmental system. It remains unclear, to me at least, why

Trump would have wanted to retain such documents and what eventually happened to them.

But even back in early 2017 it seemed painfully obvious to me: we could not trust these people with anything, not least our most sensitive secrets. What made it worse was that my reaching out to Charles Farr was clearly not the first the British government had heard about the possible links between the Trump campaign and the Kremlin. He told me that the Australian government had informed the British government about Alexander Downer's unsettling meeting with George Papadopoulos in London earlier in 2016.

I am not a politician in a position to make policy decisions and never have been. But I have spent much of my professional life in close proximity to those decision-makers, and I sympathize with how hard it is for them to give full consideration to competing interests or courses of action. But what I was witnessing was, at best, denial and, at worst, irresponsible. The British government had decided to pretend that Trump was a normal president-elect, that he had not been helped in his victorious election campaign by Russia, and that he and his team could be trusted with the most sensitive, life-and-death information that governments hold. As we later saw, they could not.

* * *

ORBIS'S FORMAL RELATIONSHIP with Fusion's client—Perkins Coie—ended once Donald Trump was declared the winner of the election. As there was no longer a Clinton campaign, the payments stopped.

We completed one full report after November 8 and one partial one, and then we stopped proactively collecting intelligence on this subject.

On one level, it was all over. Trump had won. We were no longer tasked on intelligence on his possible ties to Russia. But if anything, the stakes seemed much higher to me now than they ever had. Trump was soon to be inaugurated. I doubted anything could prevent that from happening, but I could not live with myself if I did not continue to try to get the information contained in our reports into the hands of people who might act on it.

One day in late November my friend and mentor Sir Andrew Wood, in whom I had earlier confided about the dossier, came by the office and said that he was about to travel to the annual security conference held in Halifax, Nova Scotia. "I think John McCain is going to be there. Do you want me to say something to him?" Sir Andrew asked me. I didn't know McCain, but he was widely considered a person of integrity and a true American patriot. A prominent Republican senator, McCain was then chairman of the Armed Services Committee, which enabled him to speak directly and officially to Comey, the FBI director. I knew that McCain was—like me—a hawk on Russia. He understood the threat that Putin posed. He had a long record of speaking up on matters of principle no matter the political cost to himself. And he had been, and remained, highly critical of Trump.

I told Sir Andrew I would welcome it if he spoke to McCain about our reporting.

"OK, I will try to," Sir Andrew replied.

At the conference, Sir Andrew had a discreet conversation with an aide to McCain named David Kramer, a Russia expert who had served as assistant secretary of state under George W. Bush. Wood told Kramer, whom he knew, what the dossier contained and described me as an experienced intelligence professional, a Russia expert, and a reliable source.

Kramer arranged a meeting in a breakout room with McCain. This has to be investigated further, McCain said and asked Kramer to travel to the UK to meet with me.

I picked Kramer up at Heathrow on November 28—using a rolled-up copy of the *Financial Times* under my arm as a classic recognition signal—and drove him to our home in Surrey. He had a quick shower, and then we sat down in the living room where I explained what was in the dossier and what the sourcing was. You can get a copy through Glenn Simpson at Fusion GPS, I told him. I took him to the Mill pub in nearby Elstead for fish-and-chips and then I drove him straight back to Heathrow.

When Kramer was back in Washington he visited the Fusion office. Glenn gave him a paper copy of the Orbis reports, which he took back to McCain. McCain read the dossier, put it in his safe, and called Comey's office to ask for a meeting. They settled on December 7 for a meeting at FBI headquarters.

McCain spoke to his friend and then ally, fellow Republican senator Lindsey Graham. Give Comey a copy of this report, Graham apparently encouraged his friend. The South Carolina senator took the information seriously too, whatever he has said publicly about me and it since—for obvious partisan political reasons.

In London Chris Burrows and I tried to alert the British government through another route to the threat we were all now facing of a potentially compromised incoming American president. We arranged to meet our former Crown servant colleague, Sir Richard Dearlove, who had been head of MI6 from 1999 to 2004, at the Garrick Club in central London. Sir Richard was still well-connected, and we hoped that he would communicate what we had collected to the UK intelligence community and in the British government more broadly.

We briefed Sir Richard orally on the Trump-Russia intelligence, and he asked us about the sourcing. He said it seemed credible. And that it chimed with suspicions that he already had about ties between Russia and some members of Trump's campaign team. He was particularly concerned about Trump's pick for national security advisor, Michael Flynn, who was in close personal contact with a Russian-British research graduate named Svetlana Lokhova; Flynn had met her on a visit to Cambridge University in 2014, when he was director of the Defense Intelligence Agency. Sir Richard was then master of Pembroke College and he was concerned about the interactions between Flynn and Lokhova, who had claimed to have unusual access to the archives of Russian military intelligence, the GRU.

So I now had it from both Sir Richard and Charles Farr that the UK government had questions about the trustworthiness of the Trump team. But regardless, they seemed to be doing nothing other than make the customary warm gestures toward the incoming president.

On December 7 McCain met with Comey and gave him a copy of the dossier. I've done my duty, McCain said later. It was now up to the director of the FBI to decide what to do.

* * *

TALK OF THE dossier was spreading in Washington. Some people had made copies of it—without authorization—and passed them on. Fusion apparently gave copies to the *New York Times* and to Bruce Ohr at the Department of Justice, who passed that copy on to the FBI. With our permission, Kramer spoke to Celeste Wallander, a senior security official in the Obama White House, and to Victoria Nuland, an assistant secretary of state. Kramer summarized it for Paul Ryan, the Speaker of the House of Representatives, and another Republican congressman, Adam Kinzinger. Fusion also had been approached by a *BuzzFeed News* reporter named Ken Bensinger. Kramer also spoke to Bensinger, whom I knew from earlier investigative work on FIFA.

But sadly Kramer didn't just talk to Bensinger. McCain's aide privately had decided that the world needed to know—now—about the dossier. The FBI moves slowly—and there was no guarantee it would ever make its investigation into possible ties between the Trump campaign and Russia known to the public.

So in late December 2016 Kramer invited Bensinger to the offices of the McCain Institute, near the State Department. It was just before New Year's Eve and the staff were all on vacation. The office was empty. Kramer later said that he put the Orbis reports on a table for Bensinger to read and then left the room for twenty to thirty minutes so that he could make a phone call and go to the bathroom. In other words, he left them there on purpose knowing that Bensinger likely would take photographs of the reports with his smartphone. About two weeks later *BuzzFeed* published those photographs.

Chris, Glenn, Peter Fritsch, and I all very much wanted the information in the dossier to be known by relevant decision-makers in the British and American governments. We had tried to lead journalists to do their own reporting, prompted by ours. But all along we had sought to avoid any publication of the dossier, and we had insisted to everyone we confided in that our role should not be made public.

Kramer leaked the dossier for what he felt were good reasons—his country was facing a dire threat, and he was correct in that assessment—but he violated our agreement that he would give the dossier only to McCain, and he breached our trust. He also lied to me directly about whether he had done so. I only found out several years later that he was the leaker when I was shown a legal deposition he had been forced to make on the subject.

I am reliably told he regrets his decision. I have, through intermediaries, followed his activities over the years and I wish him well. But his decision to leak the reports to a journalist— and to an arguably reckless outlet like *BuzzFeed* rather than, say, the more responsible *New York Times* or the *Washington Post*—was a mistake as well as a violation of our agreement. It has caused a huge amount of disruption, stress, and financial hardship to me and many others. More than seven years later we are still facing those consequences as we continue to fight various legal cases arising from the publication of the dossier.

And most important of all, it gave the Russians crucial clues about the identity of several of the sources of our reports. Some of these were later exposed as a result, with dire consequences for them.

I did not know Bensinger now had the dossier. And I did not know that I was spending my last few days of anonymity, after a thirty-year career operating in the shadows where discretion was fundamental to my identity and way of life.

Chapter 15

"WILL YOU LOOK AFTER MY CAT?"

SHORTLY AFTER 10 P.M. on January 11, 2017, I was upstairs at our house in Farnham when I heard Katherine calling me urgently from downstairs.

"Come down, come down here," she shouted.

I hurried down to the kitchen. Katherine was standing there looking at the TV in the corner of the room. She was tuned to CNN.

The network's anchor Jake Tapper was announcing an exclusive breaking story.

"CNN has learned," Tapper had begun, "that the nation's top intelligence officials provided information to President-elect Donald Trump and to President Barack Obama last week about claims of Russian efforts to compromise President-elect Trump. The information was provided as part of last week's classified intelligence briefing regarding Russian efforts to undermine the US elections."

Jim Sciutto, Evan Perez, and the legendary Watergate reporter Carl Bernstein joined Tapper in detailing their national security scoop.

US intelligence chiefs reportedly had presented Obama and Trump with a "dossier" of raw intelligence, they explained, compiled by a "former British intelligence officer" as an annex to their recently compiled assessment of Russian interference in the 2016 election. That assessment had concluded "with high confidence" that "Russian President Vladimir Putin ordered an influence campaign in 2016 aimed at the US presidential election. Russia's goals were to undermine public confidence in the US democratic process, denigrate Secretary Clinton, and harm her electability and potential presidency. We further assess Putin and the Russian Government developed a clear preference for President-elect Trump."

Carl Bernstein had tried to contact me the previous week through Peter Fritsch of Fusion, and again by calling Orbis's office directly. I knew Bernstein was not just going to go away. In partnership with Bob Woodward he had relentlessly pursued stories that led, ultimately, to the resignation of President Richard Nixon. So I had been mentally preparing myself for the possibility that my identity would become public.

"The allegations were part of a two-page synopsis," Sciutto said. "These were based on memos compiled by a former British intelligence operative whose past work US intelligence officials consider credible. The FBI is now investigating the accuracy of the allegations, which are based primarily on information from Russian sources, but the FBI has not confirmed many essential details in the memos about Mr. Trump."

It was deeply disconcerting. I had spent my entire professional career deliberately keeping a low profile and for thirty years I had worked in secrecy. Now my work was being discussed on the world's best-known cable news station and by one of the world's most legendary journalists—Bernstein. They knew who I was but had not named me in the broadcast and had not quoted from the dossier. I felt like I was standing on the crumbling edge of a cliff; I was still unnamed, but Bernstein in particular was describing my work and the sequence of events with great accuracy.

The information, Carl Bernstein said, "came from a former British MI6 intelligence agent who was hired by a political opposition research firm in Washington who [*sic*] was doing work about Donald Trump for both Republican and Democratic candidates opposed to Trump. They were looking at Trump's business ties. They saw some questionable things about Russians, about his businesses in Russia. They in turn hired this MI6 former investigator. He then came up with additional information from his Russian sources. He was very concerned by the implications of it. He then took it to an FBI colleague that he had known in his undercover work for years. He took it to this FBI man in Rome who turned it over to the Bureau in Washington in August. And then a former British ambassador to Russia independently was made aware of these findings and he took the information to John McCain, Senator John McCain of Arizona, in the period just after the election. And showed it to McCain, additional findings. McCain was sufficiently disturbed by what he read to take it to FBI Director James Comey himself, personally. They had a five-minute meeting, the two men. Very little was said. McCain turned it over to him and is now awaiting what the FBI's response is to that information."

I was livid. Bernstein must have received much of his information from the FBI or other US Intelligence Community sources. How could the USIC have done this to long-standing allies like Orbis without even a heads-up? We had had our parting of ways with the FBI at the end of October, but this was inexcusable.

Katherine's response was practical and much more useful

than mine. She immediately concluded that within twenty-four hours my identity as the author of the reports would surely be made public, and every journalist in the world would be prying into my professional and personal lives. We knew we would be under siege if my identity became known. This would lead to considerable intrusion by journalists but would also expose me and the family to security threats.

The evening got worse. Around midnight Chris Burrows called. "Have you seen *BuzzFeed*?" he asked.

Ken Bensinger, whom I knew from helping him with information on a book he wrote about the FIFA corruption case, had passed through London the previous week. While in town he had contacted me to ask whether I had been involved in the compilation of a dossier of intelligence on the Trump campaign's alleged links to Russia. I had promptly but politely ended the conversation there.

Katherine and I were in bed when Chris called. She had her laptop open.

"Look at this," she said. "Your reporting is all over the internet."

I could feel my heart thumping as I read the majority of our memos, almost completely unredacted, on the *BuzzFeed* website.

Katherine suggested that I phone my elder sister Alison in London. Shortly before Christmas I had gone round to see Alison and her husband, Stefan, at their flat in Kensington. "There's something I need to tell you," I said. I then explained what Orbis had uncovered about Trump and Russia.

"If this gets out it's going to be a shitstorm and I might need somewhere to stay."

We had kept our home address in Surrey off every conceivable public database but we knew that tabloid journalists paid sources within the British utilities companies illegally to leak confidential biodata about people of interest. I was also concerned about my mother. For security reasons my address was listed in public company records as being at her house in Wokingham. My sister did not think that I should tell her about the possibility that journalists might suddenly show up there, however; it would just worry her.

Katherine and I decided that we should probably leave home in the morning and that I would take my daughter, Georgie, with me. Katherine would take her daughter. "I've done some work on Trump and Russia and it's leaked," I explained to the girls, who were eighteen and sixteen at the time and were still living at home, unlike our sons. "This means that journalists are going to come looking for me and it could be unpleasant, so we think we should go and stay elsewhere for a while." I did not say that there might be a security threat; they were somewhat used to our heightened levels of security at home and there was no point in alarming them further. Besides, I felt—and still feel—that the actual chances of someone attempting to hurt me or the family were small.

The girls thought we were overreacting. "No one's going to be interested in you," responded one in typical teenager fashion. They did not warm to being told to shut down their Facebook and Instagram accounts. I scrubbed my LinkedIn profile to the bare minimum.

Our sons were away at university, so they would not be immediately affected by whatever was about to happen.

I packed a bag and tried, with difficulty, to get some sleep.

* * *

NEXT MORNING, WE had forgotten that Glen, our handyman who had been doing some tiling work in the house, was due to show up to continue the job.

I left early with Georgie, briefing my neighbor Mike on the way out that there might be some media interest coming and please not to say anything to them. I asked him if he would look after the cats. This was the only thing he did mention to the journalists who appeared on our doorstep soon after. The *London Evening Standard* the next day reported: "'Will you look after my cat' says MI6 spy as he flees home . . ."

This sentence later became the name of our family WhatsApp group.

Eventually, in the early afternoon, Katherine managed to persuade Glen to leave the rest of the tiling unfinished for another day. She then left quickly with her daughter and drove to her sister's home in Yorkshire. Georgie and I had gone to the home of Nick, my former brother-in-law. We wanted to split up and go where we hoped we would not be found.

Georgie and I spent most of the day there, but then Nick, who had of course helped set up Orbis years previously, drove me and Georgie to my sister Alison's flat in London, leaving my car behind at Nick's house. On the way we stopped at a pub for lunch. I found it difficult to focus; I had developed an intense migraine headache, I suppose in anticipation of what I assumed was about to happen.

That evening the *Wall Street Journal* named me as the author of the dossier. The backlash from Trump and his supporters began immediately. It was vicious and continues to this day.

Chapter 16

"AN ENEMY OF MOTHER RUSSIA"

IN THE DAYS that followed I felt hunted. Journalists staked out various addresses: Nick's house, a home Alison and her husband owned in the northeastern English city of Newcastle, my mother's place, a previous address we had lived in, and, of course, our home in Farnham.

Thankfully, though, none came to my sister's home in London, perhaps because the flat was registered in her husband's name. It's a wonderful place, but it became something of a prison to me. I did not want Georgie to experience that—and I was very distracted by work—so she left to stay with friends after a couple of days. I did not like letting her go; and I did not see her again for another month.

I was now alone at my sister's. Her son Dan was then about twelve, and he had to keep the secret at school that his uncle Chris was hiding out in the spare room.

Chris Burrows and the rest of the Orbis team took over nearly all the regular client work at the firm. Our company name was now widely known, and much of our newfound renown was not helpful; Trump and his supporters immediately had begun what would remain an unrelenting attack on our credibility and reputation. "Does anyone really believe that story?" Trump asked at his first press conference as president-elect, on January 11, the day after *BuzzFeed* published the dossier and the day the *Wall Street Journal* identified me as its author.

Trump played it for laughs. But his attempts at humor would soon give way to venom.

We were firefighting on multiple fronts. We soon faced legal threats from people and companies named in the reports; I had a substantial personal tax bill to pay; and our then most significant client, Bilfinger, decided to withhold payment, kicking us when we were down. I had to borrow money from Alison to pay my tax.

Meanwhile, Aleksei Gubarev, a Russian entrepreneur who is mentioned in the dossier, immediately filed a libel suit against me and Orbis in the London courts in February. More lawsuits were to follow—two from Trump himself, eventually, and a data protection complaint filed by three Russian businessmen with ties to the Kremlin.

I felt this was Putin's way of coming after me. That is what he and his obedient oligarchs do to punish their critics and enemies in the West, particularly in the UK. They do not go after their foreign adversaries with a baseball bat—or radioactive poison. They save those tactics for people they consider traitors. For the rest of us they deploy hackers, lawyers, and London-based communications and PR firms that, in my opinion, have all but committed treason in their willingness to act on behalf of Russian interests.

The Kremlin will do what it can to make its enemies' and adversaries' lives hard. In 2012 a source told Orbis that an FSB officer said I was considered by them as "an enemy of Mother

Russia." A lot of my former colleagues in Crown Service, certainly the ones who have ever worked in Moscow, have had unpleasant experiences after leaving government. One who was working for a major British manufacturing company as a senior executive went to Moscow on a business trip and signed a significant deal with Aeroflot, Russia's national airline. He was traveling with his CEO and the chairman of the board of directors. That gave him little protection, however; at Moscow airport, as they were heading home to London, my former colleague was taken to a side room and told, "Don't think that we've forgotten all the things you did against us and if you come back here we might find something illegal in your suitcase."

Putin's pressure on Orbis and on me was just beginning.

* * *

I CALLED MY sister's flat the "golden cage"; it has big rooms and beautiful art on the walls, but I did not go outside for ten days and was not sure when I could return home. My brother-in-law, Stefan, decided one evening that ten days inside was long enough, so he gave me a beanie hat and a big coat and we went for a walk around the block in the cold and dark of January.

Later they would drive me out to a house on a gated estate in Surrey that was being leased by an old friend of mine. I could not easily be spotted there and there were three exits, so if someone did stake it out, I would likely be able to get away without detection. Katherine came to stay on weekends. She and the girls moved around for a while but school was very much on, and the girls felt confused and rootless, living out of plastic bags. They eventually decided to move back into our house, where we had to have £30,000 worth of fences, tall electronic gates, and security cameras installed.

I suppose all of this might sound a little paranoid or melodramatic now, but at the time I found the public exposure and physical pursuit of me and my family members to be truly unsettling, and even shocking. I had spent all my government and subsequent career working out of sight and had kept a low profile, even in the private sector.

And there was something else my family and I were dealing with—a betrayal that had begun only weeks before the news about the dossier broke and that made us feel yet more unprotected.

Chapter 17

COLLATERAL DAMAGE

WEDNESDAY, DECEMBER 7, 2016, had begun as a normal working day for Katherine. She was, as usual, up before dawn. She put on a warm coat and took the early commuter train into London, then grabbed a cappuccino once in the office.

She had been abroad on back-to-back temporary postings to Hong Kong and Australia from the fall of 2015 to the summer of 2016, and had then taken the rest of the summer off. By the autumn, she had happily settled into her new role in government—a sensitive policy job—and was again enjoying the routine of working in London. That was about to change.

As soon as she arrived at work that day Katherine's boss asked her to come into his office straightaway.

"Oh dear, this is going to be difficult," her boss muttered, after he closed the door behind Katherine and he had gestured for her to sit down.

In what sounded like a carefully agreed form of words, he said Katherine was to be moved out of her current post because of a "perceived conflict of interest with the work of Chris's company." This had been decided following discussions held over the previous "couple of weeks" between the lawyers, vetters, and the heads of security and human resources in her government department (which I'll henceforth refer to as "the office," not least because that is how its employees commonly refer to it).

Katherine was stunned. Both she and I had been scrupulous over the years in maintaining a firewall separation between her government work and my business activities. In all the time that she had held the highest levels of security clearance and worked in the most sensitive roles, not only had there never been a suggestion of any such concern but the office only recently had sought to draw upon my knowledge of and intelligence on Russian activities in Hong Kong when I had visited her there. Her new job had absolutely no overlap with any work of Orbis.

She asked her boss what this "perceived conflict of interest" related to. He stressed that there was no question mark over Katherine's integrity but he could not elaborate further. He said the decision had been made at a senior level. Katherine assumed this was some kind of mistake. She had a hundred questions. Why had she not been part of these discussions before such a drastic decision had been made? Why had she only recently been appointed to her new job if this problem had arisen? Who was suggesting there was a conflict of interest? Her boss was a brick wall in response. He had said all he was permitted to say.

Katherine went back to her desk, feeling a rising sense of confusion and upset.

When I received a phone call from her shortly afterward, she was already on her way up to Victoria to see me. We met for coffee at the Goring Hotel and she told me about the meeting. What had Orbis been up to? Was there something I had not told her? If so, now would be a good time to fess up. But I was as dumbfounded as she was. Orbis had no business overlap with the new area she was focused on at work and had consciously avoided it.

We found out later that her office had been in secret discussions with US counterparts, specifically the FBI, about me and the dossier since at least the previous November.

Over the following weeks Katherine, refusing to be shoved out of her job without proper explanation, robustly pushed back on her management in an attempt to get to the truth of what was behind this decision. She and I did not know how worried we should be. Casting unsubstantiated claims of "perceived conflict of interest" without foundation created risk in itself, because whatever this issue was, we might unknowingly be making it worse. It is also an ominous phrase to be bandied about when you work in parts of government where integrity and discretion are paramount. The Christmas holidays approached with Katherine in a standoff with her employer.

After leaving Crown Service in 2009 to set up Orbis I had had infrequent but cordial relations with the government. I had written to them formally, for example, in 2013, to deconflict when Orbis was about to begin paid client work with the FBI, as Katherine had been working on UK-US issues at that time. There had been no objection. I also had returned there for occasional social events and family days over the years.

Then things got murkier. On December 20, 2016, I was contacted by the office. Chris Burrows and I were asked to meet up before Christmas with Cressida Dick, then a senior Metropolitan Police officer who was working in a security capacity. We agreed to meet Cressida on December 22, in a notably expensive suite at the Goring Hotel, booked at taxpayers' expense.

She wasted little time in getting to the point. The topic under discussion was the dossier and the gist was: What on earth did you think you were doing?

Rather than focusing seriously on the Trump-Russia intelligence and wanting to investigate the potential threats it might present to British national security, Cressida Dick told Chris and me that we had been irresponsible in undertaking this work and had created risk for our families. The whole tone of the meeting was akin to a headmistress-style telling off. It reminded me of the entitled sense of ownership our former employers often displayed toward us.

But there was no hint of the manipulations and deliberations that we subsequently found had been going on for some time between the British government and its US counterpart over the dossier. Just like Katherine, we were to be kept in docile ignorance while the UK government panicked about how to contain the potential time bomb of both the implications of our dossier reporting itself and the likely volcanic response of President-elect Trump should he become aware of it.

In my previous government role, any reporting we had received deemed to be politically sensitive or controversial would be called a hot potato. It was clear the office thought what was on their hands now was a hot potato of nuclear proportions. The office should have respectfully, transparently, and calmly engaged with us instead of treating us like miscreants. They would have received our willing cooperation for taking whatever steps might be necessary to limit any potential negative blowback on the UK government. We had no reason or desire to cause them—or our country—any difficulty.

But their choice was otherwise. Orbis and I were to be deceitfully manipulated by the office's joint operational collaboration with US agencies, and Katherine would effectively have a blanket thrown over her. Her bosses decided that she must be hidden away in the hope that Trump and his aides would never learn that my wife still worked in the heart of the British government. Their fear? That Trump would accuse the British government—wrongly, of course—of having had its fingerprints all over the dossier from the start. They were worried presumably that the damage to the relationship with the United States might be irreparable if Trump concluded that Britain was part of some grand conspiracy to keep him from power. The honorable and right approach by the British government would have been to stand up and make it clear to Trump that no one in government, my wife included, had had anything to do with the dossier. Instead they chose to punish a loyal government servant—Katherine.

* * *

WITH THE REST of the world, we watched the strange mix of incredulity and anticipation the upcoming Trump inauguration was provoking. We had no knowledge whatsoever of how the dossier was being handled at that time within the US government, that it had been appended to the US Intelligence Community's report on Russian interference in the 2016 election that was later briefed up to the president and president-elect, or that there was any risk of it becoming public. Katherine's employers must have known at least some of this, but they kept us in ignorance of their planning and conversations with US counterparts. By doing so they failed dismally in their duty of care to her, and arguably to me, as a spouse, former employee, and British citizen.

Although we were being kept in the dark, significant activity was going on elsewhere. And then came the CNN report on Tuesday January 10, 2017. This was followed by a telegram from the British embassy, Washington, to the Foreign Office in London carrying the time stamp 0117Z the following morning, January 11, 2017. (It may not be generally known outside government and aviation circles that to avoid confusion between local time zones, UK government communications from anywhere in the world are time stamped with "Zulu" time [also known as Z time or GMT]. So, for example, 2 p.m. in London and 9 a.m. [EST] in Washington would both be noted as 1400Z.) 0117Z came to be a time stamp of great significance to us and, to me, emblematic of the UK government's duplicitous treatment of Katherine.

We were much later to find out that on the night of January 10—the evening the story broke on CNN—the British embassy in Washington was sending a telegram back to London. Time-stamped 0117Z on January 11 (i.e., 8:17 p.m. on January 10 in Washington), the message informed the Foreign Office in London that they had briefed Trump aides Steve Bannon and Jared Kushner along the lines agreed earlier that evening on matters concerning me and the dossier. At that time, no one from Katherine's office had even given us an inkling of their deliberations with the US government concerning the dossier, or that they were already briefing the incoming US administration on "lines to take" already agreed in London. As the British government got its story aligned with Donald Trump, we were left like sitting ducks as the tsunami of media exposure was about to break over us the following day.

As I've already described, the days and weeks following *BuzzFeed*'s publication of the dossier on January 11 and my naming by the *Wall Street Journal* plunged my family into a nightmare of panic and worry, particularly for our four children. Katherine told me later that having fled to her sister's house in Yorkshire on January 11, as the media besieged our Surrey home, she felt that she had lost her husband, her family, her home, and her job in the space of a single day.

Katherine had felt guilty at having to take an unplanned day off work on January 11. But that day turned into many. Sadly she was never to return to her post again. She also subsequently discovered that in the days following the dossier's publication, the office had issued a memorandum to all staff to have no unauthorized contact with either her or me, or with Chris Burrows or his wife, Claire, for that matter. Katherine was now effectively persona non grata, after decades of loyal service.

It would be weeks before she met up again with colleagues officially, in a bizarre subterfuge that had them all gather at a provincial training location. There she was told that not only would she not be allowed to return to her job but she could not even be seen now going into the London building she normally worked in.

Instead, she was required first to travel to another central London government building, turn off her phone, and then make the rest of the journey in an official vehicle, to avoid arriving at the office on foot.

The government's concealment worked. Katherine's career as a Crown servant was never picked up on by the media or Trump.

* * *

IN THE FOLLOWING weeks and months Katherine was left in limbo. She was required to go to work each day, but once there she had no job to do. She was told her deployment was now "restricted" in terms of whom outside in wider government and foreign liaison she could contact, and she was denied any substantive role.

By the fall of 2018 nothing had changed in Katherine's work situation since that first conversation with her boss on December 7, 2016. It was not a tenable situation. The continuing stress was wearing her out. To my mind this was an obvious case of constructive dismissal, and so legal action was a potential next step. But we both knew that as well as taking years and being hugely expensive, any legal action would be met by the office with its veil of government secrecy and that would make a fair hearing impossible. The government offered Katherine another way forward: she could retire early on a reduced pension. To sweeten this, the government would add a six-figure lump sum. The bitter aftertaste was being forced to sign a strict nondisclosure agreement, or NDA, something the British government claims to disapprove of when used by others.

And so Katherine left government, signing off administrative paperwork on a Wednesday morning in a clerical outbuilding without even a thank-you from her boss or any other senior figure after twenty-eight exemplary years of service.

She walked out of the building alone and caught the bus up to Piccadilly. I had booked a table at the Wolseley, a posh restaurant. We had what we ironically called a celebratory lunch. I gave her a small present and a card "on behalf of the grateful British public" and I thanked her for her long and distinguished service.

Chapter 18

THREE STRIKES

BY THE BEGINNING of March 2017 the hunger for photographs of me—with a going price of £50,000—had abated somewhat, so I returned to living at home and reached out to an old friend for media handling advice. I had gotten to know Nick Robinson during our university years, and he was now one of Britain's most prominent journalists and broadcasters in his role as a newscaster on the BBC's *Today* program.

"I want to break out of this reclusion and do it in a way in which nobody makes any money out of it, in which we control it and in which the media spotlight goes away as quickly as possible," I told him.

Nick advised us to contact the Press Association—Britain's main press agency, whose work is syndicated to all major news outlets in the UK—and said I should arrange a photo and video opportunity outside the Orbis office in London.

So on March 7, 2017, dressed in a suit and tie, I stood outside our office in Victoria and gave a short statement to the camera saying I was glad to be back at work and thanked people for their kind messages of support. I then walked into my office

and straight out of the back door to a waiting car. My statement
was already on the radio by the time Katherine and I got thirty
minutes' drive away en route to where we were staying.

For the next few days the photographers were back outside the house again and staked out the Orbis office. The media flurry focused mainly on noting that I was alive and that
I looked like I had a 1980s-style mullet hair style. Admittedly I
hadn't had a haircut since December.

But by then, nosy journalists were the least of my problems.

* * *

I HAD MADE enemies of the presidents of both the United
States and Russia—and each of those men and their acolytes
came after me.

From early January 2017 till now I have essentially had two
jobs. My work for Orbis continues—and the company has generally thrived. The second job was defending the company—
and myself—from political and legal attacks.

I am not going to use this book to chronicle every attack
or to settle every score. Tucker Carlson, Rush Limbaugh, Sean
Hannity, John Solomon, and the editorial page of the *Wall
Street Journal* were just some of the conservative media figures
and entities who rushed to accuse me and Orbis of being unreliable and part of a Deep State conspiracy against Trump. The
likes of Devin Nunes, Lindsey Graham, and Charles Grassley
attacked from Congress; as we have seen earlier, the latter two
earlier absurdly referred me in January 2018 to the Department of Justice for a possible criminal investigation. The list of
people and institutions who failed to stand up for what is right
or raced to get in line behind Trump and Putin is long.

Orbis and I could have chosen to go entirely silent during

this period, and when it came to the press that was exactly what we did. But I felt I had nothing to hide from our allies in the US and UK governments. We are all, I kept telling myself, on the same side—against Putin's Russia. I was heartened when Rod Rosenstein, then deputy US attorney general, appointed Robert Mueller, the experienced former director of the FBI, as special counsel in May 2017. Mueller was tasked with investigating Russia's alleged involvement in the US election and possible ties to the Trump campaign. My lawyers and I decided that we should cooperate with US investigators as much as we could, without putting Orbis and myself—and, most important, our sources—in any jeopardy.

In September 2017 two FBI officials who were part of Mueller's team flew to London to interview me. I had met one of them before—an analyst named Brian Auten—at the October 2016 meeting in Rome. The other, Amy, was new to me. I have decided to withhold her surname from this book so as not to endanger her personal security, although, as we shall see, she arguably did not merit the favor. (Brian Auten's last name was made public many years ago by other people involved in the investigation.)

The meeting had been brokered by the British government and the DOJ. We agreed to it on two conditions: the fact that the meeting had taken place must never be made public; and the identities of our sources must be protected entirely. The FBI gave me—and perhaps more significantly, the British government—firm assurances that both conditions would be respected.

I suggested beforehand to the FBI agents that they book a meeting room at the then Grosvenor Hotel (now the Clermont) in Victoria, near the Orbis office. On the morning of September 17, 2017, Chris and I turned up and located the FBI team in the six-person Ghan Boardroom at the hotel. After some small talk the conversation began. Chris stayed for the first day and I continued for the second one.

Auten and Amy wanted to go through the dossier in detail. They asked me about its sources, and they were interested in any relevant new intelligence that we had come across in the weeks and months since the dossier became public. We shared that with them, such that it was.

I felt that we had a good conversation. They were professionals. And, crucially, they assured me: "We will do absolutely everything in our power to make sure none of this ever sees the light of day."

I had worked with the FBI since 2006, when I was still in Crown Service. I considered Mike Gaeta a friend. I had given the FBI information about the FIFA investigation; they had run with it, and that led to numerous indictments and convictions. I had supplied them with more than one hundred reports over the years. They had paid us for some of this information. And so, in spite of the breakdown in our relationship in late 2017, I trusted the FBI and its people. Their word, as far as I was concerned, was reliable. And it was on that basis, and the commitments they had made to the British government, that I spoke to them in such detail in London. We were, as I kept saying to myself, all supposedly on the same side.

Amy and Auten flew home. Chris and I felt we had done our duty to help an ally. And we trusted the people we had confided in.

Within weeks, however, news of the meeting in London began leaking in the American media. Evan Perez broke it first—as before—on CNN.

Amy and I had used WhatsApp to communicate in the run-up to our meeting in London. So that was how I reached out to her as the news began to spread. In early October the US media was reporting that congressional Republicans were attempting to obtain our testimony and details about our Russian sources from the FBI. This was how the conversation went from that point on:

October 6, 2017

CHRIS: Morning Amy, sorry to bother you so early. Grateful if we could have a word later today because we are obviously concerned about and keen to discuss latest developments. Many thanks, Chris

AMY: Hi Chris, apologies I'm just seeing your messages & the developments. I'm also quite concerned. I haven't been in the office yet today, as I wasn't feeling well. I'm going to go in & talk with mgt & find out what I can. I will call you before that—just give me about 45 min. Thanks

CHRIS: OK Amy. Understood. Thanks, Chris

October 13, 2017

CHRIS: Hi Amy, grateful for a call, whenever you're ready. I have some updates and issues to discuss. Thanks, Chris

AMY: Hi Chris, of course. Just at dinner with a friend & I know it's late for you. Is tomorrow ok, or if I need to step outside, I can.

CHRIS: No, please enjoy your dinner and let's speak tomorrow. Thanks, Chris

AMY: OK great, I'll call you tomorrow. Cheers, Amy

October 14, 2017

AMY: Hi Chris, just tried to call. I'm available whenever you
can chat. Thanks!

And later:

AMY: Odd, I can hear you. Let me get a new headset. One
sec.

We had no further person-to-person conversations.

On October 25, 2017, CNN broke the news that I had spoken with the FBI. "Special Counsel Robert Mueller's investigators met this past summer with the former British spy whose
dossier on alleged Russian efforts to aid the Trump campaign
spawned months of investigations that have hobbled the Trump
administration, according to two people familiar with the matter," the online story began.

More stories followed. I reached back out to Amy:

October 27, 2017

CHRIS: Hi Amy, could we speak tomorrow please? I've just
seen a media story quoting Paul Ryan saying the Bureau
have agreed to hand over to congress docs on my
relations with you and relating to the dossier (sources?)
Obviously we are very concerned about this. People's
lives may be at risk. Many thanks, Chris

AMY: Hi Chris, I'm unfortunately not in town this week—on
personal vacation with my family out of state. It will be
difficult for me to touch base until I am back & I have
no insight into this while I'm away. I can try to put you in
touch with someone else at the office, but can't be sure

I'll find them tomorrow. I hate to put it off until Monday, but there isn't much I can do at the moment. Let me know if you need me to find someone for you tonight & I can try.

CHRIS: Thanks Amy. This is important to us. Maybe I could speak to Brian later today? Best Chris

---

November 1, 2017

CHRIS: Dear Amy, I hope you had a good break last week with your family. I know things are politically hot right now but I would welcome a call. Firstly, there is the question of what might or might not be handed over by the Bureau to congress this week, especially concerning sources and my previous career/work. And secondly, our friend [Igor Danchenko] arrives here on Friday for a week, and might travel on from here to meet his friend in a third country next week. Both are interested in engaging with you too. This presents the best opportunity in our view to validating parts of the work. My former employers already know in principle this is happening. Are you and your colleagues interested in engaging with him/them at all? If so, we should make plans. We shall be going ahead with it anyway unless you have other reasons to advise against. You could meet him at least here with me introducing. We also have other significant leads we would like to share with you. Your call. Thanks and Best, Chris

---

November 7, 2017

CHRIS: Hi Amy, trying to call you. I wanted to update you on a few things. When might we speak please? Best, Chris

December 27, 2017

CHRIS: Dear Amy, I hope you had a good Christmas. We
need to talk. I am hearing some very disturbing things
from reliable contacts in the US. What they're telling
me is that highly confidential (and presumably highly
classified) information about Orbis's work with the Bureau
and associated business activities, including with your
(Special Counsel's) team, in relation to the "dossier," has
been disclosed to members of the House Intelligence
Committee who are now leaking it to the media in order to
try to discredit me, our work, and the Bureau and Special
Counsel's team. If true, the potential consequences of this
are extremely serious and risk jeopardizing the security
of both our and your ongoing operations. People's lives
may be at risk. I have raised the issue of congressional
disclosure with you before and received no response.
Given these recent developments I have to press you
again on this subject and would ask you or a colleague
to contact me at your earliest convenience to discuss it.
Many thanks, Chris

December 29, 2017

AMY: Chris, We received your message and apologize for
the delay in response. We don't believe there is a need
for further communication. If in the future circumstances
change, we will contact you. Thank you.

And that was it. The FBI was washing their hands of a
former professional and close ally with more than twenty-
five years' experience. They were doing so contrary to the
agreements that had been made with the British government
about confidentiality and assurances about the security of our

sources. And now, having betrayed us, they were shutting the door in our face.

But it gets much worse.

* * *

I'M GOING TO briefly leap ahead three years—to the point when the second explicit deal we had made with the FBI was broken. On his last full day in office—January 19, 2021—Trump ordered the declassification of a binder of documents that had been part of the FBI's investigation. Among those documents was a transcript of our September 2017 interviews with Amy and Auten. And in that transcript was unredacted information about our sources.

Soon after that two of our sources in Russia—who were named in the transcript—went silent. We have not heard from them since, nor have we received any information about them.

The FBI's promises to Orbis, to me, to the British government in the run-up to our meeting in London on September 17, 2017, were worthless. And it is important to note that unfortunately, when the chips were down in our case, the FBI could not be relied upon.

If that is how the Bureau treats an old colleague, how would they treat anyone else? If you were a source with information that could help the US government and you knew that they could not be trusted with life-and-death intelligence, why on earth would you put your faith in the FBI? That has major national security ramifications. Because the message to potential sources is: Be careful when talking to the FBI. They have no power ultimately to protect you or your information. And that only helps Russia. Not to mention other adversaries—and even possibly regular criminals.

Furthermore, the FBI knowingly deceived us. No one at the FBI or the DOJ told us that ultimately the president of the United States had the power to declassify any document and that, therefore, there was nothing they could do to protect our sources if the president decided to make such information public. Maybe we should have known that ourselves. But if we did not—and we are rather more savvy about intelligence gathering and evidence collecting than most people—then I imagine many potential sources do not know this. Chris Burrows and I simply would not have agreed to speak with Mueller's investigators about our sources if they had said: "Just one thing—we can't guarantee that the president won't make public everything you tell us."

And if Trump is reelected in 2024 it is safe to assume—because he has done it before—that he will declassify anything he feels like declassifying that he regards as useful to his partisan interests or just out of revenge.

* * *

I HAVE HAD no contact with the FBI since I received Amy's last WhatsApp message. We have occasionally fed them information indirectly through other people but not in any way that is attributable to us. They have received some of our intelligence; they just do not know it.

That is the way it has to be. I still want to help the United States, the UK's most important ally and, for now, the most powerful democracy in the world. But we would not go directly to the FBI again. And we would not be prepared to name a source under any circumstances. We have learned our lesson, the hard way.

* * *

BUT BEFORE WE came to that realization, we continued to help US investigators. In retrospect, that was also a mistake.

The next US entity that wanted to speak to Orbis was the Senate Select Committee on Intelligence. We had probably left it a little late but we decided it was time to lawyer up. It was January 2018 and I felt increasingly in need of expert, outside legal help. We hired an experienced Washington attorney named Bob Weinberg. He became our point man with Congress.

The Senate Intelligence Committee was at that time chaired by the Republican senator Richard Burr, of North Carolina. The committee got in touch to ask if I would come over and talk to them, or if they could send someone to London. Initially, I declined, due to the expense this would incur and the time it would take.

Bob explained to the committee staffers that we would engage with them but only in written form—and in return they would have to suspend any subpoena they might be issuing against me and Chris.

This was largely symbolic. Such a subpoena would not have been enforceable because the US Congress has no jurisdiction over the UK, but I did not want to be portrayed as having anything to hide.

So they sent over forty questions. Some of them covered areas where I just could not comment, particularly ones about my career as a Crown servant. They asked other questions about sources and leads. We were able to help them with some of these. We shared both Project CHARLEMAGNE reports with them.

One Trump-Russia lead we shared with the Senate Select Committee at this point concerned the role an American businessman resident in Russia, David Geovanis, who allegedly had been Trump's fixer and facilitator there around the turn of the millennium, played in any Russian compromise of Trump. As CNN reported later, in February 2019, Geovanis had a reputation for the high life in Moscow and organizing wild parties. He appeared as an early lead in the Trump-Russia investigation. He was photographed calling on the deputy mayor of Moscow with Trump in 1996, despite Trump's claim that he had never met officials when visiting Russia. But attempts by the media, Special Counsel Robert Mueller and Senate Select Committee on Intelligence to contact/subpoena him to give testimony in their respective investigations proved fruitless. Geovanis lay low throughout the Trump presidency, apparently moving to a remote part of Russia and never returning to the US, where he had close relatives. This spoke volumes to us as intelligence professionals but apparently has never been followed through by the media, congress, or the US government. You have to wonder why not.

In exchange for our cooperation they agreed to the following: There should be no publicity around our cooperation or publication of the material by the committee without our consent. And after we had submitted our written answers, they would then leave us alone.

Burr breached all of those agreements. He talked loosely to a journalist and confirmed that the committee had spoken to me and indicated that I could have been more forthcoming. When the committee's report came out, extracts from our answers were included in it. Every undertaking they had made to us was violated.

* * *

THE AMERICAN GOVERNMENT does seem to like investigating themselves. In 2019 we were faced with another request for an interview, this time from the Office of the Inspector General of the Department of Justice. Inspector General Michael E. Horowitz was charged with investigating whether political bias within the FBI had spurred on the opening of the Crossfire Hurricane (Trump-Russia) investigation.

We were tipped off by knowledgeable US sources that the Office of the Inspector General would criticize us heavily in their report if we refused to engage with them. So eventually, with Bob's wise counsel, we agreed to speak to the IG as well.

A team of four investigators flew to London in June 2019. We met in a nearby US embassy–occupied building.

The tone was hostile. And eventually they made an accusation that I had a rather good rebuttal for: You had it in for the Trump family from the beginning, they declared, admit it.

"Hang on a second," I said, "there's something you need to know." And I explained that I had in fact known Ivanka Trump for several years, had visited Trump Tower, had hoped to do business with the Trump Organization, had briefly met Don Jr. and held his baby for a moment—and so it was ridiculous to suggest that I had a long-standing animus toward the Trump family.

They turned white and looked a bit lost.

On the eve of publication, in December 2019, the OIG's office called Bob and told him that previously redacted parts of the report—details about Igor Danchenko, it turned out—had been declassified and would be in the report. Furthermore, it would contain derogatory material about me and Orbis. Previously the OIG had pledged to give us time to rebut anything about us or our work before it was published in report form. But that was clearly not going to happen. We believed it was for this reason: we had effectively rebutted all their other allegations against us, and wrong-footed them with the Ivanka

Trump friendship revelation, and so they needed to hit us with something below the belt. This was no way to treat well-meaning and long-standing allies of the US.

That was the third time we had tried to help American investigators. And it was the third time we had been burned. That was enough. We were done cooperating with our supposed allies—allies we had tried to help by warning them of a potentially grave threat to their country.

Chapter 19

THE DURHAM FARCE

AND SO THE fourth time we said no.

Of all the various iterations of Donald Trump's desire to abuse the US executive branch and legal system to wreak revenge on his political enemies, the investigation led by Special Prosecutor, later Special Counsel, John Durham was by far the most egregious.

In May 2019 Trump's partisan attorney general, William Barr—who has now turned on his former boss—appointed Durham, a formerly respected federal prosecutor from Connecticut, to lead a probe into what had prompted and motivated the FBI to investigate the possible Russian interference in the 2016 election. (And yes, that was exactly what the Office of the Inspector General had examined. But Durham's probe, unlike the OIG investigation, was a criminal inquiry that could lead to prosecutions.)

The Durham investigation was based on the absurd notion that there was some kind of political conspiracy cooked up by the Hillary Clinton campaign, the FBI, and associates of both—including me—to fabricate intelligence on the Trump campaign's ties to Russia in order to smear and discredit the Republican Party candidate and later ruin his term in office.

Durham set about his business and continued for nearly four years. His deputy, Nora Dannehy, who had worked closely with Durham for many years, resigned from his team in the run-up to the 2020 presidential election reportedly because she could not tolerate the politicization of the US justice system that his investigation represented.

In late 2019, about a year before she resigned, Dannehy called our lawyer, Bob Weinberg, to ask him if I would be willing to be interviewed by the Durham team. Bob advised me strongly against it. This investigation was different, he said. It was politically partisan. We politely declined.

* * *

EVER SINCE IGOR DANCHENKO had been effectively unmasked by Senator Lindsey Graham in the summer of 2020 for, in our view, clearly partisan political reasons, even though Graham apparently must have known he was working as an undercover asset for the FBI, we had been worried about Igor. The FBI had cut off contact with him from that point and had not paid him any compensation for the obviously sterling operational work on Russia he had done for them, including helping them conclude that a Russian woman named Maria Butina, who was living in Washington, DC, was a Russian asset operating in and around Republican Party leadership circles in Washington.

We had asked a close American associate who had good US Intelligence Community and political ties in Congress to look after Igor during the tough period after his unmasking, something that the FBI should have been duty bound to do but did not because they were too afraid of Trump and his Republican sycophants in Congress. Our American associate had been doing a great job in finding Igor work and had grown close to him and his hugely supportive and impressive wife, Kristina, and had given them some degree of peace of mind.

But that was all to change in October 2020 when Durham indicted Igor on five separate charges of making false statements to the FBI during interviews about the sources for the dossier. Durham charged Igor under Section 1001 of Title 18 of the US penal code. There is no similar law in many other countries, including the UK, and it is commonly seen as a last resort for prosecutors wanting to indict targets when everything else has failed.

I lost many nights' sleep worrying about Igor, not least because we all had had to break off contact with him due to potential legal jeopardy, doubtless one of Durham's objectives. I felt—and feel—a great responsibility to him. He was also the means by which our Republican adversaries could uncover our subsource network in Russia, which was vulnerable to coercion and repression by the Russian security services and our oligarch litigation plaintiff adversaries.

The judge was clearly unimpressed by Durham's case. He dismissed one of the charges against Igor and the jury quickly delivered a unanimous not guilty verdict on the other four. Durham had taken one other case to trial and had lost that one too. He had now lost two out of two.

Igor's acquittal did not erase the hell that Durham had put him through. Igor had had to wear an ankle bracelet for a year, was not allowed to leave the greater DC area without formal permission, and had racked up huge legal expenses. He found it difficult finding work for a while and still lives in fear of physical attack from either Kremlin agents or MAGA Trump fanatics. The FBI, which promised him substantial compensation and a retirement payoff as recompense for being unmasked, disgracefully abandoned him for fear of incurring the wrath of Republicans in Congress.

And there was another unpleasant bit of blowback from the trial, in spite of Igor's full acquittal. Durham's groundless and vindictive indictments of Igor changed the prevailing US news media narrative around the dossier. The coverage became overwhelmingly negative overnight. On the day Igor was indicted the front page of the Murdoch family's partisan tabloid, the *New York Post*, featured a banner line: "The *Real* Collusion Case." The headline and subhead read: "Lie, Cheat, Steele. Russian who invented fake dirt on Trump for Hillary-funded dossier arrested." The front page featured photographs of Igor and myself.

But it was not just the trashy newspapers and the Murdoch-owned *Wall Street Journal* that fell into this trap. The coverage of Orbis and our work by normally respectable outlets like the *Washington Post* and the *New York Times* also changed. They seemed to accept Durham's indictments of Igor as the conclusive assessment of our unreliability.

The US media pendulum never swung back after Igor's acquittal, and that has been a puzzle to me ever since. Setting the record straight here has been one of the reasons I wrote this book.

The irony is that although Durham failed in court, his own professional milieu, he did succeed in his aims to smear us all via the US media.

* * *

FINALLY, IN MAY 2023, after nearly four years of work and after spending more than $6.5 million of US taxpayers' money, the Durham investigation was wound up and issued its final report. The entire investigation resulted in only one conviction: a junior FBI lawyer pled guilty to altering an email—about Carter Page's relationship with the CIA—an act the judge described as "an inappropriate shortcut." The lawyer concerned pleaded guilty and was given twelve months' probation and four hundred hours of community service. I wonder if there has ever been a special counsel who failed as dramatically as Durham did.

All Durham had left was his report. When it eventually appeared, the document repeated many of the same conspiratorial arguments and used congressional privilege in doing so, allowing Durham to make defamatory statements about me and other people involved in the case in the knowledge that there would be no legal recourse for any of us.

After reading the report I sent out a series of tweets that summarized my views on it. They were sent in the raw aftermath, but now I realize there is one yet more important point to make: If Trump is reelected, he likely would unleash more highly politicized Durham-like investigations. They would be a powerful, intimidating way to cow his critics and punish his perceived enemies. And his abuse of power—he would surely command his supposedly independent attorney general to initiate such investigations—would further undermine American democracy and its separation of powers.

This is some of what I said at the time, and I stand by these tweets, posted on May 17, 2023:

> John Durham's long-awaited report merely repeats the allegations he failed to prosecute in court. It reveals further an investigation driven by a partisan conspiracy theory to which he bent unclear testimony. It also contains various factual errors 1/4

Our reporting in 2016 was objective and not politically motivated. The allegation in Durham that our intelligence was Kremlin disinformation is also without foundation, unless you believe Putin wanted to damage Trump to assist a Clinton victory 2/4

But, as we know, Putin admitted in Helsinki he wanted Trump to win in 2016 and Trump's assertion there was no evidence of Russian interference spoke volumes.... 3/4

Finally, our 2016 Trump-Russia reporting has not been "discredited." In fact its main tenets continue to hold up well and almost no detail has been disproven, including through numerous court cases. It's high time serious American journalism put the record straight on this. 4/4

* * *

THERE IS A notable footnote to our reporting on alleged connections between Russia and Trump. This concerns Michael Cohen, Trump's former personal lawyer and fixer.

One of the 2016 dossier memos reported that Cohen allegedly traveled that year to Prague to meet with Kremlin representatives on behalf of the Trump campaign. There has been much debate around this since. We are aware of subsequent intelligence geolocating one of Cohen's mobile phones in the Czech Republic in August 2016. The McClatchy newspaper group reported in April 2018 that Mueller's team had evidence that Cohen had entered the Czech Republic in August or early September. And in December 2018 the same McClatchy reporters wrote that Cohen's phone had "sent signals ricocheting off cell towers in the Prague area in late summer 2016" and that an Eastern European intelligence agency had eavesdropped electronically on a Russian saying that Cohen was in Prague during the relevant time.

More generally, Cohen's turning against Trump made him something of a hero to those seeking to attack the former president. So there is now a tendency by liberals to view everything he says as fact. But let's not forget—Cohen is a convicted perjurer. He has lied repeatedly.

Chapter 20

THE LONG ARM OF
THE KREMLIN

THE PERIOD AFTER January 2017 was relentless. By November 2018 Katherine and I badly needed a vacation. For more than a year our lives had been upended. Every day, without fail, my name had appeared in news media. Katherine was in a constantly stressful and disempowering situation as she was having her career ripped away from her by her office. The backlash from the Trump administration, from Republican members of Congress, from the Kremlin, and from many other people wielding power and influence had been unrelenting. So we booked a vacation in Antigua.

It was the first time we had been outside Europe since the news of the dossier broke, and I was a little concerned for our security. So I called the hotel we liked the look of. They assured me the resort was very private and secure. It had a fenced perimeter and guards. I felt reassured.

But were we really at risk from the Kremlin? I thought at the time—and continue to hold this view—that Putin would not give an order physically to harm me. The former lieutenant colonel in the KGB has, so far at least, apparently heeded to a convention that goes back decades: intelligence services do not, by and large, physically attack their opposite numbers in foreign governments.

People considered traitors, however—most of them Russian citizens—are vulnerable to attempts on their lives. I knew this rather intimately because of my involvement in the investigation into the murder of Alexander Litvinenko. And I had watched with horror if not surprise as details of another assassination attempt—of former Russian military intelligence (GRU) agent Sergei Skripal and his daughter, Yulia, in the English cathedral city of Salisbury—emerged in March 2018, several years after I had left government service. This time the assassins—believed to be officers from the GRU—had used the nerve agent Novichok. Investigators concluded that both operations most likely were ordered and/or approved by Putin. But Litvinenko and Skripal were, in the eyes of the Kremlin, traitors. They had defected and used their knowledge of the workings of the Russian security state to hurt the Kremlin. That made them, in the calculus of the Russian intelligence services, entirely legitimate targets for physical attack.

I, however, had always been on the opposing side. I'm an adversary, not a traitor. So I think I'm relatively safe.

I think.

During the week we were there, it was the Antigua Yacht Show, a large regatta event, and several Russian oligarchs had sailed in to show off their superyachts. On day five of our holiday a black-hulled, 269-foot-long yacht named *Alfa Nero* moored offshore in the bay. *Alfa Nero* belonged to Andrey Guryev, an oligarch who owns Witanhurst, the second-largest house in London, after Buckingham Palace. (The yacht is currently being sold by the Antiguan government because Guryev abandoned it there after he was sanctioned by the UK government following the full-scale Russian invasion of Ukraine in 2022.) The *Alfa Nero* then left, and soon after another yacht turned up, a 360-foot-long white yacht. It was even more spectacular than the black yacht; a sleek, fast-looking bullet of a vessel with a helicopter landing pad to the aft.

It was the penultimate day of our holiday. In the afternoon we took a launch from the dock to go on a snorkeling trip along the coast. Snorkeling and scuba diving have been among my favorite activities since my youthful days in Cyprus. The sea was rough outside the bay, but when we finished snorkeling, I was still sorry to get out of the water and onto the boat and head back to land.

In retrospect I realize that our apartment at the resort, facing the half-moon bay where the big white yacht was moored, was fully within an easy line of sight from the vessels anchored there. We could have been easily observed walking along the dock and onto the launch and then out of the bay.

On the way back we asked the pilot of the launch to take us nearer to the white yacht so that we could see its name. It was called *Anna*.

Our launch pulled up to the hotel's white wooden dock and we walked back to our room. Once there I Googled the yacht. "Oh wow, it's Rybolovlev's," I said to Katherine. Dmitry Rybolovlev is a Russian oligarch with close ties to the Kremlin. In 2008 a trust that benefits Rybolovlev's older daughter, Ekaterina, bought a mansion in Palm Beach, Florida, called Maison de l'Amitie for $95 million. The seller: Donald Trump. That sale generated a profit of $55 million for Trump, who had bought the property in 2004 for only $40 million.

Orbis had done work on Rybolovlev in the past. The appearance of his yacht was a bit of a strange coincidence, but I didn't think much more about it.

Two hours later Katherine went into the bathroom of our suite. "Chris, come in here," she said, with urgency in her voice.

She was standing and looking into her brand-new washbag.

Inside were two wedding bands—one slimmer, one wider. Presumably one for a man, the other for a woman. They were not ours and they had not been there that morning. How could they have been put there? And by whom? What did this mean?

My mind immediately ran through various possibilities of what could be going on here. Were they a calling card? Were they poisoned? Had they been stolen or taken off people who had been murdered—as planted evidence that preceded the police showing up at our door or our being arrested at the airport on the way home?

We plucked the rings out of Katherine's washbag using a facecloth and took them down to reception. "This is very strange," we explained to the staff. "Someone's been in our room and has put something in my wife's toiletries bag."

The people at reception assured us that it was a fireable offense for any of the hotel staff even to touch a guest's washbag.

The manager on duty later assured us that he had checked the CCTV footage and no one other than staff members had been in our room. We decided not to make a fuss; we no longer had the rings, having given them to the hotel manager. But we now felt a bit spooked and just wanted to get home.

To my mind, a likely explanation seems that the Russian government might have known from their signals monitoring that we were at the hotel and had an operational team deploy to the bay. There were obviously lots of Russians around the island that week, so a few more undercover would go unremarked. Perhaps they carried out the ring trick on our last night so that we would not notice the rings and could be pulled aside at the airport—or maybe just to freak us out. What other credible scenarios could explain such an odd thing?

Some time later I called the hotel general manager from London to ask whether they had uncovered anything further about the ring incident. No, she told me—and then asked me the name of the manager who had been on duty at the time. "He's left the hotel," the general manager told me. "He no longer works here."

Were all these things coincidental? I do not think so. The prospect of future exotic vacations certainly came to seem less appealing.

So, if this was a cryptic message, what exactly was its purpose? Was it a warning that they (whoever they were) could get to me and my family—even harm us—whenever they felt like it, in Londongrad or at a supposedly secret and secure holiday location three thousand miles away? Were they telling me that I could be watched wherever I went in the world, for the rest of my life? That, by placing wedding rings in my wife's washbag, they could invade my family's most private spaces—and that if I thought I had not made my own family vulnerable by my actions against the Russian state, I was deluding myself?

I do not know. But at the very least the fact that we even asked those questions then—and again now—is a victory of sorts for them. You can laugh it off, take modest precautions, get on with your life—and you have to, because otherwise you would be living in an exhausting state of paranoia. And on some level, you know that if they did want to hurt you, they could, pretty much at any time. So you hope that the old rules still apply and that people like me remain out of bounds.

But to be honest, that is of only modest comfort to me when I look at how the Russian intelligence services have changed their way of operating over the past thirty years. And this is an important point: Russia, and the Soviet Union before it, has not always operated on foreign soil in the way it has come to operate now. And it is intensifying, dangerously, and Western governments must recognize that threat and devote appropriate resources and political attention to combating and deterring it.

Chapter 21

LAWFARE

YOU MIGHT THINK that in the summer and autumn of 2023 Donald Trump had other things on his mind than Orbis Business Intelligence. He had been indicted in four different criminal cases in American courts and was facing more than ninety charges. If convicted of even a handful of those charges he faced the prospect of spending the rest of his life in prison. In a separate civil case, a New York judge had ruled in September 2023 that Trump had committed such a serious fraud that he might have to relinquish all his properties in New York state, including his home base of Trump Tower. He was running out of money to pay the legal fees of the former associates who were in legal trouble alongside him. A judge had decided in a civil case that he had sexually abused the writer E. Jean Carroll. And he was, in the meantime, running for president again. But somehow Trump still found the time to pursue a civil suit against me and Orbis in the London courts. It did not seem to matter to him if he won; what he wanted was to tie up a perceived enemy in legal proceedings and saddle that adversary with costs.

This is what is known as "lawfare." And we have been on the receiving end of it since 2017.

Trump had already included me in a specious RICO—or antiracketeering—lawsuit that he filed in Florida, alongside a star-studded list of other opponents including Hillary Clinton, James Comey, Jake Sullivan, Andrew McCabe, and John Podesta. The judge in the case dismissed it in 2022 and ordered sanctions against Trump and his lawyers, but Trump appealed. Meanwhile, in October 2022, Trump filed a writ against Orbis in the UK claiming that we had breached UK data protection laws and inflicted "personal and reputational damage and distress" to him by, as he claimed, producing the dossier.

On February 1, 2024, Judge Karen Steyn threw out Trump's lawsuit on the basis it was time-barred. It was a huge relief and a victory that was certainly sweet but was also important for other whistleblowers. If Trump had prevailed, it would have set a dangerous precedent in the UK courts.

This is the front line of lawfare. This is where extremely wealthy individuals or corporations use their limitless funds to crush people who dare to face up to them. The London courts are the most plaintiff-friendly in the world and so any wealthy, litigious individual with a desire to punish and silence an adversary will look to here as the venue of choice for pursuing a legal vendetta. It is, in my opinion, a national disgrace for Great Britain.

Of course people like Trump would like to win these battles—but victory in court need not be their primary objective. Rather it is enough for bad actors with deep pockets to cripple their opponents with up-front costs and to upend their lives and working practices by tying them up in legal battles that distract them from doing their jobs. I speak from experience. Orbis has spent hundreds of thousands of pounds on lawyers and months of work on building our case when we should have been investing that time and money in the business. The Trump case in London has caused much stress and loss of sleep to me, to the extent that I have now developed high blood pressure in the process, despite being fit for my age.

Trump would probably consider these victories even though he lost the case. That is the pernicious nature of lawfare.

* * *

IT IS NO small irony that the people who have pursued Orbis and me in the same legal venues and with similar legal tactics, and often using the same attorneys, are Donald Trump and Russian business oligarchs, some of whom have now been sanctioned for their support of Putin and his illegal war in Ukraine.

In particular we have had to defend ourselves in England in two cases, which both came to trial in 2020 but that had been filed in the aftermath of the dossier's publication.

The first of these trials got underway in March 2020, just prior to the first Covid lockdown in the UK.

The case was a data protection lawsuit brought by the three Russian oligarchs who owned Alfa Group—Mikhail Fridman, Petr Aven, and German Khan. These three men also had tried to sue us previously for defamation in the US District Court in Washington, DC, but had the case quashed at the first hurdle by the judge there on First Amendment (free speech) grounds.

Fridman, Aven, and Khan had been partners in the Russian joint venture oil company TNK, with British energy giant BP. Each of them had made billions of dollars from the 2012 sale of TNK and been able to invest the proceeds abroad, something which in modern Russia is unlikely to have been possible without the approval of President Putin, given it was contrary to the policy of keeping Russian capital in-country.

The Alfa UK data protection case had been in preparation for over two years before it finally came before the High Court in London. But a fortnight before the trial opened we were called into our solicitors' office to be told that our lead lawyer on the case had been suspended. It later transpired that she had forged a High Court judge's signature on a court order to avoid being blamed for incurring extra fees for us due to her incompetence and negligence. She was later struck off as a lawyer by the Bar Council.

So that was not a good start. When we finally got into court in mid-March 2020, I was subjected to a two-day cross-examination by Hugh Tomlinson KC, some of whose questions strayed into my previous role as an intelligence professional and Crown servant. I had received instructions before the trial from the Foreign Office Legal Department that I was not permitted to discuss my government service in court under any circumstances (even though doing so might have helped our case by further establishing my expert knowledge of modern Russia and my bona fides).

On the second day of my testimony, when I was still sworn in as a witness, Katherine stayed at home, sick in bed but downplaying the seriousness of her illness so as not to destabilize me. The guidance on Covid at that early point in the pandemic—before the first lockdown—was that its principal symptom was a fever and, as Katherine did not have one, I did not imagine she had caught the virus.

But when I came out of giving testimony that morning, I was informed that Katherine had been taken to the hospital in an ambulance. She was barely able to breathe and was now in the same hospital near our home in Farnham where Laura had died eleven years previously. The judge, Sir Mark Warby, had to decide whether to release me from my testimony prematurely or have me carry on. There was chaos in the court. People assumed, probably correctly, that I might also have Covid and could be infectious to everyone else in the court.

Despite the fact that Katherine was potentially critically ill, Hugh Tomlinson initially would not agree that Justice Warby should dismiss me as a witness—and not before he had finished his cross-examination. By any stretch that was inhuman of Tomlinson, and in my view unforgivable. I was, therefore, ushered into an empty adjacent courtroom, and the cross-examination continued on an old-fashioned telephone landline, the connection to which kept dropping. Justice Warby soon decided, however, that enough was enough and kindly dismissed me as a witness so that I could go back to the hospital in Surrey to be with Katherine. By the time I arrived there, she was thankfully breathing more easily and I was able to take her back home that night. It was another couple of months before she had made a full recovery.

We waited until July for Justice Warby to issue his ruling. The three Russian billionaires each had complained about assertions in one of the dossier's memos concerning their supportive relationship with Putin and the Kremlin. We could not prove that any of these were true at trial, but succeeded in persuading the judge that we had taken reasonable care over the accuracy of almost all of them so that in the end Mr. Justice Warby found for Aven and Fridman only in respect of one allegation about illicit transfers of cash. The damages he awarded them were limited—£18,000 each to Aven and Fridman, but due to a quirk of English law, we also had to pay the majority of their costs (£1.2 million). Two years later, after Russia's invasion of Ukraine in 2022, the British government, in addition to the EU and later the US government, sanctioned Fridman, Aven, and Khan for their close political affiliation with

Putin and support for his regime. The cherry on the cake for us, however, came in 2023 when I was reliably informed that the British government's case to sanction Fridman, Aven, and Khan had drawn on evidence we had presented against them at the data protection trial in 2020.

Fridman, Aven, and Khan have all now been sanctioned by the EU and the US as well as by the UK. They have had billions of dollars of assets frozen, and their ability to travel is restricted. They have all been named as allies of Putin.

* * *

WHEN OUR SECOND London High Court trial took place in July 2020, during a partial lifting of the Covid lockdown restrictions, we were chastened by the earlier experience but much better prepared. I had undergone one long cross-examination and knew there would be another to come.

This case was a libel—or defamation—suit brought by another Russian, Aleksei Gubarev, whom I have mentioned before and who had featured, along with his IT companies, in another Trump-Russia report we had produced in late 2016.

Gubarev moved to file suit against us very soon after the Trump-Russia dossier was published without our knowledge or permission by *BuzzFeed* in January 2017. Our lawyers immediately smelled a lawfare rat. Our barrister, Gavin Millar KC, told us at our initial meeting that no normal plaintiff would have filed such a libel suit without establishing from media reporting (and correspondence with us) whether we had been responsible for or involved in publishing the particular memo in question. Of course, we were not responsible for publishing the memo, and that led to Gubarev's seemingly inevitable defeat in the High Court when the judge, once again Sir Mark Warby, issued his ruling.

Covid was by this stage a part of everyone's lives, and so this meant that we had several witnesses who were not able to attend in person and were given special dispensation by the judge to do so remotely by video link. This technological shift provided an intriguing window into the forces we were really facing. It happened during my cross-examination, this time by Gubarev's KC.

During a break in the middle of my testimony the judge asked his technical team at the court to test the video link in preparation for our defense witness, Sir Andrew Wood, and for one of Gubarev's witnesses. When they did so, multiple faces appeared suddenly on the Zoom-like box screens on the monitor in court. Each witness's remote connection to the court had had to be approved by the judge, who signed a separate court order for each one. This was meant to be a tightly controlled communications environment. But it became clear that the proceedings were being accessed by a number of unauthorized viewers.

Moreover, it quickly was established that some of these unauthorized viewers were in Russia.

Justice Warby was furious. He left the court to retire to his chambers so that he could consider how to respond to this seemingly unprecedented situation.

We were being watched from afar—certainly from Russia. And I knew that meant our viewers could well have included the Russian government and its various intelligence and security services.

I was left in the witness box for over an hour before Justice Warby returned to the bench and continued the proceedings. He announced that he was thinking of reporting Gubarev and his legal team—from the London office of the Chicago-based international firm of McDermott Will & Emery—to the Crown Prosecution Service. It transpired that Gubarev's legal team had been fully aware that a link to the video streaming of the trial had been circulated to other locations and had in fact permitted it. Ultimately the lawyers were reported by the judge to the Solicitors Regulation Authority (the professional body of English lawyers).

When Justice Warby eventually issued his judgment on October 30, 2020, he only gave the two parties access to his ruling one hour before it was made public, rather than the customary several working days. Given the plaintiff and their lawyers' previous, arguably illegal conduct in court, you could hardly blame him. But it made the stress of it much worse for all of us at Orbis—the sense that we would have no real opportunity to prepare our game plan if we had lost. Unlike with the Alfa data protection case, I was personally being sued by Gubarev alongside Orbis. And because the suit had dragged on for so long, we had exceeded our professional indemnity insurance ceiling. This meant that I faced potential financial ruin if Gubarev prevailed.

When the email came through to my computer from our counsel with the judgment attached, our IT security had to scan it before we could access it. However, sitting in our living room in Farnham, I was able to see the top line of the covering email, which read "Many congratulations, you won," which was enough for us. A three-and-a-half-year legal ordeal was over. Justice Warby had ruled in favor of Orbis and me, noting that "Mr. Gubarev's claim must be dismissed" because he had failed to prove that either Orbis or myself had intended for the dossier to be published. It was an immense relief. We were able to walk away and regroup.

But not long after, as is almost inevitable with lawfare, another case emerged. This was the absurd Trump RICO case. And then, in 2022, came Trump's more worrying data protection suit in London, where the courts tend to favor the plaintiff.

In February 2024 the judge ruled against Trump and in favor of Orbis in the former president's protracted data protection law civil case against us in the English High Court. The case was struck out and Trump was later refused the right to appeal this judgment by the head of the appeals court, Lord Warby, who coincidentally had presided over both the Alfa Group and Gubarev cases against Orbis in 2020. The judge ordered Trump to pay us an initial costs order of £300,000, with probably a similar amount on top of that to be awarded later.

At the time, Trump through his English lawyers accepted that he was fully liable to pay our costs but has prevaricated and become uncommunicative thereafter. Orbis's uninsured bill for this ridiculous case reached $1 million and is still rising. Classic "lawfare," the very thing Trump complains of himself so often in the US. He still had not paid up at the time of writing, two months later, and appeared to have no intention of doing so. This put Trump, a former US president, in breach of an English High Court order, underlining his contempt for the rule of law and, I would argue, toward the UK, the place of his mother's birth. It cements his place right at the center of what I have referred to as the "New World Disorder."

* * *

WHY DOES LAWFARE matter?

Imagine you receive an email with a legal threat that guarantees—no matter how specious the accusations contained in it—that the next move you make will be to find and then call a lawyer. You will likely feel scared and vulnerable, no matter how resilient you think you are, how righteous your cause is, and how sure you are that you have not infringed the law. And you would be right to feel scared.

Because, putting aside for one minute the issue of a judgment in a trial that may ensue, you are almost immediately racking up legal bills that will run to the tens of thousands, if you are freakishly fortunate, and almost certainly in the hundreds of thousands. And if you lose, you'll have to pick up the other side's tab—so we could easily be talking over a million here.

Such a case consumes your life. It takes you away from your family and your career. It hammers your reputation and damages your ability to make a living. You worry about your children's education or what will happen if you or your spouse gets unexpectedly unwell. You think about declaring bankruptcy; and if you do not think about it, you should be.

I share Orbis's and my struggles with lawfare here not because I feel we deserve special sympathy. I share them purely as an example. I believe that Orbis and other whistleblowers, leakers, journalists, human rights investigators, and other private intelligence companies have a role to play in helping to maintain the rule of law and democracy by exposing wrongdoing. And I have found through experience that there is no greater current threat to those who hold the powerful to account in this way than lawfare. Specifically, the legal system of my own country has long since become a weapon in the hands of wealthy bad actors. When oligarchs and despots and would-be autocrats habitually turn to the English courts and hire the best British lawyers to fight their battles to suppress critics, dissenters, and whistleblowers, it is a problem that threatens our very freedoms.

Part Three

THE QUIET FIGHT

Chapter 22

SILVER LININGS

I DID NOT much like the consequences of having the presidents of both Russia and the United States—and their proxies—put me high up on their enemies list. But the publication of the dossier had an unexpected upside. Overnight, unwittingly, I had become a globally recognized former British intelligence officer, and Chris's and my firm had become the world's most famous private intelligence company.

This had several unforeseen consequences: once the initial storm had passed and a few supposed friends and fair-weather clients had abandoned us in our time of greatest need, others stepped up.

Some did so out of support for what they thought was an important battle we had enjoined. Those clients were often wealthy individuals who wanted us to continue our political work too. They had nothing to gain financially from it; they simply wanted us to stay afloat and to continue the work, using our connections and sources to report on what was going on in Putin's Russia, and to share what we learned with politicians, journalists, and—through intermediaries—with the general public. These wealthy clients—who were more often than not donors, really—felt and continue to feel that their investment in us is a small price worth paying for helping to defend our democratic and tolerant way of life.

Other new clients reached out and wanted to work with us for their own, more orthodox business or investment-oriented reasons: they realized that we had good access to reporting inside the Kremlin and the upper echelons of Russia's political and business elites. Those new clients wanted the sort of intelligence about what was going on in Russia, Ukraine, and elsewhere that would enable them to make better-informed strategic business decisions.

There has always been overlap between these two worlds in our work. As I have said, when the work for our business-minded clients unearths information that we feel has relevance to national security, we will ask those clients for permission to disseminate that reporting to the appropriate authorities. Very often they are happy for us to do so. In the aftermath of the publication of the dossier the Venn diagram between these two worlds saw ever-greater overlap. And rather than feeling intimidated by what had happened to Orbis after January 2017, I, Chris Burrows, and our colleagues became ever more determined to keep reporting on Putin's Russia and on other threats to our way of life—including from China, the Middle East, and beyond.

In this section of the book I will be sharing for the first time some of the work we have done since 2017 to help quietly inform our private clients, national governments, and journalists. This is the tip of the iceberg; we have produced hundreds of reports in the postdossier era of Orbis. I hope they have provided insight into key geopolitical events—and also to explain how former intelligence officials now in private practice, including those at Orbis, quietly work to help protect Western democracy and the rule of law in ways that governments cannot, or will not.

Orbis does not do this alone. Chris and I and our colleagues have extensive contacts around the world who collaborate and share information. Some are former FBI and CIA officers. Others worked for intelligence services in the UK, France, Germany, and, of course, Russia and the CIS. We have contacts in the Middle East, in numerous European countries, in Asia, Australasia, and Africa. We are paid professionals, but we also all care about the same things—combating the growing number of autocrats, despots, corrupt politicians, amoral billionaires, oligarchs, and organized crime figures who have growing influence over our lives and who do all they can to undermine the rule of law.

It is tempting to ask: what wins has this network notched up? The world in 2024, after all, looks pretty bleak at this point in time. I would argue that the dossier and related events were, in fact, a significant win. Without it, Trump could have begun his presidency without a cloud of suspicion and scrutiny of his connections with Russia hanging over him. He could have done his worst, ending sanctions, cooperating with Putin, and undermining Ukraine's valiant efforts to fend off Russia after Moscow's partial invasion of the country in 2014. But for three years Trump was tied up with investigations and he was burdened by the—in our view, well-founded—suspicion that he was too close to the Kremlin. In shining a light on this, Orbis potentially contributed to stopping Trump from doing his worst and to preventing Putin from being able to exert greater influence on the incoming president of the United States.

But notching up wins is not our primary goal at Orbis.

We have a more subtle approach, and we know the limits of our ability to help shape policy. We inform and, therefore, we influence—in a similar way to how national intelligence agencies inform and influence their masters in government. The difference is that we are not constrained in the same ways national intelligence agencies are to fit into a foreign policy framework or diplomatic strategy. We can do more. We can dig deeper.

In the pages that follow I shall share examples of what we have done and what we have found and how we continue to operate. We have a library of intelligence reports on corrupt Western politicians and business leaders, on China's intelligence gathering and political influence in the West, on the Kremlin's support for extreme right- and left-wing Western European politicians and political parties, and on much more. But I am going to focus here on the Kremlin's misdeeds, internal battles, and plans as they relate to American politics—because that is where the stakes are arguably the highest.

In particular, I will describe some of our reporting on the 2020 US presidential election, none of which has been made public before. What matters so much about this intelligence is that it shows that Putin was not done after his remarkable "win" in 2016, in helping Trump get elected. He tried again to assist his preferred candidate in 2020—albeit in rather different ways. Feel free, if you would like, to hope that Putin has decided to call it a day and not to interfere in the 2024 election—but I would caution that that is a fantasy, and a very dangerous one.

Our 2020 reporting was funded by a small number of high-net-worth individual donors, mainly in the United States, and it was shared with former government officials there. We did not pass our reporting directly on to the United States government, however. Our relationship with the FBI was broken and, more important, Trump was still president. Sadly, we simply did not and could not trust the people who most needed to see our intelligence.

Chapter 23

2020

THERE IS A simple reason many people barely remember whether Russia tried to influence the 2020 US presidential election: Putin's preferred candidate, Donald Trump, lost.

To so many people, including me, the election result felt like an almost transformative relief. We had made it through a chaotic and nightmarish four years but now there was a reasonable and competent person—Joe Biden—taking over the most powerful job in the world. And then we were all distracted by the shocking, alarming drama of the losing candidate apparently trying to subvert democracy, overturn the choice of the people, and instigate a violent attack on Congress on January 6, 2021.

Russia's interference in American democracy seemed to be distant, toothless, and a thing of the past. Putin had failed this time. And his apologist—Trump—had been defeated.

But the Russian government had—albeit with a different strategy—tried to repeat the successful interference of 2016. And one setback did nothing to deter them. The Kremlin did not shut up shop and decide that its attempts to sway foreign elections were over simply because it failed in 2020. On the contrary, since 2020 Russia has taken interfering in other countries' self-determination to a new level: in February 2022 Putin ordered the Russian military to invade Ukraine, a nascent but pivotal European democracy. He had substituted subterfuge with invasion. It was a catastrophic mistake, as history will show. And so he is now, as I said at the start of this book, fighting for his survival and for his life. He will do whatever he needs to do. If he is willing to invade a country roughly the size of Texas with a population of more than 40 million, then he will not hesitate to try to help Trump get reelected in November 2024.

* * *

PUTIN UNDERSTOOD, IN the last year of Trump's presidency, that there is no one in the world more powerful than a second-term American president.

"*Putin knew that if he were re-elected, Trump would be much freer to act in Russia's favour than he had been in his first presidential term*," I wrote in an intelligence report in mid-August 2020, less than three months before the election, citing "*a senior Russian intelligence officer*" who had outlined to an Orbis collector "*the current Kremlin thinking on interference in the 2020 US presidential election.*"

In a subsequent report a month later, I cited a senior Kremlin official as telling our collector:

In the event that Trump won the election, Russia was hoping to get his assistance in further talks with Zelensky [sic]—over the occupied Crimea and Donbas (recent rioting in the East Donbas was of concern to Putin). Also, Putin was certain that, beginning immediately in a second term, Trump would have every interest in releasing Russia from Ukraine-related sanctions and also would compel Zelensky to make agreements with Putin which had been long sought after by the Kremlin.

Putin was not the only person to draw those conclusions. The world knew all too well what a second Trump term could look like. His final year in office saw him jettison or part company with the so-called "adults in the room" who had made up much of his cabinet during the first part of his presidency. Gone were the generals he had surrounded himself with and who, it seems, had taken those jobs in part to try to contain Trump. Other officials and aides who had acted as restraints on Trump had been fired, had quit, or had lost their influence. The Mueller investigation was complete, and on February 5, 2020, the Senate voted to acquit Trump on two articles of impeachment relating to soliciting foreign interference to help himself win the upcoming 2020 election. The Republicans had the majority in the Senate, and acquittal was almost inevitable. Trump was finally unbound.

Throughout 2020, as media reports emerged of the Kremlin's efforts to help Trump beat Biden, and as some US national security figures warned members of Congress that Russia was again meddling, we produced dozens of detailed reports about the Kremlin's fresh attempts to keep Putin's man in the White House.

Private individuals funded these reports because they wanted us to help shed light on the Kremlin's attempts once again to undermine American democracy. We readily agreed to send all the reports to two well-connected people in the United States, one Democrat leaning, the other Republican leaning.

Each of them had worked in government and retained close ties to and relationships with the US Intelligence Community and to members of Congress. All our reports were sent through these channels. We don't know, for sure, whether those reports made it to the right people in Congress and the US Intelligence Community, but we presume and hope they did.

I'm sharing some of the intelligence from these reports here to illustrate three key points.

The first is that the team at Orbis had acquired—and retains—reliable direct access to Russian sources, allowing us to illuminate the workings of Vladimir Putin's autocratic and closed regime.

The second is that the story of the Kremlin's more subtle, sophisticated, but no less determined attempt to help Trump get reelected in 2020 allows us all to see how Putin will have tried once again in 2024. This will be the Kremlin's third dance. Putin and his aides now have deep experience of influencing US and other foreign elections. No other state actors in history have such a track record, and we should fear them.

And the third point is this: The portrait painted by these reports helps us to understand our adversary. Written in the run-up to the 2020 election, they depict a Kremlin that makes numerous audacious plans but veers between being surprisingly cautious to behaving in an alarmingly and criminally cavalier manner. It's a Kremlin that can appear extremely sophisticated and focused one moment and then, suddenly, ill disciplined and brutal.

Since the campaign described below, Russia has had a further four years to develop its influence and interference plans. It has had more than two years of war in Ukraine to further accelerate and hone its tactics, including hacking, blackmail, human intelligence gathering, disinformation, propaganda, and murder. The West's chief adversary in this year of multiple elections around the world is as determined and malign as ever.

* * *

LET'S GO BACK to the summer of 2020. At that time we learned of an operation that proved to be central to the Kremlin's plans.

In a report written in late July 2020, we cited a senior Russian source engaged in political influence operations against the West. They were involved in the Kremlin's efforts to influence the outcome of that November's US election. We also cited a lower-level operative connected mainly in the operational aspects of Russia's foreign influence operations.

Both sources reported "*a high level of confidence in Kremlin circles that Donald Trump would win, based partly on the expectation of a 'late development' that would undermine Joe Biden's candidacy in the closing stages of the campaign.*"

Our source claimed that kompromat on Biden was deliberately being held back and would be unleashed near the end of the campaign. The source repeated what other Kremlin insiders were telling us: "*Putin considered that a Trump victory would enable the final negotiation of a new bilateral relationship and a revised international order on Russia's chosen terms.*" In other words, Putin expected Russia and the United States to find accommodation on Ukraine and other points of tension between the two nations in the event of a Trump victory. To many mainstream policymakers and experts in the West—myself included—any accommodation with Putin would amount to appeasement and a betrayal of our national interests. It would be catastrophic.

In a report in mid-August, I cited a Russian intelligence officer as telling our collector:

[Russian intelligence] was plotting a decisive offensive against Biden. It would be ready to be deployed from September. There were several new documents which, mixed up with compromising data against his family and son, both genuine and fake, could comprise a serious blow to his (Biden's) presidential ambitions. They would be rolled out from Ukraine, by Russian agents and the Russian political allies there. The Ukrainian MP Andriy Derkach was at the forefront of this operation.

It's worth pausing here briefly to revisit what the so-called Burisma scandal was all about, as it was central to the Kremlin's bid to prevent Biden from winning.

The conspiracy theory alleges that Biden, while vice president, used his political influence to help his son Hunter from being investigated and potentially prosecuted for alleged wrongdoing in Ukraine. Specifically, the allegation is that Biden withheld a loan guarantee to pressurize the Ukrainian government to fire a prosecutor—Viktor Shokin—in order to prevent that prosecutor (who, in the real world, was notoriously corrupt) from investigating alleged corruption at a Ukrainian gas company called Burisma where Hunter Biden was on the board.

Joe Biden did, indeed, withhold the loan guarantee to Ukraine—but he did so on the advice of the State Department, with the approval of the White House and in accordance with bipartisan policy.

But as early as 2014 pro-Russian Ukrainian figures and politicians, coordinated by the Kremlin, began pushing the conspiracy theory as a way to undermine Biden and the Obama administration more generally.

One of the most influential proxies for the Kremlin was a colorful pro-Russian Ukrainian politician and businessman named Andriy Derkach, who has since fled to Russia and has been charged with treason by Ukrainian police and prosecutors.

Derkach reportedly met with Trump's personal attorney Rudolph Giuliani in Kyiv in December 2019. Then, in May 2020, he released heavily edited recorded clips of Joe Biden speaking on the phone with the former president of Ukraine, Petro Poroshenko, discussing the loans and the removal of Shokin. However, despite selective editing, these recordings failed to incriminate Biden or his son.

We were getting almost real-time reporting about Derkach, Giuliani, and the drive to embarrass Biden from inside the Kremlin.

In a report in mid-September we cited a Russian intelligence officer speaking at that time:

despite having been sanctioned by the US Treasury just a few days previously [this was publicly known], Ukrainian figure Andrei Derkach would remain the leading anti-Biden political hit man in the near future. [Russian intelligence] had been surprised that the US action to counter Derkach had been taken only now, and not much earlier....

Continuing on this theme, the [Russian intelligence officer] reported that for over a year, Derkach had been cooperating closely with [Russian intelligence] on an anti-Biden dossier/discourse. And even after Derkach's direct dealings with Trump's lawyer, Rudy Giuliani and

several US Republican senators had gained him noto-
riety as a recognized source of political dirt on Biden
and former Ukrainian president Poroshenko, he had
continued to work closely with [Russian intelligence].

In a separate report, also dated mid-September, a different Russian source fleshed out the picture. The source, a senior
Russian intelligence officer, told our collector:

> A few days before the US Treasury sanctioned
> Ukrainian anti-Biden figure Andriy Derkach, [Russian
> intelligence] had orchestrated the publication of a well-
> structured and highly detailed anti-Biden and anti-
> Democrat kompromat tract in English [our report cites
> the URL of the Google Drive made public at the time].
> The Kremlin had thought this tract would attract the
> attention of the US media and thus become the basis
> for further attacks on Biden. For its part, [Russian intel-
> ligence] reckoned such a "systematized database" also
> would embarrass those in the US who had attacked in-
> ternational corruption, including several Republicans
> who were included in the table.

And then, on cue, a "late development"—the supposed anti-
Biden kompromat, as our sources had foretold—landed on October 14, in the form of a front-page *New York Post* story with
the headline "Biden Secret Emails." The story was purportedly
based on data obtained from the hard drive of a laptop the
paper claimed had belonged to Hunter Biden. Giuliani apparently had given a copy of the hard drive to the Murdoch-
owned, Trump-friendly tabloid on October 11. Staff members
of the *New York Post* apparently knew the story could be deeply

flawed; some reportedly refused to work on the story or have anything to do with writing it. The journalist who did end up writing it reportedly demanded that his byline be removed from the story.

A few days later fifty former senior US intelligence officials signed a letter that described the *New York Post* story as having "all the classic earmarks of a Russian information operation."

Later, in March 2021, the US National Intelligence Council (under the Office of the Director of National Intelligence) made public a redacted Intelligence Community Assessment titled "Foreign Threats to the 2020 US Federal Elections." This concluded:

> A key element of Moscow's strategy this election cycle was its use of proxies linked to Russian intelligence to push influence narratives—including misleading or unsubstantiated allegations against President Biden—to US media organizations, US officials, and prominent US individuals, including some close to former President Trump and his administration. . . .
>
> We assess that President Putin and other senior Russian officials were aware of and probably directed Russia's influence operations against the 2020 US Presidential election. For example, we assess that Putin had purview over the activities of Andriy Derkach, a Ukrainian legislator who played a prominent role in Russia's election influence activities. Derkach has ties to Russian officials as well as Russia's intelligence services.

The echo in the US intelligence report is gratifying in the sense that it confirmed our reporting that this plan had indeed been the Kremlin's big gambit. But, in other ways, it was frustrating: our reporting could have made a more useful contribution in real time if we had still had direct channels into the State Department and the FBI.

* * *

THE DERKACH-FRONTED CAMPAIGN to portray Biden as corrupt and willing to use his influence to help his son was not the Kremlin's only tactic.

The more senior of our two sources for the late July report told our collector that the Kremlin was confident Trump would win for other reasons also: because the US economy was strong and because Trump had set himself up in opposition to the Black Lives Matter movement, and this *"would enable him to mobilize white voters on the basis of fear and prejudice. Biden was expected to reinforce this divide with the 'genius idea' of picking a Black woman (Kamala Harris) as his running mate. The late withdrawal of Biden's candidacy, if it happened, would make Trump's re-election a certainty on the basis of the Kremlin's assessment that American voters would never elect a Black woman to the White House."*

Say what you like about the accuracy and astuteness of the Kremlin's analysis of American politics in 2020—Biden and his running mate, Kamala Harris, did of course win—but our source showed that Putin's people were again deeply engaged with what was happening in the United States. And US officials told the *New York Times* in 2020 that the Russians were stoking racial hatred and anger in the US.

The March 2021 report released by the Office of the Director of National Intelligence noted, in relation to Russian online influence operations: "In addition to election-related content, these online influence actors also promoted conspiratorial narratives about the COVID-19 pandemic, made allegations of social media censorship, and highlighted US divisions surrounding protests about racial justice."

As before, our collectors and sources had been gathering information from the Kremlin that would subsequently be confirmed by the US government.

* * *

AND THEN THERE was the renewed push to influence American voters online, and to create further division within the US to help Trump's chances.

In a report in mid-August 2020, we wrote that a senior Russian intelligence officer had reported on the Kremlin's online interference operation in the 2020 presidential election. This report noted that

the main recent development in terms of social media manipulation had been that in addition to Facebook, Twitter, Instagram and other western platforms, Russia also would, and in many cases primarily, utilize platforms and media that were based in the CIS. These were much less accessible to US law enforcement and regulators and included platforms like Rambler, Lenta, vKontakte, Odnoklassniki etc. On these platforms not only Russian- but English-speaking and Spanish-speaking voters were to be targeted, with the intention of stimulating them to create the same and often more advanced instruments as the ones the US [social media] giants possessed. Groups, pages, movements etc. were being set up in order to proliferate (dis)information outwards through sympathetic or unwitting users, with the added opportunity for such users to receive payments online and hold secret chats. . . . [Russian foreign intelligence/ the SVR] had created a special department for these activities at its Yasenovo headquarters and established some secret 'bases' in the surrounding Moscow Oblast (region). From July 2020 onwards, [Russian intelligence] officers were using their own databases and working through their agents working undercover as bankers, insurers and local and international services providers. These agents and their contacts were facilitating the targeted engagement of (social media) audiences in the US, EU and UK. They offered users various opportunities to both earn and raise money, in exchange for either their confidential or public pro-Trump and anti-Biden interventions. Many thousands of Russians abroad had been contacted already in this regard. Most of these had significant connections with the US, but not all of them.

The Kremlin was now operating at a level of sophistication that went far beyond troll farms in Russia flooding Facebook with disinformation. One source, a well-connected Russian political operative, had shared with a professional associate a great deal more detail about how the Kremlin was using disinformation online. In a report in early September we wrote:

According to [source], Yevgeniy Primakov Jr. (grandson of the late Russian Prime Minister, Yevgeniy Primakov, in office 1998–99), was appointed head of Rossotrudnichestvo (the public agency responsible for cultural diplomacy and contacts with "compatriots" abroad) in June 2020 with a mandate to expand its role as a deniable cover for influence operations against the West. The agency accordingly had been "purged" of old personnel and restructured with an increased budget. It would now report directly to president Putin instead of the Foreign Ministry....

[Primakov] had been appointed as Head of Rossotrudnichestvo after submitting a paper to Putin offering sharp criticism of Russia's foreign influence operations in recent years. In particular, the paper argued that the activities of Yevgeny Prigozhin and his "Olgino center" had been crude, ineffective and counter-productive. In [source's] words, Primakov concluded that: "90% of Russia's problems are due to Prigozhin and his people."

For context, the chef-turned-mercenary-leader Yevgeny Prigozhin had established and run the "Olgino center"—officially the Internet Research Agency (IRA)—and it had been a major but crude source of online disinformation that was particularly active in 2016. (Primakov, of course, was not the only senior Kremlin official who grew to dislike Prigozhin. Prigozhin was an outspoken and ruthless figure whose Wagner mercenary group helped shore up the faltering Russian military in Ukraine, which gave him yet more confidence to speak his mind in public. Prigozhin's open contempt for senior Putin aides contributed to his decision to mutiny in 2023. He died soon after when his small plane, very conveniently for the Kremlin, exploded in midair and crashed.) The source then described how

"the various foundations and organizations that had been operating separately and independently abroad would be brought under the supervision of a single structure..."

According to [the source], the intention was to create a more effective network of friendly social media and IT structures using connections with emigres from the former Soviet Union. This network would be used to spread messages to more specific target audiences. The use of emigres from the former Soviet Union would allow cyber operations to be conducted in a way that appeared more organic and would be harder to detect than the use of bots and troll farms as favored by Prigozhin. As the agency responsible for maintaining contact with "compatriots" (Russian nationals, ethnic Russians and Russian speakers living abroad), Rossotrudnichestvo was the perfect vehicle for building and maintaining such a network....

In Primakov's assessment, Prigozhin and his team had over-bombarded US audiences with (dis)information in 2016. The effectiveness of these (dis)informational waves, however, was very low because the audience was fragmented according to race, religion, wealth, ideologies, etc. As [source] had said: "It has to be subtle. If one has databases with e.g. specific goods/services buyers and specific church parishioners, they can use a much more effective, individual, targeted approach. Also, there's a drastic difference between the information originating from one server and information from 80 different countries...."

[Source] had reported that social media messaging about the "pedophilia scandals in the Democratic Party" [an apparent reference to the QAnon conspiracy theory] and "Bill Gates' plan to reduce the US birth rate" [another conspiracy theory] had served as a test run in evaluating the new system's capabilities: "As one can see from experience, the internet is the most effective tool for spreading (dis)information. Moreover, with micro-targeting, it's possible to sell any absurdity to people, and they will buy it."

It's unclear if Primakov was justified in his criticism of the Internet Research Agency and the 2016 campaign; after all, Russia prevailed that time but did not in 2020. But it is also possible that he was right in his approach and that the Kremlin needed to become more sophisticated with its disinformation strategy. Either way, Primakov succeeded in one clear way—he is still alive and working for Putin, unlike his rival Prigozhin.

On February 25, 2023, however, Primakov's postjournalism career finally caught up with him: the EU placed him on a list of sanctioned individuals. He "has clearly manifested support for Russia's war of aggression against Ukraine. He is therefore responsible for supporting and implementing actions and policies which undermine and threaten the territorial integrity, sovereignty and independence of Ukraine."

* * *

SOME OF OUR collectors' reporting during this time was alarming and to Western eyes possibly far-fetched, but it was hard to assess how seriously the plans apparently being discussed in the Kremlin actually were. One of our established Russian sources reported:

The GRU also was scoping possible assassinations on US territory of people regarded as Russian state enemies. Among the most prominent were (Oleg) Kalugin and Rodchenkov [the Russian Olympic Athletics doping program defector]. And Bill Browder in the UK. Also in the US, assassination plans were constantly being reworked against Mikhail Khodorkovsky and his son Pavel (who was living there). The idea was to carry out an assassination in the US with apparent traces leading to the Democrats, perhaps connected to them through their supporters in the USIC [US Intelligence Community]. Among the potential assassins being considered for deployment were pro-Putin Chechens resident in the US.

The above-described active measures however were still not finalized or approved. However, [the source] opined that there was considerable appeal in them for Moscow and they were supported in Russia by Putin's closest associates like [National Security Council Secretary] (Nikolai) Patrushev, if and when an escalation (in US election interference) was required.

For context, Oleg Kalugin is a former KGB general who lives in exile in the United States and is highly critical of Putin. Grigory Rodchenkov was a leading figure in Russia's state-run doping program for athletes. He went public about the doping regime and now lives under witness protection. His story was told in the award-winning documentary *Icarus*. Bill Browder is a US-born British financier who is a leading anti-Putin activist. And Khodorkovsky was Russia's richest oligarch who became a critic of Putin, was sentenced to prison in Russia, released in 2013 prior to the Sochi Winter Olympics, and now lives in Europe. In my estimation, Putin would be unlikely to

hurt Browder, who is a foe but not a traitor. And he is also unlikely to go after Khodorkovsky's son. The rest of the men our
source mentioned, however, are very much at risk—which they
are all very aware of.

And then the source changed the topic, from murder and
assassination to a relatively granular understanding of American electoral dynamics that prefigured much of what was to
happen after the election in states like Georgia:

> Meanwhile [Russian intelligence] was focusing ev-
> ery effort on known US battleground states which, on
> the basis of conversations with Trump administration
> or administration-connected figures, Russia currently
> considered to be Florida, Georgia and Wisconsin. The
> aim was to create uncertainty around the legitimacy
> of the elections in those states. But it was also to es-
> tablish in advance grounds for contesting the results
> there in the event he (Trump) lost them.

We do not know if Russia aided Trump in a bid to overturn
the election result in states that included Georgia, where the
former president subsequently has faced charges of trying to
change the outcome of the 2020 election. But as we can see,
it was the Kremlin's full intention to help—long before Trump
did exactly what the Kremlin predicted he might.

* * *

ONE MESSAGE WE kept receiving from our sources in the
months leading up to the 2020 election was that Putin had
decreed that "2020 should not be 2016." In other words, the
Kremlin and its allies would push hard to help Trump but they

would not be excessive; they would not pursue the aggressive approach they had taken by hacking the DNC's emails in 2016 and then releasing them through a willing partner like WikiLeaks. That approach had been rather primitive in the sense that it was almost instantly traceable to Russian hackers. It was too obvious and had been embarrassing to the Kremlin, even if it had delivered the desired result.

Instead, this time they would rely on more subtle tactics—disinformation campaigns online and, primarily, by planting anti-Biden news stories. Putin, it seemed, was concerned about the backlash from Biden, if the Democrat ended up winning, and so he apparently made it clear that the Kremlin should have a softer and less obvious role in influencing events this time.

"In their intervention in the US 2020 election process," a Russian official told our collector for a report in mid-August, *"all Russian actors were first and foremost concerned with not leaving any evident traces."*

The more cautious approach continued, and in a report in mid-September we described tensions in the Kremlin about how aggressive Moscow should be. A subsource who was a senior Russian official speaking in confidence to our collector in early September reported:

> Within the Kremlin itself, the [source] reported that [Foreign Minister Sergei] Lavrov's overall (pragmatic and restrained) approach to the US was strongly supported by Russian Presidential Administration (PA) chief Anton Vaino....
>
> In the opposite, interventionist camp however Putin's Press Secretary Peskov was now at the pinnacle of his influence in the Kremlin. He thought Russia should

be more active in supporting Trump and "dumping shit on Biden and the Democrats." Peskov was convinced that relations with the (US) Democrats were completely beyond salvation in any event and, if they won, the Kremlin would have to make new efforts from scratch to re-establish a minimal working relationship with Biden....

Meanwhile, according to the Russian official, Putin was currently not declaring openly and clearly to policy-making officials his position on the US elections, whom to support and how.

In a further September 2020 report, another Kremlin source speaking early in that month to our collector recounted that Moscow *"would use soft and indirect measures"* to help defeat Biden, *"as long as the leadership could be confident there was no direct evidence that these originated in Russia."*

A senior Russian official repeated that Lavrov *"was now closer than ever to Putin"* and that he

> "thought it was likely that Biden would win" the election. Lavrov had recently repeatedly told Putin and Kremlin colleagues that "he had enjoyed a good working and personal relationship with Biden since 2016, and that this relationship should be carefully maintained whatever the outcome (of the elections)...." Within ruling Russian circles, Lavrov regularly had stated that Biden was a very clever and experienced diplomat who would not be keen to confront Russia, even verbally. Consequently, he should be neither directly provoked, nor bullied.... According to reports

provided by the RIS [Russian intelligence services] at
[a meeting of the Russian National Security Council]
Trump's chances of losing the presidential election
were growing. Consequently, there was discussion on
how the Kremlin could take care not to make Biden a
full-on enemy in the event that he won.

* * *

AT THE MORE bizarre end of the reporting range, in early
October 2020 a senior Russian intelligence officer shared a
plan with our collector that showed how at least some elements within the power structure in Moscow were considering a radical, highly risky last-minute operation to help
snatch victory from Biden in the last days of the campaign.
The report reads:

> During at least the past week and no more than the
> past two weeks, in the (GRU) head-quarters in Mos-
> cow a small and highly secret group detached from all
> other tasks has been meeting on a sole mission; to in-
> stigate the kidnapping or hostage-taking of US citizens
> in either Iraq or Syria....
> The aim of this plot is to create a distracting event
> just before the US elections and either to:
>
> - allow Trump quickly and successfully to
>   settle the hostage situation and use it to his
>   political advantage, or (the Kremlin's preferred
>   method);
>
> - to resolve the situation in a joint operation between
>   Russian military forces and the US military. In

the event of a joint operation being too complex to organize, only Russian forces would be used for the rescue mission.

The aim is to fake a situation and then to "resolve" it with the effect that Russia appears as a friend to the US, and Trump's relationship with Putin has all been worth it. A side issue would be a future relaunch of US-Russian relations, at least in the field of security. The aim is not to turn a hostage situation into an actual crisis, just a perceived crisis as far as the American people are concerned. In any event, it would be solved quickly and easily with no complications. Risks that are normally associated with hostage situations occasions [sic] are to be avoided.

The action (if it occurs) is planned to take place sometime before October 20. And it would provide the opportunity for Trump and Putin to react forcefully and effectively over two to three days, leaving as little time as possible for any effective action from the media, or even for the media to digest what is actually happening.

The two countries most likely to be targeted are Iraq or Syria. In both countries both US and Russian forces can quickly make decisions and take action, whether separately or together.

This particular "October surprise" obviously never happened, but is an indication of the kind of warped thinking that is common currency within the Russian intelligence services. Approaching the 2024 election, and with all restraints off Putin, we must be alert to the potential for operations that could be even more aggressive, ambitious, and outlandish than this. Putin may feel he has nothing to lose—and everything to gain.

* * *

EVERY TIME WE receive intelligence suggesting that Russia may be intervening to help secure Trump's reelection or may have leverage over him, I think about the two hours Trump and Putin spent alone in Helsinki on July 16, 2018, with only their interpreters for company. Only those four people know what was really discussed during those two hours. Trump's interpreter has never spoken publicly about what transpired.

In the press conference the two men held after the meeting and the working lunch that followed, Trump was asked who he believed—"every US intelligence agency" that had "concluded that Russia did" interfere in the 2016 election or Putin, who had just denied that Russia had any role in trying to shape the outcome.

Trump rambled a bit and then said: "My people came to me, [Director of National Intelligence] Dan Coats, came to me and some others they said they think it's Russia. I have President Putin. He just said it's not Russia. I will say this: I don't see any reason why it would be."

To be clear: in that moment the president of the United States was publicly declaring that he believed the words of Putin rather than the assessment of his own intelligence community.

Both men were also asked if the Kremlin held any kompromat, a reference to the allegations in the dossier: "I did hear these rumors that we allegedly collected compromising material on Mr. Trump when he was visiting Moscow," Putin said. "Well, distinguished colleague, let me tell you this: When President Trump was at Moscow back then, I didn't even know that he was in Moscow. I treat President Trump with utmost respect, but back then when he was a private individual, a businessman, nobody informed me that he was in Moscow."

Putin continued: "Well, let's take St. Petersburg Economic Forum, for instance. There were over 500 American businessmen, high-ranking, high-level ones. I don't even remember the last names of each and every one of them. Well, do you remember—do you think that we try to collect compromising material on each and every single one of them? Well, it's difficult to imagine an utter nonsense of a bigger scale than this. Well, please, just disregard these issues and don't think about this anymore again."

In the aftermath of the Helsinki summit some leading US political figures voiced their profound concerns about what they had seen and heard.

"Millions of Americans will continue to wonder if the only possible explanation for this dangerous and inexplicable behavior is the possibility—the very real possibility—that President Putin holds damaging information over President Trump," Senator Chuck Schumer said.

"I think it's likely" that Russia did have compromising material, Senator Jeff Merkley, a Democrat, told *BuzzFeed News*. "It's the standard strategy of Russia when people visit there who are important, to try to get compromising information on them, to set them up with hookers, to tape everything that goes on in their room. So it's likely that they have that."

It wasn't just Democrats who voiced their concerns after Helsinki. Charlie Dent, a former Republican member of the

House of Representatives, told CNN's John Berman: "It makes me think the Russians have something."

In the face of the outrage that followed his summit comments and apparently under pressure from officials, the following day Trump issued an unconvincing "correction" of his stated support for Putin over the US intelligence agencies, claiming that "the sentence should have been 'I don't see any reason why I wouldn't or why it wouldn't be Russia.'" It was obvious that this "correction" was both disingenuous and not credible. Indeed, in early 2024 in a Truth Social post, Trump returned to the subject of the Helsinki summit:

> Remember in Helsinki when a 3rd rate reporter asked me, essentially, who I trusted more, President Putin of Russia, or our "intelligence" lowlifes. My instinct at that time was that we had really bad people in the form of James Comey, McCabe (whose wife was being helped out by Crooked Hillary while Crooked was under investigation!), Brennan, Peter Strzok (whose wife is at the SEC) & his lover, Lisa Page. Now add McGonigal & other slime to the list. Who would you choose, Putin or these Misfits?

Why would Trump draw attention to this again more than five years later, after he had "corrected" his comments at the time? If the suspicions of Dent, Schumer, Merkley, and many other people are well-founded and the Kremlin did have compromising information on Trump, then they will, of course, still have that. Putin has, to date, revealed nothing. The stakes in the 2024 US election are even higher for both men. It could be argued they are existential. If Trump wins he can put off the criminal cases against him for at least four more years. If he loses he could face going to prison for the rest of his life. Without Trump in the White House Putin would face a newly empowered second-term President Biden, determined to contain Putin and perhaps see an end to his regime. Goodness knows what either Putin or Trump might do in such circumstances.

Chapter 24

THE CHINA CHALLENGE

WHILE RUSSIA STILL generates the most work for Orbis, another country now takes up a growing amount of our time: China. That is because China is a rising global superpower and a potential threat to our way of life, and it also increasingly calls the shots in Moscow. Russia, squeezed by sanctions and with many markets off-limits, now depends on China economically. And the Russian military increasingly relies on Chinese technology and weapons, and on China giving North Korea the green light to ship weapons to Russia. There is no one in the world Putin can less afford to alienate than Chinese leader Xi Jinping.

In the years leading up to 2020, Orbis had done fairly conventional enhanced due diligence projects and reporting on China, as well as intellectual property investigations—especially in the pharmaceuticals sector, where Western firms' patents worth eye-watering amounts of money were being routinely stolen. But this was a modest and unremarkable part of our business.

That changed in 2020 when one of our clients (an American political activist and philanthropist) approached us with a request: could we contribute to an intelligence report on the Chinese telecoms giant Huawei and the wider issue of Chinese elite capture in the UK? ("Elite capture" is the term used to describe the corrupting of powerful figures within society by an outside power, largely through financial manipulation.)

The British government had recently decided to allow Huawei to participate in the rollout of Fifth Generation mobile phone communications infrastructure in the UK. This cost-orientated approach was very much at odds with the policy adopted by the White House and Congress, which was to regard Huawei as an arm of the Chinese security state and a potential Trojan Horse within Western economies. Like many right-minded people in the US, our client was extremely concerned that the United States' closest ally was essentially allowing the Chinese Communist Party to place key hardware inside the British telecommunications network. The potential for the Chinese to monitor communications within that network was obvious to everyone—apart from, it seemed, the key decision-makers in the UK government itself.

Chris Burrows and I had not developed a high-level Chinese capability up to that time but had previously worked with and knew well various leading sinologists, both in the UK and US, from our time as Crown servants. I had visited China only once, in 2015–16, when Katherine was undertaking a temporary posting at the British Consulate General in Hong Kong.

That happened to be just prior to the 2017 introduction of a key piece of Chinese legislation, namely the National Security Law. This law obliges all Chinese companies to provide proprietary commercial data to the security authorities in Beijing on demand. Whatever Huawei's protestations to the contrary, it was obvious to us that if the Chinese government asked

Huawei for sensitive commercial or political data, the company would have no option but to comply.

We worked on our contribution to this project in partnership with several experts, academics, and journalists through the summer of 2020, as the debate in the UK Parliament on Huawei intensified. We quickly discerned that while there was some overlap with the modus operandi of Russian influence operations in the UK—for example, a number of powerful people were clearly being co-opted to the Beijing cause through significant financial inducements, just like many prominent figures had been corrupted by Russian wealth—there were also distinct differences in the way China went about this.

One of these was Beijing's focus on targeting the British academic community. UK universities had become increasingly—and dangerously, from a national security perspective—dependent on fees from Chinese overseas students and for Chinese research money. That dependence had led to growing self-censorship within British academia and a reluctance to criticize the policies or conduct of the Chinese government.

We also found evidence that a number of influential figures around the then prime minister Boris Johnson had likely been targeted by Beijing when Johnson was mayor of London. At that level of government, Johnson and his inner circle were not subject to the extensive vetting and Security Service oversight that central government officials are.

The report was also shared with the British news media. And, predictably, several of the leading public figures who were then serving on the Huawei board and were mentioned in the report promptly threatened Orbis with legal action. As is almost standard now, they didn't bother with a libel claim but used—or abused, as I would argue—the poorly drafted British data protection laws in their attacks. Given that the report did not belong to us and was not stored on our IT servers, they were forced to back off.

Unfortunately, reaction to the report also took the form of press stories that referred to the Trump dossier in unhelpful and distracting ways. The *Daily Mail* headline was: "Trump Dirty Dossier Spy Reveals How China 'Targets British VIPs.'" In typical British tabloid fashion, the *Mail* journalist with whom we had worked seriously on Chinese UK elite capture issues said she had had the copy taken out of her hands, sensationalized, and reorientated back toward Trump, me, and the dossier.

Thankfully, the BBC's flagship current affairs program *Newsnight* addressed the issues seriously, and its excellent feature on the report included a contribution from our former government colleague and China expert, Charles Parton. That shifted the story back to where it should have been all along—on the issue and details of the clandestine operations and political influence in the UK of a newly aggressive China under Xi Jinping.

We believe that this report helped moved the dial on the Huawei issue and contributed to a change in UK government policy, in line with Washington's and our own Security Service's concerns. In retrospect it seems extraordinary that the policy would ever have been otherwise. Our client was pleased as, we were told, was the US government—including on this occasion, ironically, Donald Trump and his closest aides. Needless to say, he did not send us a thank-you note.

* * *

OUR CONTRIBUTION TO the Huawei/UK elite capture report prompted the strategic decision within Orbis to develop a greater Chinese intelligence capability and expert analytical skill set. With an increasing workload on China ever since, we are now engaged in both conventional commercial projects and gathering political intelligence on the regime and its proxies.

The report also led us to draw several significant political and economic lessons about the direction of travel of Xi's China. The most important of these was that parts of the British establishment had been or were in the process of being, in our view corruptly, cultivated by the Chinese government, often masquerading under the cover or guise of private corporations or academia.

As with the Russian influence threat, the British Security Service did not appear to have the resources or expertise to tackle this problem effectively—having pivoted much of its resources and efforts toward counterterrorism in the early 2000s—and the threat appeared to be more subtle and closer to the center of British power than even Moscow's UK agents of influence were. Suspicions of Chinese leverage sometimes fell on the same individuals who we suspected of having been corrupted by the Kremlin. One particular senior Labour MP, and several members of the House of Lords, repeatedly appeared in our reporting on both Russia and China, to the extent that we began wondering if the Russian and Chinese intelligence services were not in some way collaborating in targeting such people.

Certainly the Russian foreign influence playbook had provided a successful template for other authoritarian states and undemocratic governments to adopt. Furthermore, the potential extent of Chinese resources available to achieve Xi's political influence objectives also likely far exceed those at the disposal of the Kremlin, especially over the longer term.

Another focus of malign Chinese state influence and activity has been the international Olympic movement, where Beijing has in recent years procured hosting both the summer and winter Olympic games. The administration of the IOC, particularly the award of the 2022 Winter Games to Beijing, has been questionable to say the least and never properly investigated to our knowledge by state-level authorities. In a little-known but significant episode, the IOC vote in 2015 to award the 2022 Winter Games to Beijing was marked by a first paper ballot (in which China was losing to Kazakhstan) being canceled without proper explanation. It was then superseded by backroom haggling and an electronic revote, in which Beijing unsurprisingly came out on top.

Later, the scandal surrounding the alleged sexual abuse of the Chinese women's tennis player Peng Shuai by Zhang Gaoli (a senior Chinese Communist Party official who is reportedly close to Xi and was the lead Central Committee official responsible for liaison with the IOC) again demonstrated the inability or unwillingness of the IOC to recognize and confront matters of evident misconduct by Chinese government officials.

Why does this matter? Authoritarian regimes love to exploit the prestige of international sporting events to reinforce domestic political legitimacy, present a happy and competent face to the global audience, and at the same time effectively undermine the institutional governance of the organizing bodies, as the FIFA corruption scandal amply demonstrated. And they're good at stifling criticism and chilling the will of governments and private individuals to investigate through the routine threat of political pressure and litigation respectively. This modus operandi reinforces wider political corruption and elite capture within our democracies and has been accommodated or ignored for far too long.

These international sporting events should belong to us all, not just to unaccountable plutocrats in cozy relationships with repressive regimes to which they are happy to give succor. If we let them continue to corrupt our greatest sporting spectacles, this will only reinforce their appetite to influence and corrupt our political leaders more generally. In retrospect it seems incredible that a head of state of a leading Western democracy, President Emmanuel Macron of France, would have attended the soccer World Cup Final in Moscow as Putin's guest in 2018, four whole years after Russia's illegal occupation of Crimea.

* * *

THERE IS NOW a risk that China could become a rogue authoritarian state on the world stage akin to Putin's Russia. This would be catastrophic, not least for the world economy. Arguably, unlike Russia, China is just too much invested in the West's economic and political spheres for us not to engage with them going forward on issues like climate change and pandemics at the very least.

However, being overly accommodating of China would be a mistake, as it was with Russia in the early years of Putin's leadership. If Beijing chooses, it could become as much of a threat to our elections as Moscow is.

We must not make the same naïve mistakes with China that led to the ruinous consequences of our failed engagement with Putin's Russia post-2000 and the effective collapse of deterrence.

* * *

FOLLOWING THE FULL-SCALE Russian invasion of Ukraine in February 2022, China became even more of a concern and a target of work for Orbis (and for our political research offshoot entity, Walsingham Partners). From the outset it was no secret to Western governments and journalists that Beijing was Putin's main backer and that China represented a potential life jacket for the Russian economy as the Kremlin attempted to withstand Western sanctions. But our work has shown that it's not quite that simple.

The conventional wisdom in much of the Western media—and the line pushed by both Russia and China—is that the two countries are united and that Putin and Xi are unusually good friends and allies. Our sources on Russia and China tell a much more nuanced story, and one that is essential for policymakers and media in the West to better understand.

China and Russia have long been geopolitical rivals. The Far East, which is rich in minerals and raw materials and also provides access to the Arctic, has caused significant tension between the two leading Asiatic military powers, especially in modern times. Beijing's split from Moscow in the 1960s during the Cold War was a major coup for US diplomacy and followed a hot war, albeit limited in scope, between the two powers over their border along the Amur River in the late 1960s. There also had been a tug-of-war between them for influence and control over communist Mongolia at the time, in which Moscow prevailed. None of this history has been forgotten by either side, nor have the underlying issues been fully resolved.

Russian Far East territories contain most of the region's natural resources, including more than 20 percent of the world's fresh water in the remarkable Lake Baikal, while over the border China must cope with providing for its huge population and would dearly like to exploit the region's resources, especially in the longer term.

I would also argue that many Russians have had a political

and cultural fear and loathing of China ever since the brutal Mongol invasions and occupation of large parts of Russia from the thirteenth century onward.

To put it mildly, there are very significant historical, political, and economic barriers to these two great powers' friendship and cooperation with each other.

Beijing also sees Russia as setting a shockingly bad example of how an autocratic superpower should go about its business. The Chinese Communist Party leadership views Mikhail Gorbachev's democratic reforms and the consequent collapse of the Soviet Union as precisely the sort of fate the CCP would like to avoid at all costs.

But even a dysfunctional, autocratic Russia that unwisely allowed its people to hope for a representative form of government is better than a genuinely democratic Russia, in China's view. Putin's Russia is useful to China as a fellow block on the democratic world's agenda. Moscow's veto on the UN Security Council and its role as a foil and a distraction for Western democracies helps to deflect the West's attention from the corrupt authoritarian regime in Beijing and its obvious expansionist ambitions. It is essential to Xi and his allies that even Putin's shabby version of Russia is not allowed to be defeated in Ukraine or on the world stage. That would leave China to face off alone against the richer and more powerful NATO and Western allies.

And so it was with the knowledge that "my enemy's enemy is often my friend" that Putin kicked off his reckless and illegal full-scale invasion of Ukraine in February 2022.

Beijing and Moscow go to great lengths to present a united front, but our Russian and Chinese sources have given us and our clients unique and almost real-time insights into the thinking and actions of the two regimes.

Our sources have made it repeatedly clear that Xi and his

regime regard Putin as a reckless, irresponsible adventurer who cannot be trusted. Some of our intelligence reporting since 2022 has even suggested that in his bilateral meetings with Putin, Xi has hinted heavily that this might be a good time for the veteran Russian leader to step down, or at least move aside. In other words, Beijing wants Russia to remain autocratic—but not necessarily with this particular, unpredictable autocrat running the show.

In a report in October 2023, we cite "two well-placed Russian political sources" as describing what was to Putin and the Kremlin a profoundly disappointing visit to Beijing by Putin that month:

> Significantly, according to one source, Xi had hinted that Putin should consider whether to serve another term. Xi was paraphrased as saying: The great Mao could be the leader of China for 27 years, the great Stalin leader of Russia for 32 years. But who are we against them? In our age, it is not people that matter, but procedures. Three terms is enough for me, four for you, let others try. This was taken as a signal that Xi thought Putin should step aside, expressed in allegorical form.

There are, our sources tell us, clear reasons for this deep ambivalence about Putin in Beijing.

One key point is that the Chinese regime is determined to maintain and operate within the existing international order. It highly values the structures and agreements that provide stability to the world—especially the United Nations, the World Trade Organization, and numerous other bodies and treaties. These structures give China considerable influence.

Furthermore, the Chinese hold more than $750 billion worth of US Treasury bonds. They prioritize economic development and influence, especially their flagship Belt and Road Initiative. Global trade and geopolitical stability is essential for Chinese economic growth and political stability at home. All of this is incompatible with Putin's threats to expand the Ukraine war and to use nuclear weapons if the Russian army falters on the battlefield.

Beijing also wants Belarus and the former Soviet Central Asian states to develop and prioritize their relations with China—inevitably at Moscow's expense—and for Belarus in particular not to be absorbed by Russia as Putin clearly desires. Our October 2023 report also states:

> Xi had indicated that he was not enthusiastic about Putin's plans to incorporate Belarus into a "Union State" with Russia. He had told Putin that he considered Belarus (and Lukashenko) to be under his own political protection.

I'm going to quote six of the key findings in this report here because they flesh out exactly how imbalanced the relationship between Putin and Xi was described as, and what the points of disagreement are:

> 1. According to [two well-placed Russian political sources], President Putin's recent visit to China was judged a failure by Kremlin strategists, with results falling significantly short of intended goals. Neither of the two priority objectives set in advance of the visit were met. In other areas, Russian aspirations were dismissed or side-lined in favor of Chinese priorities. The

overall message was that China considers Russia to be a junior partner.

2. Firstly, Putin had hoped to persuade President Xi to increase Chinese purchases of Russian oil and gas, using the argument that supplies from the Middle East could not be considered reliable. In return for meeting a larger proportion of China's energy needs, it was hoped that . . . Xi would agree to a major increase in bilateral trade. The current turnover of Russia-China trade ($200bn) was much lower than China's trade with the US ($1.5tn) and less than half the value of its trade with the EU ($530bn). Even China's trade with Taiwan was higher at $300bn. Putin however had failed to secure agreement from Xi on either objective.

3. Secondly, Putin had proposed to buy back from China stocks of redundant Soviet/Russian military equipment currently mothballed in Xinjiang and scheduled for destruction. It was hoped that this equipment could be used to meet Russia's immediate operational needs in Ukraine. Although Xi had agreed that the topic could be "examined," he had made it clear that this would not happen within the coming year. This was understood by the Russian delegation as a diplomatic way of refusing Putin's request.

4. On Ukraine, Xi told Putin that China intended to uphold its position as a country that supports the resolution of international disputes through diplomacy rather than military force. China might be willing to recognize Russian territorial gains, but only as part of a comprehensive settlement agreed by other major powers and only if Ukraine were offered some form of compensation.

5. Putin had emphasized that three points were important to him: a) Ukraine must be a neutral state; b) Ukraine must recognize the territorial realities created by the war; and c) there must be regime change in Ukraine. At the same time, Putin had stated that EU membership for Ukraine and Moldova would not, in principle, be opposed by Russia. According to one source, the Kremlin assessed that Ukraine's integration actually could be used to destabilize the EU.

6. Xi had informed Putin that a decision on the northern branch of the Belt and Road Initiative would depend on how soon Putin found a compromise on Ukraine. China was interested in the transit of goods to Europe, and a lifting of sanctions on Russia would help. However, China considered this impossible without an end to the war.

To be clear, this is just one report of many on Russia-China that we have from Russian sources. Our China reporting is noticeably different in tone. Our reporting from sources on China around the same time reflects a more confident regime, focused on numerous policy details, navigating a complicated relationship with Russia as China pursues its economic and political interests in multiple arenas and territories. The tone and content shared by our sources, as might be expected from the dominant and more functional partner in the relationship, is less anxious and confrontational, and more confident:

SUMMARY

- Senior source on China gives overview of leadership views on Ukraine war

and managing relations with Putin/Russia
worldwide

- Beijing understands its modus vivendi with Russia
  as one in which both countries avoid confronting
  each other and encroaching on the other's internal
  affairs or "reserved areas"

- China and Russia also seeking to co-operate on
  mutual interests in third countries and regions

- The biggest strategic tensions between Beijing and
  Moscow concern China's relations with Central
  Asian countries and Russia's Far Eastern border

China's red lines are, to some extent, working as a restraint
on Russia, especially in the Ukraine war. Putin will, of course,
have his own reasons for not using nuclear weapons and not
targeting civilian areas more than he currently is. But he has
repeatedly received warnings from Beijing to hold back, and so
far, knowing that he can't survive without Beijing's support, he
has done what he has been told.

China has several key reasons for wanting to shape the
course and outcome of the war in Ukraine.

One of those motives is an issue that is particularly sensitive in Beijing—Taiwan. Xi and his allies are reportedly
concerned that the international community will continue to
make comparisons between Putin's territorial ambitions in
Ukraine and what Xi regards as his legitimate ambition to reunify Taiwan with mainland China. If China invades Taiwan,
Xi would do all he could to sell the invasion internationally
as a righteous reclaiming of Chinese territory rather than the
obviously rapacious, revisionist land grab that is Russia's war
in Ukraine.

Beijing reportedly also wants to see a peaceful end to the war because it wants to trade with Ukraine and has an eye on winning significant postwar reconstruction contracts there. That requires Xi and his colleagues maintaining good relations with Kyiv and Ukraine president Volodymyr Zelenskyy. And for their part—for similar reasons—the Ukrainian leadership has no wish to offend or criticize publicly the Chinese regime.

Of course, China is benefiting from the war in Ukraine in many respects, not least in terms of discounted Russian oil (exports to China increased by 25 percent to 75 million tons in 2023) and liquefied natural gas, neither of which Moscow can any longer easily trade directly with the West. China also profits from supplying Moscow with embargoed high-tech dual-use or pure military-application equipment.

But there are clear limits to all this. Beijing does not want to be seen by the rest of the world as Putin's arms supplier and would prefer North Korea to be perceived as the main exporter of military hardware, including missiles and shells, to Russia. In a report we issued in November 2023, which focused on Putin's visit to Beijing on October 18 for a summit to celebrate and promote China's international infrastructure project, the Belt and Road Initiative, we reported

> that China had committed to continue supplying dual-use goods, including parts for drones, to Russia. This would continue on a very secretive basis rather than in open cooperation, Russia's preferred scenario. [Senior Russian officials] had confirmed in talks that China also would continue to supply occasional batches of arms via North Korea when Russia was in urgent need. China also said it would encourage Kim Jong-un to supply Russia on a bigger scale and that

it would facilitate indirect payments from Russia to North Korea for these supplies.

A different Russian [source] reported that China wanted to maintain control over Russia's arms trade with North Korea but that it wanted to avoid being publicly linked to it.

The media coverage of this summit portrayed Putin as being greeted as an equal and "given the red carpet treatment," as the BBC reported. But behind the scenes Xi was reportedly communicating that this was absolutely not a meeting of equals. Putin came away essentially empty-handed, as our report describes:

12. The first Russian [source] reported that Xi was not enthusiastic when discussing the Sino-Russian relationship. He had reacted positively when Putin reported on the growth of bilateral relations, but without enthusiasm. When Putin discussed the potential for Russia and China to create a zone of joint technologies and developments within the BRICS [Brazil, Russia, India, China], as an alternative to dependence on Western countries, Xi had nodded but said this should be discussed by their respective delegations. This concluded the talks and the delegations continued on absent Xi and Putin.

13. The Russian [source] said that China was not keen to grant any more major commodities contracts because it did not want to be seen to be providing new funds for Putin's war machine. China would not grant anything further as a result of this fear of the optics. This included any progress on the Power of Siberia II

gas pipeline. The Chinese had told Russia they did not need the pipeline, though the parties were negotiating on the cost of the gas that would flow through it. As this was the main project the Kremlin was interested in involving China, it was very disappointing for Russia.

But for all China's caution, no one should be in doubt that Beijing is arming a faltering Russian military that needs all the help, weapons, and technology that it can get. The summary of an Orbis report from March 2023 citing "a senior Russian source" notes:

- Russia-China military co-operation increasing and intensifying as Ukraine war unfolds but Beijing reluctant to make this public, despite Moscow's urging it to. This may change if hostility with the US continues to increase

- Secret protocols in Russia-China bilateral agreement already in operation allowing supplies of ammunition, rockets and military grade drones. One shipment in January 2023 comprised 90 million bullets and 240,000 shells. China also facilitating arms supplies to Moscow from DPRK [North Korea]

- Importance of alumina, especially white fused alumina, in Russian military production underlined and importance of RusAl as interface with China to evade sanctions and exploit other non-sanctioned production sources

- For Russia, supply of Chinese drones with military application a priority. Rostec hopes to be importing 100 such Chinese drones a month by the autumn

- Quite sophisticated masking operations underway to disguise military exports from China to Russia, including doctored customs papers, bills of lading and markings on military products

- Rostec and China's Poly Group important in this growing bilateral weapons trade, with military-application drones and helicopters, some production of which has been offshored by Russian Helicopters to China, both high priorities

Some of the detail in this report shows how crucial China's restraint of Russia is—but also how significant a threat the partnership could pose to the United States, the West more broadly, and global peace. The report states that Russia has essentially wanted to be much more public about the military cooperation between the two countries, and for that cooperation to be expanded:

Up to now China has refused officially to endorse such close strategic cooperation, at least publicly as Russia wished. The Chinese have explained their position by the necessity to avoid direct military confrontation with the US and NATO. However, the Chinese are also keeping these talks open and ongoing, around the possible parameters of such an arms trading deal to be announced publicly. For Putin this was primarily about delivering an open snub to the US and NATO. He wanted it to be known that the Chinese were supplying arms and materiel to Russia. But the Chinese were still reluctant and dragging their feet on this.

4. In [Kremlin] discussions, however, it was believed

China was likely to accept such cooperation soon, and even publicly, as part of a deliberately antagonistic ramping up of tensions with Washington. The Chinese decision on this point was assessed by [Moscow] to depend on when China-US relations had deteriorated to the extent that China had decided to take a definite decision to attack Taiwan. In the second half of 2022 Russia had assured China of its full support several times—including militarily—in settling the Taiwan "problem," even if that meant a direct confrontation with the US.

5. According to a separate source . . . the Kremlin was actively looking now for direct confrontation with the US. China knew this and was wary of these motives. However, Russia's cooperation with China over Taiwan had been agreed in talks between the foreign ministers and defense minister of the two countries, and at least once by Putin directly with Xi Jinping. Overall, the Kremlin was trying to persuade China to take a more aggressive stand against the US and NATO in every possible way. Russia's urgent interest to enter into a close military cooperation with China was obvious in Kremlin policy-related discussions.

The overall picture is clear: Moscow has effectively become a supplicant of Beijing, which must be obvious and culturally and politically very unwelcome to the Russian elite and wider population. This greatly weakens Putin and it makes China ever stronger. The war in Ukraine has served to accelerate China's rise and Russia's decline—both overall and relative—in political, economic, and military terms. This leaves the West with a huge problem. We are, to a great extent, now depending on one ambitious, expansionist autocrat to restrain another. The risks are obvious and very considerable. In the longer term, China is much more of a potential strategic challenge and threat to the West than Putin's dysfunctional, impoverished Russia has ever been.

Chapter 25

THE NEW WORLD DISORDER

THIS YEAR, 2024, could well mark a tipping point in the conflict between corrupt authoritarian nationalism and liberal democracy. By year's end, more than half of the world's population will have had the opportunity to vote. Many of those elections—in countries like the US, India, Mexico, and the UK—will be hugely consequential. Particularly in the United States, I would argue, the outcome of the presidential election will have reverberations for at least one generation, either for good or bad.

The foremost challenges to liberal democracy and the rule of law, which are ultimately inextricable, will be played out on the battlefields of Ukraine, in the Taiwan Strait, and in the ballot boxes of countries where there is an internal, nonsystemic (extreme) political challenger. We can say little for certain at this point, but the optimists among us will hope we may have already seen the high watermark of creeping authoritarianism. In my opinion, the principal challenge in Europe will be defeating Russia in Ukraine and deterring it from other neo-imperialist land grabs. In many ways the performance of the

Ukrainian army on the battlefield, albeit strongly supported by Western money, weapons, and (doubtless) intelligence, has to a considerable degree degraded the threat Russia poses to others, at least in the short term. According to US government declassified estimates, and Orbis's own intelligence, by the two-year point Russia had suffered at least 300,000 casualties (killed and seriously injured); it has lost about 2,200 (or 60 percent) of its battle tanks, 4,400 (30 percent) of its armored personnel vehicles, 539 planes and helicopters, and 16 (20 percent) of the naval ships in its Black Sea Fleet. In manpower terms, this amounts to more than the whole original Russian force of around 180,000 men that invaded Ukraine in February 2022.

So Putin's Russia is in many ways already a spent force, militarily, although its ongoing possession of a strategic nuclear arsenal and an unstructured, psychologically unstable top political leadership—increasingly isolated from objective reality—is of major concern. Also significant here are the lessons that China and other authoritarian regimes will have learned from Putin's Ukraine misadventure. These are, first and most important, that such military engagements against closely related neighbors who are highly motivated to fight and enjoy strong Western support are not to be undertaken lightly; and, second, that although there are ways of circumventing Western economic sanctions, the idea that NATO, the EU, and other such Western organizations are too weak, selfish, and divided to stand up to defend fellow democracies is simply wrong.

Russia, going forward, now has to contend with an extensive new northern border with NATO in the form of Finland—and now, thankfully, Sweden—which is the real long-term strategic consequence and downside for Moscow of Putin's adventurism. It is also hard to envisage Russia as a serious economy or trading power going forward, as the confiscation of foreign and Russian businesses for the benefit of Putin's gangster cronies becomes ever more common and visible, spreading the cancerous corruption that eats away the potential for national prosperity.

Xi's China is, of course, massively larger and shrewder, and thus a more formidable adversary than Putin's Russia, a country that was already in serious decline in terms of population and dynamism well before 2022. Regardless of whether the Chinese economy becomes technically bigger than that of the US (or the EU), Beijing will become increasingly powerful on the world stage. China is already the biggest creditor of the Global South, has extended its authoritarian tentacles into many international institutions—the World Health Organization being one good example—and has fostered economic dependency upon it among a disparate swath of countries, from Brazil and Argentina to South Africa and Saudi Arabia. Whether we like these trends or not, they do mean that China will have a significant and growing stake, unlike Russia, in the existing international order. Managed skillfully, however, this could be a positive development.

That is not to say Xi will not be tempted or forced—perhaps as a result of provocative action by the new Taiwanese president, Lai Ching-te, or by serious economic downturn at home— into taking reckless action against Taiwan or more broadly in the international community. There is much latent popular hostility in China, for example, toward Japan, which could easily be whipped up as nationalist fervor by Xi and other hawks inside the Chinese regime. The social contract in China, which in recent times has comprised pragmatic government and trickle-down economic prosperity in return for the mass voluntary suspension of political and legal rights, does risk breaking down due to an unbalanced economy, aging population (as the one-child policy of the late twentieth century bites), a degraded natural environment (exacerbating vulnerability to pandemics like Covid-19), and shrinking diversity in the top political leadership.

Another element of constraint on Chinese adventurism, and of following Putin's Russia down the full-on rogue state route on the international stage, is the inexperience of the Chinese armed forces on the battlefield. The People's Liberation Army has not fought an external war since 1979, two generations back, and then was in reality defeated by a Vietnam still reeling from a war with the United States, which had concluded only five years previously. This must have been a terrible shock to the Chinese Communist Party leadership at the time and will prey on Xi's mind even now. For if an invading Chinese fleet were to be sunk in the Straits of Taiwan, of which there must be at least an even chance, that would be the end, I believe, for both Xi and the CCP overall. Conventional defeat in any Chinese war against Japan, or even South Korea, also would be likely and would have similar political consequences.

All this suggests that, although we are right to focus attention, policy, and resources on managing, constraining, and deterring the world's leading authoritarian states, our economies, military capabilities, and political alliances are well capable of surviving and flourishing. Under the likes of former German chancellor Angela Merkel, President Trump, and a succession of Italian political leaders, none of these attributes were fully engaged to protect our system of government and economic well-being. However, I would argue that events have forced their successors to do so at this current juncture.

So that brings me to the major conclusion I, and my close associates, have drawn from our journey of professional discovery since the late 1980s: that the main threat to Western democracy and the rule of law actually lies *within* our own societies, and especially since the pivotal political year of 2016, which saw the triumph of Brexit and, even more significantly, Donald Trump.

For, let me be clear, the rise of the populist authoritarian Right is not yet spent in either Europe or the United States. Indeed, in the US, it seems to have metastasized into the Republican Party as a whole, which is currently clearly unfit either for government or to oversee the defense of the West, America's indispensable historic role in the late twentieth century and early in this one. The dominant global role of the United States was indeed the rock on which my career as a Crown servant and intelligence professional was based. Republicans in Congress, like Senator Lindsey Graham and Representative Elise Stefanik, who previously at least seemed part of rational political reality, have now abandoned this for the Trump personality cult. In this topsy-turvy, make-believe world the January 6 US Capitol rioters are described as "hostages" rather than the criminals they are (as many have confessed to being at trial) and claims that the 2020 presidential election was rigged can still be asserted, despite being disproved in court in more lawsuits launched by Trump and his supporters than I have had hot dinners.

And so the US Republican Party has become the cheerleader for a parallel universe in the same way as, and possibly on the very model of, Putin's Kremlin lying machine led by his longtime media spokesman, Dmitry Peskov, who dissembles daily almost as a reflex. I firmly believe that if Trump wins the 2024 US presidential election or the Republicans come to control Congress, then all bets for Western democracy are off.

Ukraine would be surrendered to Putin, NATO mutual

defense guarantees among member states under Article Five would likely be suspended, and countries like Israel and Saudi Arabia would be freed up to conduct themselves in whatever (brutal) manner they wish. This would not just be catastrophic for Western democracy and world peace, but also for the fight against climate change, which, unlike political systematics, is irreversible. It is arguable that a belligerent and nuclear-armed Putin, or even Xi, could be the most dangerous person who has ever lived. This may be true right now, but, if he is reelected president, I would put a reckless, isolationist, autocratic, volatile, and impulsive Donald Trump ahead of them both.

In Europe, I see the major country of concern as France, one I know well and care about deeply from my time posted as a diplomat in the British embassy there. It has a powerful executive presidency like the United States, but fewer checks and balances than Washington, especially in terms of the weaker powers assigned to the French legislature—the Assemblee Nationale and Senat. There is a real risk that even the first past the post system in France could enable a victory in the 2027 election for the extreme right party, Rassemblement National (formerly Front National), which is led by Marine Le Pen.

Le Pen is an avowed isolationist and pro-Russian, especially pro-Putin. As has been widely reported, her party was involved in taking opaque loans from Kremlin-linked Russian banks in the run-up to the 2017 presidential election, the first one in which she ran. Le Pen has shown consistent opposition to economic sanctions on Russia and the provision of heavy weapons to Ukraine. She has called for a referendum on France exiting the EU and believes France also should leave NATO. A victory for Le Pen in the 2027 French presidential election would also be one for Putin, Xi, and other authoritarian adversaries of democracy around the globe.

I am less concerned about the UK, now the execrable Boris Johnson, Liz Truss, and Jeremy Corbyn have been consigned to the dustbin of history. Each of these, in their own way, was a gift for Putin, Xi, and Britain's other adversaries. But while I firmly believe that Brexit was the worst self-inflicted wound in British peacetime history, and that the UK is a weakened shadow of the country it was a generation ago, the current political leadership of both main parties has swung back to the center and to pragmatism. In particular, the strength of consensus and support between the ruling Conservative and opposition Labour parties over assistance for Ukraine has been deeply impressive and made me proud once again to be British.

In many ways, the key issue for Britain, as a democracy with integrity and credibility on the world stage, is coming to terms with the insidious corruption from abroad which started in the permissive, so-called light touch regulation of the 2000s. During this time, numerous highly dubious foreign business conglomerates were encouraged to list on the London Stock Exchange without proper due diligence having been conducted by the regulators. The move provided them with unmerited respectability and thereby unnecessarily increased shareholder risk.

Separately, Boris Johnson supported the highly questionable ennoblement of Yevgeniy Lebedev, the son of the KGB officer Alexander Lebedev, who earlier had been permitted to purchase several major British media outlets (including the *Evening Standard* and *Independent* newspapers) despite opposition from the security services. Yevgeniy Lebedev was later appointed to the House of Lords as a *Life* Peer, reportedly also against the advice of the UK Security Service, a truly shocking turn of events.

The lack of proper due diligence of the funding of British

political parties and manipulation of our plaintiff-friendly civil courts by foreign bad actors also urgently need to be tackled. What matters in party political funding is not the technical British nationality of the person making the donation, but the ultimate origin of the funds and motivation behind them being proffered. The until recently governing Conservative Party, the priority target of Russia-linked individuals and entities, has been particularly disingenuous and negligent on this. Its reluctance to address legitimate concerns was exemplified to me by the suppression by then prime minister Boris Johnson of the Intelligence and Security Committee of Parliament's Russia Report in 2019–20. This had called for better due diligence over and greater transparency of party political donations.

There are many senior and influential Conservative politicians who share our concerns for democracy and with whom I have worked closely over recent years, and continue to do so. However, although not a Conservative supporter myself, I was invited in the autumn of 2023 to speak to a London borough Conservative Party association on the subject of "Londongrad," a term used to describe the dubious Russian financial and political operations conducted in the UK after 2000. I was told there was considerable interest among local party members in hearing me speak on this subject, but the event was canceled at the last minute without proper explanation. To my mind this was clearly a sign of the ruling party's oversensitivity and even denial about these important issues. They undoubtedly have much to hide.

So what should we be concerned about going forward, and what do we need to do to guard the integrity of our democracy and safeguard and improve the rule of law in Western societies? First and foremost, we must expose and defeat populist authoritarian politicians running for office with covert Russian,

Chinese, or Gulf support. Recent talk by some MAGA US Republican supporters about the need for a "dictator president" and the abolition of term limits is particularly dangerous. There are no simple solutions to complex problems like economic inequality, environmental change, or mass immigration, and politicians like Trump and Le Pen who claim there are should have their simplistic and base lies exposed and challenged at every opportunity. For example, contrary to Trump's repeated claims of having forced the Chinese to pay greater duties on goods they export to the United States, it is not them but rather American consumers who have to pay the resulting import tariffs.

Second, we should recognize that it is the rule of law and independent judiciary that form the bedrock of our democracy, rather than elections per se. It has been the US judicial system, rather than executive or legislative branch safeguards, that has most effectively blunted Trump's destructive policies, apparent criminality, and recklessness. But also, we need to recognize the need for freedom of speech and investigation and protect these precious rights from "lawfare," as I have described earlier in this book. Wealthy foreign bad actors, often operating out of the unsafe jurisdictions of our authoritarian adversaries, must not be allowed to stifle the due diligence and investigative journalistic work so vital to the health of our economy and political life by exploiting loopholes in our laws and the greed of unscrupulous lawyers.

I am unashamed in saying that the US, not the UK, has the model legal system for defending the freedom of speech. Jurisdictions like England and Wales should emulate the First Amendment to the US Constitution and the rights to freedom of speech that the amendment confers. These include requiring a higher bar of proof for those declared to be public figures when pursuing litigation. In these cases, the putative plaintiffs must be able to prove "actual malice"—in other words, that the defendant has knowingly told lies about them—in order to prevail in the courts.

Britain and Europe need anti-SLAPP (Strategic Litigation Against Public Participation) legislation and a fast-track (and therefore reasonable-cost) mechanism for striking out malicious and frivolous civil cases pursued by the likes of Trump. We also need stronger whistleblowing protections and financial rewards to encourage people to expose wrongdoing, especially by government and by big corporations.

The UK and Europe need also to apply "public figure" defense statutes to data protection law, which has become the new front line of the "lawfare" battle. British judges should be able to fine lawyers when they act in such frivolous "lawfare" cases, and it should not even need saying that no sanctioned individual or entity should be granted a license to initiate civil proceedings in our courts. That is not, believe it or not, currently the case.

Parliamentary privilege and immunity, which unbelievably have been under pressure from homegrown bad actors of late, also should be strengthened, codified, and preserved at all costs.

The American judicial system, however, does have something to learn from English common law: in the US full costs should be awarded to defendants if and when they win at trial, as is the case in England.

So, what should we advocates of liberal democracy and the rule of law be aiming to achieve? First, we have to strive for a tolerant, transparent society, open to free trade and immigration in line with our principles and which serves our economic interest in the era of aging developed-world populations. But that openness should have limits. Governments and leading corporations of corrupt authoritarian countries should not be allowed to buy influence in our politics or own key strategic parts of our economies. All cases of foreign strategic investment should be fully transparent and based on reciprocity. If China or Russia do not allow us to invest or own designated assets in their countries, we should insist on the equivalent. Our financial and business regulatory and investigatory bodies should be properly funded and empowered. These arguably are in the United States, with the likes of the Office of Foreign Assets Control and the Securities and Exchange Commission being effective and, therefore, feared. This is not the case in the UK or Europe, where we should aspire to establish such strong institutions.

It is also vital, of course, that economically and politically Western democracies stick together. This is a fundamental strength, especially in areas like defense and intelligence, which require levels of trust that autocratic states like China, Russia, and Iran have never and could never engender between one another.

Britain needs an ever closer economic and security relationship with Europe, something that cheap populists like Boris Johnson never accepted and indeed actively worked against.

We also should use soft power to its best effect. The globalized English language, our liberal higher education systems, the strength and influence of nongovernmental institutions and civil society—our authoritarian adversaries are largely lacking in all of these. However, Western political hypocrisy, such as Washington and London giving unconditional support to the ruthless and vengeful Israeli operation in Gaza while arguing in favor of respect for international law and national sovereignty in, for example, Ukraine, undermines our credibility, particularly in the increasingly important Global South.

* * *

THERE IS ONE other pivotal part of any functional democratic society that we must protect: the news media. I have come to greatly value an industry I once stayed clear of as a UK Crown servant and that I have some cause to be wary of. In fact I now engage with it frequently.

During my twenty-two-year career as a UK Crown servant, I was all but invisible to the wider world and, especially, to the media.

All that changed after the Trump-Russia dossier story broke in early 2017. I no longer had the option of avoiding engagement with the media, not least to push back against the avalanche of lies, half-truths, and ludicrous conspiracy theories being touted about us.

I had been deluged with requests for interviews from mainly British and American journalists. I began to engage with several of them off the record. When the Skripal poisoning scandal broke in the UK in early 2018, I decided this was a subject on which I wanted to engage directly, and it was to Deborah Haynes of Sky News that I spoke. By 2019 I also had met George Stephanopoulos, the prominent American journalist from ABC, when he transited through London in early January of that year.

I finally sat down to do my first two full TV interviews with George (for ABC/Hulu) and Deborah (for Sky News) in September 2021. At first it was profoundly unsettling to have TV cameras and lights pointed directly at me. Deborah at one point asked me if I *was* a "fraud" like my critics claimed.

No legal threats were issued after these initial interviews for ABC and Sky—a significant concern at that time—and so my Orbis partner, Chris Burrows, other senior colleagues, and I decided that I should keep talking in public.

I realized I had no reason to be afraid and that I had a public platform I could use to some good effect, not least in articulating how important it is to defend the integrity of democracy.

And then, with Russia's full-scale invasion of Ukraine in February 2022, the media approaches became very frequent. As outraged as everyone else, I had a lot to say. The world now seemed to be entering a very dangerous phase, and it was vital that a properly informed understanding of Putin, Russia, and the corrupt international oligarchy was conveyed by the media. I eventually joined Twitter/X, where there is still serious comment and debate to be sought out among the trolls, chatter, propaganda, and misinformation.

I use my media appearances and social media not just to give analysis but to share, albeit suitably sanitized, intelligence that our sources have given us in the course of our commercial and political project work. I do this with the support of our clients, who generally approve of using the media in this way to feed out important information about what is going on inside Russia and, to some extent, China and elsewhere. My appearances are expressly designed to share valuable information and, gently but surely, hopefully, to exert influence on policymakers who sometimes would rather take the easy way out when it comes to the West's antagonists.

I also engage with the media as an act of support for the mission of journalism itself. And I do so in spite of my past experiences with journalists whose judgment and integrity I have cause to question. My encounters with a small number of flawed individual journalists have not shaken my own belief that a free press is an essential part of democracy.

My old Crown servant self, of course, would have been horrified that I am now in frequent and public contact with journalists.

* * *

CHRIS BURROWS HAS always accused me of seeing the glass as half full, and it is true that, by nature, I am an optimist. I believe in the fundamental strengths of democracy, the rule of law, and a vibrant civil society. And I believe that if people are given a fair choice, they will always choose democracy, fairness, and togetherness over authoritarianism and corruption. But I also believe that we cannot be complacent. We must redouble our efforts without hesitation or delay in order to secure a peaceful, prosperous, and safer world for future generations. We face a grave threat. We must prevail. And I believe that we can. If this book moves the needle even a little in the right direction, then it and my professional work and career will have served their purpose.

Epilogue

2024: HIGH NOON FOR WESTERN DEMOCRACY

WILL PUTIN'S KREMLIN try to interfere in a US presidential election for a third time? How will Moscow have tried to influence the July 2024 UK general election, held in the same year as the US poll for the first time in a generation? (It is notable in this regard that the now former British deputy prime minister Oliver Dowden alleged during the campaign that Russian bots were bolstering the far-right Reform UK party of Nigel Farage on social media.) But with a major war to fight in Ukraine and a shaky economy to shore up, has Putin perhaps decided that meddling seriously in American and British politics is not worth the effort? Can Americans, and to a lesser extent Britons, once again have confidence that their fundamental rights as citizens—to choose their own leaders in a transparent and even-handed way—will not have been impeded in July and November? And then there is the question of Moscow's potential interference in the snap French legislative elections of June/July 2024, in which the Russia-supported and -financed Rassemblement National (RN) had a realistic prospect of victory and taking power at a national level for the first time.

The answer to this central question was addressed by a knowledgeable former Russian intelligence officer in early 2024. He, like many others now effectively unable to travel to or operate in the West, claimed the Kremlin was exploring an approach that would benefit Putin's Russia no matter who won the American presidential election in November. It was one of the most chilling insights we have gained on Moscow's intentions toward US electoral politics. It showed us a Kremlin that is adjusting to new realities, morphing into a fresh threat. According to the former Russian intelligence officer, the Kremlin had asked for a detailed analysis of which American figures would likely occupy key positions in the future administrations of both Trump and Biden. Kremlin officials were instructed to focus on the likely candidates for each position. And then the Russians should look to begin cultivating those people—before they were appointed to positions of significant power with a security cordon, both physically and metaphorically, surrounding them.

However, according to our other reporting and analysis, the Kremlin's wish was to appear and remain at arm's length from interference attempts, working as much as possible through proxies, especially from non–former Soviet third countries. The Kremlin wanted to help worsen the migration crisis on the border between Mexico and the United States in the hope that social tensions would increase as a result. If successful, both Russia and China would be ready to amplify the expected resulting popular discontent in America via social media platforms. Increased chaos around the border would not be helpful to Biden (or any other Democrat) in an already uphill reelection campaign.

A further key point to emerge has been that Russia was now actively cooperating with China and Iran on attempts to destabilize the West in 2024. Ministers of state security from the three countries had held a trilateral meeting in spring 2024—bound together by the shared goal of undermining NATO. From the Russian perspective, the trilateral meeting was a success; all three countries undertook to continue sharing information and would hold regular meetings about the US elections. Nikolai Patrushev, a long-time close security aide to Putin (but since demoted), had emerged from this meeting confident that NATO would become weaker after the US elections. This would, in part, lead to the end of the war with Ukraine in 2025—and favorably for Russia. The United States would have to accept that Ukraine could not win back its lost territory. This would constitute a major defeat for Washington, Patrushev believed. It is not clear whether or not Patrushev and other senior Kremlin officials were explicit in stating that Russia was much more likely to prevail in Ukraine with Donald Trump in the White House. But as I have mapped out in this book, this is a barely contestable fact.

One last key strategic point worth highlighting is that Russian policymakers have considered the "price ceiling" adopted by the G7 countries for Russian oil to be ineffective and believe that Putin could use his personal relations with the leaders of Saudi Arabia, the UAE, Venezuela, Iran, and other oil-producing countries to agree a cut in global production levels that would force price increases in September and October and push up inflation, just prior to the US presidential election. They have attached more significance to this as a potential driver of US public opinion than the effects of other issues, like Ukraine and the Middle East, combined.

Whether or not this happens, and whether or not Putin actually has the clout to pull it off, our assessment that the Kremlin was exploring this approach as early as spring 2024 is a deeply unsettling sign that this time they are prepared to use everything—even the global markets—to influence the outcome of the election. And if Russia's newfound commitment to working with other authoritarian states hostile to the West was not yet clear enough, it is now.

According to our reporting, this time round the Kremlin has also produced relatively sophisticated and nuanced analysis, displaying a good understanding of how different communities in the US might lean politically. This analysis has not overstated its own authority; it accepts that the Kremlin had more work to do to understand the political inclinations of certain ethnic populations within the US. Young people from Cuba, Nicaragua, Venezuela, and Bolivia—countries that have had socialist or communist governments in recent years— tended to have antiestablishment views and potentially could become willing activists.

My inference from all of this is that the Kremlin is looking for groups and people within the US to cultivate and to recruit as agents of destabilization, whether they are conscious of being this or not. Some of the Russian analysis of the US is, I would argue, blinded by racist and xenophobic sentiment. But much of it is remarkably well-informed. Our reporting suggests that the Kremlin is in the process of obtaining sophisticated polling data on the key 2024 American policy issues, political figures, and voting intentions, much like it reportedly did from Trump's 2016 campaign manager, Paul Manafort, back in 2016.

It is worrying that Kremlin analysts are drawing some of the same conclusions as America's best pollsters. So, yes, the Kremlin will try to interfere a third time. It is already doing so. But this time will not be the same as before. And as Putin's tactics change, so must ours. It is no exaggeration to say that our way of life depends on adapting quickly, anticipating Putin's new tactics and defeating this generational threat.

Separately, in mid-2024 we received intelligence suggesting that relations between Russia and the West had deteriorated to the point where the Kremlin had ordered a new program for kinetic operations; i.e., assassinations and sabotage against the leading NATO member states. An FSB scientific research institute near Moscow had been revamped for training and planning purposes in this regard. The direction of travel is clear. We in the US and UK have entered a pre-war phase with Vladimir Putin's Russia. It is a frightening prospect for sure but needs to be recognized and addressed by our politicians and military leaders without further delay.

And over the summer of 2024 we received further intelligence This outlined how the Kremlin thought the 2024 American election would be a win for Moscow either way because if Trump won, they expected him to abandon Ukraine and lift sanctions on Russia but if Biden were reelected, there would be civil strife and internal instability in the US. Furthermore, a top-level Kremlin official, deputy head of administration Sergei Kiriyenko, had been put in overall charge foreign election interference, indicating its "increased status and importance to Putin."

But as this new intelligence starts to come in, sadly our bitter past experience makes us hesitate before sharing the details of it with the USG, our strategic ally but one we could not trust at all were Trump to return to power and his acolytes to go through the US intelligence community's files. Trusted journalists are an alternative option, but not with the same direct impact (for effecting countermeasures) and carrying with it the risk of hostile "lawfare" being unleashed upon us again at some point by our many adversaries. At the time of writing (early

July 2024) we are currently considering the alternatives for follow-up action. Our old professional mantra remains as true as ever. There is no point taking the time, risk, and expenditure of gathering intelligence if you are not going to use it, and ideally with highest impact and to best effect. It is just that within this "new world disorder" it is far from clear anymore just where we should go with such intelligence. In the end it may have to be to the USG and HMG (in the UK) once again, albeit with more caveats and more heavily sanitized than before to protect sources and methods from any political backlash.

* * *

I WANT TO finish this book with one final thought.

In the course of our work in 2016 and after, we learned of independent reports on Trump's activities in Russia, including the alleged existence of further "kompromat" sex tapes of Trump in Moscow. This reporting was entirely separate from anything that had appeared in the "Steele Dossier."

This subject was referred to in a classified Mueller Investigation interview note of their meeting with Chris Burrows and me in London. The "Official Record" of the FBI's interview with Chris and me in September 2017 in connection with its investigation were declassified by Trump and made public in the days before he left office in January 2021. As described in those interview notes, the FBI was investigating both the dossier and the alleged existence of further "kompromat" sex tapes of Trump in Moscow, including allegations contained in an unverified memo referred to by the FBI as the "Cody Shearer memo" that are separate from Orbis's reporting in the dossier. The descriptions contained in the Cody Shearer memo are shocking and graphic—worse than anything depicted in the first report of the dossier.

As we told the FBI at the time, this was not reporting from our sources and we therefore could not vouch for it. There were, however, obvious similarities between some of it and what we had reported in Orbis's Trump-Russia dossier. The FBI interview record shows we stated our view that this independent source reporting on Russian-Trump kompromat "chimed with the [Orbis] Miss Universe reporting, the Ritz-Carlton reporting, and the Agalarovs." But we also noted that the ultimate source was "neither the most sophisticated nor impressive person" and that his "Russian language skills were not that great." The FBI report goes on to note what we had heard about a suspected FSB operative who "was offering to provide tapes of President Trump. At least one of those tapes was related to the Miss Universe event." And, worryingly, there was also the suggestion that some of this kompromat material may have reached the Russian and other, third-country governments.

The FBI told us at the time that they took this reporting seriously and intended to investigate it further. We do know they had a follow-up meeting with at least one of these independent sources in Europe, though we were not privy to the outcome of it.

I genuinely wonder what the US intelligence community knows about all this. We, at Orbis, did not and do not have the resources or capability to verify any of this additional reporting properly. Someone who might be able to comment authoritatively on it, however, is a former senior Russian official, Oleg Smolenkov, whom the CIA reportedly exfiltrated from the country via Montenegro in June 2017 and resettled in the US. Smolenkov had served in Washington when Yuri Ushakov was ambassador there, and subsequently worked under him after the latter returned to Moscow in 2008 as Putin's Foreign Policy Advisor. In this position, Smolenkov must have had access to and knowledge of any Kremlin files on Trump (as well as on leading congressional Republicans) and Russian interference in the 2016 US election. But most oddly and inexplicably, this (Smolenkov) angle never seems to have been visited or addressed by the multiple US Trump-Russia investigations. Why would that be?

The stakes in 2024 are arguably even higher than in 2016. Putin is desperate to influence US foreign policy given his catastrophic full-scale invasion of Ukraine, from which he needs a face-saving escape. Trump has claimed he could end this war in a day, but presumably only with a settlement favorable to Moscow. That would only boost Putin. There is also the increasingly suspicious role as intermediary between Putin and Trump being played by pro-Russian Hungarian premier Viktor Orban, an authoritarian populist leader on whom Trump regularly heaps praise. It is therefore more important than ever that Western intelligence continues fully to investigate what influence our greatest adversary—Vladimir Putin's Russia— may have over Trump now.

The future integrity of Western democracy may well depend on it.

Acknowledgments

THERE ARE MANY people without whose contribution, advice, loyalty, kindness and support this book would never have been written. Some of them, either through choice or necessity, should remain anonymous. They know who they are and must stay safely in the shadows. As for the others, aside from my wife, Katherine, and business partner, Chris Burrows, my children deserve special mention given all that I have put them through, as do my Orbis Business Intelligence colleagues, especially since the Trump-Russia dossier was published in January 2017. The endless media inquiries, threatening phone calls and emails, hostile targeting on the Dark Web, trolling on social media, and occasional Russian or MAGA visitor banging crazily on the office door in London. This has not been normal professional fare and I am immensely grateful to them for just keeping calm and carrying on.

Over the years I have particularly benefited from the Soviet/Russia expertise and more general advice of Peter Oppenheimer, Ed Lucas, Sir Andrew Wood, Catherine Belton, and Strobe Talbott. And on other key subjects covered in this book—China, the US, France and civil law—John Gerson, Charles Parton, Mark Medish, Jon Winer, Glenn Simpson, Mark Stephens, and Pulina Whitaker.

Then there are the journalists I have been interviewed by and worked with, especially George Stephanopoulos and Jane Mayer in the US—Nick Robinson, Tom Bradby, Beth Rigby, Luke Harding, Christian Fraser, Deborah Haynes, and the pioneer and conscience of investigative reporting, John Sweeney in the UK.

My Oxford and Cambridge universities alumnae "faction" have always been true and valued friends and have brought their various professional skills to bear in my support when called upon. Neil Sherlock, my media coach Graham Davies, Richard Klein, Nick Robinson (again), and the various other "knights called Nick," all members of my very own Praetorian Guard. As are Rob, Aled, Andy, Graham, and George from my earlier school years in England and Cyprus. And, of course, my sister Alison and her husband, Stefan, who have always been there for me.

I am also eternally grateful for the team that promoted the idea of this book, stuck with it through the multiple iterations and edits, and have had the courage to publish it into a turbulent and potentially hostile political world—Laurie, Matt, Peter, and Clare. And especially to Lucinda, my peerless chief of staff, who has consistently exhibited the patience of a saint.

And finally relatives, friends, and former colleagues who are no longer with us, but who played a formative role in my life and career. My father, Perris; university friend Tim Bass; and former professional colleagues Stuart Gibby, Nigel Backhouse, and Charles Farr. I often wonder what they would have thought if they had lived to see the disordered state of our world today and had had the chance to read this book. I hope it does their memory and legacy justice.

—Farnham, Surrey, England, July 2024